Praise for
Unmistakable Impact

A true master of "walking his talk," Jim Knight humbly shares what he has learned about establishing environments characterized by empowerment, authenticity, joyfulness, equality, respect, and learning. He offers many powerful resources to guide principals and coaches in their transformation efforts.

—*Stephanie Hirsh*
Executive Director, Learning Forward

A must-read for anyone who cares about learning—this book is from the heart. Knight uses his own experiences to describe processes and strategies for impacting student and adult learning in today's schools.

—*Sandee Crowther, President*
Phi Delta Kappa International

Jim Knight's work has had a tremendous impact on the quality of our professional development practices that are job-embedded and meet the *real* needs of our teachers. He is a consummate relationship builder who models how to establish the types of relationships necessary for second-order change to occur.

—*Carolyn J. Teigland, Associate*
Superintendent for Education Services
Cecil County Public Schools, Elkton, MD

Jim Knight outlines a clear path to success for educators to make sense out of the complex nature of external mandates, competing initiatives, and prevailing traditional models found within many schools and districts around the nation.

—*Ken Geisick, Superintendent*
Riverbank Unified School District, CA

UNMISTAKABLE
impact

This book is dedicated to my parents, Joan and Doug. I've always known that my parents loved me, believed in me, and supported me. The rock-solid foundation my parents gave me has made it possible for me to create this book and do most of the work I do. If this book is any use to you at all, you can thank my parents for making that possible.

UNMISTAKABLE
impact

A Partnership Approach for Dramatically Improving Instruction

jim knight

Foreword by Michael Fullan

A JOINT PUBLICATION

CORWIN
A SAGE Company

learningforward

For information:

Corwin
A SAGE Company
2455 Teller Road
Thousand Oaks, California 91320
(800) 233-9936
Fax: (800) 417-2466
www.corwin.com

SAGE Ltd.
1 Oliver's Yard
55 City Road
London EC1Y 1SP
United Kingdom

SAGE India Pvt. Ltd.
B 1/I 1 Mohan Cooperative
    Industrial Area
Mathura Road, New Delhi 110 044
India

SAGE Asia-Pacific Pte. Ltd.
33 Pekin Street #02-01
Far East Square
Singapore 048763

Printed in the United States of America

Library of Congress Cataloging-in-Publication Data

Knight, Jim.
Unmistakable impact : a partnership approach for dramatically improving instruction / Jim Knight ; foreword by Michael Fullan.
        p. cm.
"A Joint Publication With Learning Forward."
Includes bibliographical references and index.
ISBN 978-1-4129-9430-9 (pbk.)

    1. Teachers—In-service training—United States. 2. School improvement programs—United States. I. Learning Forward (U.S.) II. Title.

LB1731.K5733 2011
370.7'155—dc22   2010037117

This book is printed on acid-free paper.

13 14 15 16 17 10 9 8 7 6 5 4

Acquisitions Editor:	Dan Alpert
Associate Editor:	Megan Bedell
Editorial Assistant:	Sarah Bartlett
Production Editor:	Melanie Birdsall
Copy Editor:	Adam Dunham
Typesetter:	C&M Digitals (P) Ltd.
Proofreader:	Wendy Jo Dymond
Indexer:	J. Naomi Linzer
Cover Designer:	Scott Van Atta
Permissions Editor:	Karen Ehrmann

Contents

Resource A: Impact Toolkit can also be accessed at the
Unmistakable Impact companion website at
www.corwin.com/unmistakableimpact

Foreword

The beauty of *Unmistakable Impact* is that it moves effortlessly back and forth from the big picture to micro application. It does so because the author, Jim Knight, is clearly deeply immersed in making the big ideas work.

He makes the case that "dramatically improving instruction is a matter of focus, simplicity, precision, leverage, and a cut across humanity that infuses all of this work." Knight then builds a powerful case on ideas that work through "partnership principles," "the role of the principal as lead learner," and grounds this work in "the Big Four" ideas that incorporate content planning, formative assessment, instruction, and community building. This set of ideas, clearly depicted early in the book, provides a comprehensive agenda for what school improvement should focus on, but Knight does not stop there.

He then proceeds to furnish us with high-leverage strategies to get there. We get ideas and tools for "creating the Target," "observing and monitoring progress," and how the principal as lead learner needs to work closely with teachers while getting support from central office.

Building on his already impressive work on instructional coaching, we see how the key components of coaching work in practice to achieve results. *Unmistakable Impact* drills into the role of workshops and follow-up based on equality, choice, voice, reflection, dialogue, and praxis. But these are not just normative niceties. They are buttressed by incorporating key impact factors like intensive learning teams, principals as first learners, coaches as integrators, and detailed design principles that provide clear guidelines for taking specific action.

Unmistakable Impact is a treasure trove of ideas in two ways. It contains scores of ideas for "going deeper," which Knight presents at the end of each chapter, complete with a short list of best source books. Second, each concept in the chapters is accompanied by a tool or checklist to carefully guide action. These practical tools are complete and invaluable. In addition, the Resources offer the whole Toolkit.

Jim Knight models his advice to be a lead learner. He clearly constantly draws on recent best sources in the literature and makes them accessible to the reader. He holds up high but specific expectations for action within a framework of respect for practitioners. *Unmistakable Impact* contains the best of both worlds—compelling ideas and reader choice.

The ideas in this book are entirely compatible with our own recent work in Ontario and elsewhere. We have found that good ideas, high expectations, precise application, leadership support from principals and coaches, and multiple partnerships produce amazing results in teacher engagement and student achievement (Fullan, 2010a, 2010b). *Unmistakable Impact* takes us deeper into the realm of grounded school improvement—a great contribution to the field.

—Michael Fullan
Professor Emeritus
Ontario Institute for Studies in Education
University of Toronto

Preface

*Every student receives excellent instruction
every day in every class.*

Since the publication of *Instructional Coaching: A Partnership
Approach to Improving Instruction* in 2007, my colleagues and I at
the Instructional Coaching Group have been fortunate enough to
work with school districts across most of the states and provinces in
the United States and Canada. During our visits, we've had the good
fortune to work with many, many great people who are deeply
committed to improving student learning by improving instruction.

Each visit, of course, is unique, but certain themes seem to surface
repeatedly. Generally, instructional coaches love their work, and they
are motivated by their ability to make a difference—every time they
help a teacher to become more effective, they help every student that
teacher will teach in the future. Instructional Coaches tell us that the
partnership principles provide a solid foundation for instructional
coaching. And, most important, we frequently hear that coaching is
leading to real, significant improvements in teaching and learning.

At the same time that we hear about the rewards and successes of
coaching, we also hear about common roadblocks that many coaches
and instructional leaders are encountering. In the majority of districts
we visit, workshops, professional learning communities, and
instructional coaching are all offered as supports for teacher
professional learning, but those offerings are not sufficiently aligned.
Districts are trying all kinds of different approaches and programs,
but often each is implemented separately, with the net result being
that teachers are overwhelmed by demands on their time, and
coaches are underutilized as supports for implementing those
programs.

Additionally, we have found that school improvement plans are
not used effectively to shape and propel positive changes in teaching.

In truth, in most of the districts we visit, what theoretically should be the centerpiece for professional learning, the school improvement plan, is too long, too complicated, and understood by too few to be implemented with any kind of success.

Finally, we have found that principals are underprepared to be the kind of instructional leaders they must be if their districts are to flourish. Principals need to understand good instructional practices, know how to observe teachers to gauge how effectively teachers are using those practices, and know how to design and coordinate professional learning that makes it possible for teachers to master those practices. Nevertheless, despite their need for extensive professional learning support, principals often receive less professional development than anyone else in a district.

I wrote this book to address these issues, to build on the successes and address the roadblocks. This is my attempt to provide a simple map so that educators (central office staff, principals, instructional coaches, teachers, and all other educators) can align and integrate all professional learning for impact. A teacher should only be asked to attend a workshop, participate in a professional learning community (PLC), partner with a coach, or be observed by a principal, if those events will have an unmistakable impact on teaching and student learning. My goal here has been to create a map that is simple enough to be understood but sophisticated enough to guide schools to their real destination.

Acknowledgments

My own journey writing this book has been taken with many fellow travelers, people who have inspired me, kept me on track, and given me fuel for the expedition. I am tremendously grateful to all the people whom I mention below, and the many others who have dedicated their lives to creating outstanding learning experiences for our children.

The person who had the greatest influence on my writing of this book is Michael Fullan, who was also very generous with his time to write the foreword. I recently read a quotation that accurately summarized how I feel about Michael's contribution to this book. When Dizzy Gillespie was asked to describe the impact Louis Armstrong had on him, he gave a great, concise response: "No him, no me." I don't want to suggest that I'm in anyway like Dizzy, one of the greatest jazz innovators of all time, but Mr. Gillespie's comments nicely capture the impact Michael Fullan has had on my research and writing. *Unmistakable Impact* would not exist were it not for Michael's brilliant work in more than a dozen books on educational change and leadership.

At the Kansas Coaching Project at the Center for Research on Learning at the University of Kansas, I've been fortunate to work with outstanding researchers and colleagues. Don Deshler, my mentor, and the director of the center, has taught me an enormous amount about being a researcher and author and even more about how to be a decent person (still a work in progress, for certain). After close to 20 years of working with Don, I still *always* walk away from our conversations happier, more inspired, and—if I listened carefully enough to Don—smarter.

Jean Schumaker, the former associate director of the center, dramatically improved the quality of my writing during our many one-to-one sessions at KU. Even more important to me, though, Jean has become an incredibly important friend to my family and me.

My longtime colleague and friend Mary Brieck has done a fantastic job of doing the wonderful magic act of making most of the problems we faced on our project disappear. Together, we have won several grants; kept those grants in compliance; and, most important, shared a passion for the blues, especially Stevie Ray Vaughn.

At the Kansas Coaching Project, while writing this book I have been working with two fantastic research teams. Indeed, many of our findings mentioned in this book were arrived at through the efforts of my colleagues. On the Teacher Quality Study of Coaching, funded by the U.S. Department of Education Institute of Education Sciences, Mike Hock, Irma Brasseur-Hock, Tom Skrtic, Barbara Bradley, Jana Craig Hare, Jake Cornett, Michael Kennedy, Leslie Novosel, Belinda Mitchell, and David Knight have deepened my understanding of what effective coaches do, who they are, and what impact they can have on student learning.

The Pathways to Success project, funded by the U.S. Department of Education GEAR-UP Program, provided the setting for much of my foundational work on instructional coaching. My colleagues Devona Dunekack, Bill Towns, Lynn Barnes, Shelly Bolejack-McBeth, Stacy Cohen, Jeanne Disney, Marti Elford, LaVonne Holmgren, and Ric Palma and I have worked together for more than 10 years, and I am very fortunate to work with such a great, positive, high-energy team. I am also especially indebted to Ethel Edwards, an honorary member of the Pathways Team, who collaborated with me to develop the first intensive learning teams, which were implemented as a part of the Pathways to Success project.

Two people at the Kansas Coaching Project have been especially helpful as I've written this book. Carol Hatton has completed many, many important tasks, such as refining the reference section of the book and overseeing multiple edits, and her efforts have allowed me the freedom to write the book. Marilyn Ruggles has sought out references and summarized multiple books that were necessary resources for this publication.

My colleagues at the Instructional Coaching Group always push my thinking and help me to ensure that our ideas and not merely conceptual but also practical. Along with Lynn, Devona, and Shelly from the Pathways to Success project, I'm fortunate to work with Ann Hoffman, Ruth Ryschon, Tricia Skyles, Conn Thomas, and Sue Woodruff.

I'm also tremendously grateful to the following reviewers who took a great deal of time to read early manuscripts and then provide excellent advice on how I could improve this work. Thanks to the following reviewers' comments, this work is easier to understand, more meaningful, and more useful: Stephen Barkley, Katherine C. Boles, Donald Deshler, Michael Fullan, Ken Geisick, Carolee Hayes, Shirley Hord, Charlotte Ostermann, Dennis Sparks, Bill Sommers, Vivian Troen, Carolyn Teigland, Georgia Wentzell, Doris Williams, and Sue Woodruff.

I've been fortunate to work with many outstanding colleagues who have supported me as I've written this book. Kirsten McBride is a gifted copyeditor who has found hundreds, possibly thousands, of ways to simplify, clarify, and improve my writing. I've yet to write a page that Kirsten couldn't improve! At Corwin, Megan Bedell has done a fantastic job coordinating my very complicated review process. Sarah Bartlett has provided great assistance (and patience!) readying the manuscript for production, and Melanie Birdsall has been a wonderfully creative colleague shepherding the book through production. Dan Alpert, my editor at Corwin, has been provided daily support and encouragement as I've written this book. Dan is always gracious, attentive, and insightful, and I've been fortunate to be guided through the book publication process by such a professional and warmhearted editor.

As much support as I've received professionally, I've received even more at home. My children, Geoff, Cameron, David, Emily, Ben, and Isaiah, inspire me and encourage me. What a joy it has been to watch my children grow into adults, having their own unmistakable impact on the world. My wife Jenny is the love of my life, my thinking partner, my motivation, and as anyone who knows me can tell you, I struck gold when after over a hundred marriage proposals, Jenny finally said yes.

Publisher Acknowledgments

Corwin gratefully acknowledges the contributions of the following individuals:

Steve Barkley
Teacher and Principal Trainer/Education Author
Performance Learning Systems
New Hope, PA

Katherine C. Boles
Director of Learning and Teaching Program and Senior Lecturer
Graduate School of Education
Harvard University
Cambridge, MA

Donald Deshler
Professor of Special Education and Director of the Center for
    Research on Learning
University of Kansas
School of Education
Lawrence, KS

Carolee Hayes
Co-Director
The Center for Cognitive Coaching and Kaleidoscope
    Associates, LLC
Highlands Ranch, CO

Shirley Hord
Scholar Laureate
Learning Forward
Dallas, TX

Tricia McKale Skyles
Educational Consultant
Safe and Civil Schools
Eugene, OR

William A. Sommers
Principal
Spring Lake Park High School
Spring Lake Park, MN

Dennis Sparks
Leadership Development Consultant
Ann Arbor, MI

Vivian Troen
Lecturer and Senior Education Specialist
Brandeis University
Waltham, MA

About the Author

 **Jim Knight** is a research associate at the University of Kansas Center for Research on Learning and the president of the Instructional Coaching Group. He has spent more than a decade studying instructional coaching and has written several books on the topic, including *Instructional Coaching: A Partnership Approach to Improving Instruction* published by Corwin and Learning Forward (2007). Knight co-authored *Coaching Classroom Management.* He also edited *Coaching: Approaches and Perspectives.*

Knight has authored articles on instructional coaching in publications such as *The Journal of Staff Development, Principal Leadership, The School Administrator, Kappan,* and *Teachers Teaching Teachers.*

Several research projects directed by Knight include an Institute of Education Sciences–funded qualitative and quantitative assessment of coaching and Pathways to Success, a comprehensive, districtwide school reform project for the Topeka Public School District in Kansas. Knight also leads the coaching institutes and the Annual Instructional Coaching Conference offered by the University of Kansas.

Frequently asked to guide professional learning for instructional coaches, Knight has presented and consulted in more than 35 states, most Canadian provinces, and in Japan. He has a PhD in education and has won several university teaching, innovation, and service awards. He also writes the popular radicallearners.com blog. Contact Knight at jimknight@me.com.

Core Questions for Impact Schools

School
- Do we have a one-page instructional improvement plan that clearly describes the critical teaching behaviors that are most important for our students and teachers?

Principal
- Do I know precisely what it looks like when the teaching practices on the instructional improvement plan are used effectively by teachers?
- Do I know exactly how well each teacher is doing in implementing those practices?
- Do I know how to prompt teachers to use the school's professional learning opportunities to master the teaching practices in the Target?
- Do I know how to communicate clearly and positively so that staff are motivated to implement the Target?

Teacher
- Is the content I teach carefully aligned with state standards?
- Do I clearly understand how well my students are learning the content?
- Do my students understand how well they are learning the content being taught?
- Do I fully understand and use a variety of teaching practices to ensure my students master the content being taught in my class?
- Do my students behave in a manner that is consistent with our classroom expectations?

Workshops
- Do workshops focus exclusively on the teaching practices in the instructional improvement plan?
- Do workshop facilitators use effective teaching practices?
- Does each workshop conclude with teachers planning how to use their coach to implement the practices learned during the workshop?

Teams
- Do teams and professional learning communities focus exclusively on the teaching practices in the instructional improvement plan?
- Do teachers use coaches to help them implement the methods and materials developed during team meetings?

Coaches
- Do I have a deep understanding of *all* of the teaching practices in the instructional improvement plan?
- Can I provide sufficient support (precise explanations, modeling, observation, feedback, and questioning) so teachers can implement the practices?

1

Impact Schools

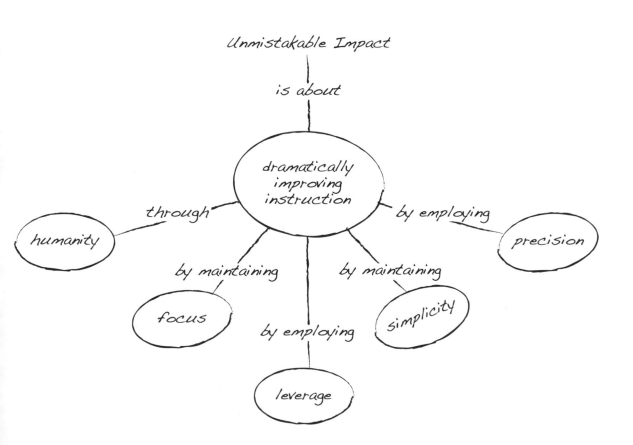

I've had the pleasure of working with some astonishingly good people from the Beaverton, Oregon, School District. Three times a year, on their own time, instructional coaches Susan, Michelle, Jenny, Lea, and Rich come to the Kansas Coaching Project at The University of Kansas Center for Research on Learning to collaborate with my colleagues and me. They come for one reason: they want to become better instructional coaches.

Our meetings are highlight days for me even though what we do is fairly simple. Most of the time, the coaches watch themselves doing their work on video[1] and discuss the strengths and weaknesses of what they see themselves doing. This work is not easy. The conversations demand that the coaches be courageous, supportive, open-minded, reflective, and above all, committed to learning. Together, we take an honest look at what is working and what we can do better. They watch themselves coaching; our research team watches our ideas in action to see what works and what needs to be refined. Each day is filled with substantial reflective comments, kind words, hard truths, laughter, fun, energy, and, mostly, learning.

During one of our meetings, I decided to document what was happening, so I asked everyone to write down a few words that described how they felt. What they wrote offers some insight into what we experience.

- Learning, exploration, humbling, in awe, affirming, reflection, imperative for growth/change, helpful
- Sweaty, shaky, good, validation, curious, aha moments, respected and collegial, safe, insightful, nervous
- Pride, laughter, nervousness, sincerity, humility
- Sweaty, nerve-wracking, exposing, vulnerable . . . yet comforted, validated, supported, encouraged, learning a ton, silence is golden

Their words surface what makes our sessions together so significant—we are energized by learning with each other. Since we cannot avoid reality (it is right on the screen for all to see in the recordings of coaching sessions), our talk focuses on issues that really matter. However, because we like and respect each other, because as a community of learners we have a stake in each other's well-being, we treat each other kindly and supportively, and that tenderness toward each other makes it possible for us to feel safe

---

1. As part of our design study of coaching, the coaches use micro cameras to record every minute of their coaching practices and then review the video.

together. With a clear picture of reality and a safe setting, we learn an enormous amount.

The experiences of the Beaverton coaches put professional learning at the heart of our talk. We leave our conversations smarter, more empowered, and more aware of our mutual humanity. Learning fuels our talk and makes us more alive. This kind of learning—learning that is safe, humane, empowering, and guided by a vivid awareness of current reality—should be a driving force for humanizing professional learning in schools. Indeed, I believe that schools will only become the learning places our children deserve when our professional learning embodies this kind of humane learning. I've written this book to suggest how such learning might occur.

The Best Jobs

Most of us can think of a few elements we'd like to experience in a fulfilling, productive, and happy career. The best jobs involve frequent, supportive, encouraging, and warmhearted conversations like those created by the instructional coaches from Beaverton. The best workplaces are electric with learning, with the buzz of new ideas, the inherent joy of growth. In the most rewarding work, we use our knowledge, minds, and hearts to do something that contributes significantly to the greater good.

Teachers should have many opportunities for this kind of meaningful work, involving positive conversations, personal learning, and contributing to the greater good. By continually exploring new ways of reaching students, teachers can see their classrooms as learning laboratories where their own professional learning mirrors their students' academic and life learning. By empowering students to be masters of language, to transcend their social status, and to love learning, educators have a marvelous opportunity to create a brighter future for their students and society at large.

Unfortunately, far too often, teaching does not feel like the best job in the world. Too frequently, conversation between educators is negative and unpleasant, with more eye rolling than nods of appreciation. Too often, educators, worn down by continual social and professional criticism (from politicians, journalists, parents, administrators, students, and others), slowly stop trying to improve. Defeated by the roadblocks that keep them from having the impact they hope to have on students, and naturally determined to protect their self-esteem, educators may adopt a defensive stance, blaming others for their lack of success rather than asking what they and their peers can do to reach more children. Feeling frustrated and defeated, many of these educators give up and stop their own learning. When teachers stop learning, so do students. When schools stop learning, our students and society as a whole suffer.

The Failure of the American School System

During my workshops, I often play a recording of a 15-year-old ninth-grade student, Tyshon, as he struggles to read a few hundred words written well below his grade level. Tyshon is able to sound out most of the words, and bit by bit, word by word, he makes his way through a paragraph about a family of geese, each syllable another mountain to be climbed. At times, Tyshon sighs deeply as he struggles through or mispronounces words such as *signaled, immediately, trio, waddle,* and *children.* While Tyshon eventually gets to the end of the paragraph, he has little understanding of what he has just read.

When workshop participants listen to Tyshon read, they quickly become silent. They know that Tyshon, even if he is totally committed to learning, is up against an enormous challenge. Every day, when he sits down to read—and he'll need to read almost every day in every class—he is reminded of his reading challenges. It is quite possible that he will fail a pop quiz after spending hours on preparatory reading, only to be told, "If you want to pass the class, you'll need to do the reading."

I think the workshop participants fall silent when they listen to Tyshon because they know that they have students like him in their school. They also know that he probably isn't going to make it. Even if he is very committed to graduating high school, he will eventually find his failure too frustrating, and he will drop out.

Unfortunately, Tyshon is not an isolated case. The statistics on students in American schools are frightening. Numerous extensive and comprehensive studies of the U.S. school system make it clear that our schools are not preparing our students to graduate and succeed. Here are just a few of the findings:

- Every year, over 1.2 million students—that's 7,000 every school day—do not graduate from high school on time (Alliance for Excellent Education, 2005).
- Nationwide, only about 70 percent of students earn their high school diplomas. Among minority students, only 57.8 percent of Hispanic, 43.4 percent of African American, and 49.3 percent of American Indian and Alaska Native students graduate with a regular diploma, compared to 76.2 percent of white students

and 80.2 percent of Asian Americans (Alliance for Excellent Education, 2005).

- Only 29 percent of America's eighth-grade public school students meet the National Assessment of Educational Progress (NAEP) standard of reading proficiency for their grade level (U.S. Department of Education, 2007).
- About two-thirds of prison inmates are high school dropouts, and one-third of all juvenile offenders read below the fourth-grade level (Haynes, 2007).
- The Organisation for Economic Co-operation and Development (OECD) reports that the United States ranks 16th out of 21 OECD countries with respect to high school graduation rates (Kirsch, Braun, Yamamoto, & Sum, 2007).
- Among U.S. students, 71 percent told the Public Agenda Foundation that they only do the bare minimum to get by (Hussey & Allen, 2006).
- Fewer than half of all high school graduates are prepared for basic college-level math (Kadlac & Friedman, 2008).
- According to several studies, only one in five minority students who receive a high school diploma are ready to go to college (Williams, 2009).
- Too many new teachers, 14 percent, leave by the end of their first year; 30 percent have left within three years; and nearly 50 percent have left by the end of their fifth year of teaching (Alliance for Excellent Education, 2005).
- Unless current trends change, more than 12 million students will drop out during the course of the next decade—at a loss to the nation of more than $3 trillion (Alliance for Excellent Education, 2005). To put that number into perspective, the president's proposed fiscal year 2009 budget for the entire federal government—including defense spending, Social Security, health care, education, NASA, and everything else—was $3.1 trillion (Stout & Pear, 2008).
- If the nation had graduated 100 percent of its high school students 10 years ago, the money the additional graduates would have put back into the economy would have covered the entire cost of running the federal government in 2009 (Amos, 2008).

Unmistakable Impact

These data are overwhelming, disturbing, even frightening; and not surprisingly, they have prompted many to seek someone to blame.

Democracy, after all, as Laurence J. Peter has stated, is "a process by which the people are free to choose the person who will get the blame" (Lummis, 1996, p. 6).

When it comes to the crisis in schools, most of us have been indicted. Parents, television, central office, the government, the unions, teachers, we are all blamed, and of course the blame is usually misguided and unfair.

Rather than pinning the blame on someone, a more productive approach is to look for ways to make things better. One area we can improve in schools is professional learning. In interviews with more than 300 teachers about professional learning across Canada and the United States, the one finding that surfaces from those conversations is that traditional forms of professional learning (workshops without follow-up) do not make an impact on teaching or student learning.

This book proposes Impact Schools, where every aspect of professional learning is designed to have an unmistakable, positive impact on teaching and, hence, student learning. I am convinced we can radically improve how well our students learn and perform if our schools become the kind of learning places (for students *and* adults) our students deserve. Students will not be energized, thrilled, and empowered by learning until educators are energized, thrilled, and empowered by learning. When all educators engage in humane professional learning that empowers them to embrace proven teaching methods, we can move closer to the goal of every student receiving excellent instruction in every class every day.

Core Concepts of an Impact School

This book provides a simple map for creating the kind of schools our students and our teachers deserve. The professional learning occurring in Impact Schools is built around the following five concepts: humanity, focus, leverage, simplicity, and precision.

Humanity

When leaders and policy makers come face to face with the challenges that exist in American schools, many are tempted to propose and promote draconian methods designed to force teachers to learn new programs and hold teachers accountable for implementing them. Driven by their noble, passionate desire to improve children's lives, people talk tough about school reform. "We don't have time to ask for input; our teachers just need to follow the same script," they might say. "The program provides the script and the pacing guide, and teachers just need to do it exactly how it is spelled out with fidelity." "Teachers should be ashamed of these scores, and if they refuse to adopt this program, there is no place for them in this school."

I understand the power of the moral purpose behind these comments, and I share the leaders' desire to move schools forward as quickly as possible. However, I fear that the strategy of telling teachers what to do and making sure they do often by punitive measures is one of the reasons why schools do not move forward (Payne, 2008). When we take the humanity out of professional learning, we ignore the complexity of any helping relationship, and we make it almost impossible for learning to occur.

Humanity is not a concept we hear a lot of when people talk about professional learning, but I believe the absence of humanity within professional learning is precisely why it frequently fails. What is humanity? We can get a better understanding of the concept by looking at its opposite. According to the standard U.S. dictionary, to dehumanize means to "deprive of positive human values." Similarly, the *Oxford English Dictionary* defines *dehumanize* as "to deprive of human character or attributes." Wikipedia, on March 5, 2010, defined *dehumanization* as

> the process by which members of a group of people assert the "inferiority" of another group through subtle or overt acts or statements. Dehumanization may be directed by an organization (such as a state) or may be the composite of individual sentiments and actions.

The opposite of dehumanize, then, is to recognize the inherent value of others and to celebrate positive human values, such as empathy, support, love, trust, and respect. Margaret Wheatley (Wheatley & Kellner-Rogers, 1996) describes what a humane way of organizing might look like:

> There is a simpler way to organize human endeavor. It requires being in the world without fear. Being in the world with play and creativity. Seeking after what's possible. Being willing to learn and be surprised . . . This simpler way summons forth what is best about us. It asks us to understand human nature differently, more optimistically. It identifies us as creative. It acknowledges that we seek after meaning. It asks us to be less

serious, yet more purposeful, about our work and lives. It does not separate play from the nature of being. (p. 5)

Professional learning that dehumanizes its participants carries the seeds of its own failure. When a select few do the thinking for others, when people are forced to comply with outside pressure with little or no input, when teachers asking genuine questions are labeled resisters, when leaders act without a true understanding of teachers' day-to-day classroom experiences, those dehumanizing practices severely damage teacher morale. And when teachers feel disillusioned and damaged by the professional learning they experience, their disappointment, hurt, and unhappiness surface in the classroom and inevitably damage the very children they are there to educate and inspire.

The necessity of putting humanity at the heart of professional learning was well stated by Parker Palmer, in his introduction to *The Courage to Teach: Exploring the Inner Landscape of a Teacher's Life*:

> In our rush to reform education, we have forgotten a simple truth: reform will never be achieved by renewing appropriations, restructuring schools, rewriting curriculum, and revising texts if we continue to demean and dishearten the human resource called teacher on whom so much depends . . . [nothing] will transform education if we fail to cherish—and challenge—the human heart that is the source of good teaching. (2007, p. 3)

In Impact Schools, educators nourish humanity by working from foundational principles that lead to respectful interchange. When people act on the partnership principles described in Chapter 2, they foster humanity by recognizing everyone's value, by encouraging and listening to others' voices, by providing real choices, and by learning in the context of real-life work. Most importantly perhaps, people working from the partnership principles see themselves as learners as much as teachers in any helping interaction.

Focus

Two interrelated components are essential for schools to achieve their potential as authentic, meaningful, joyful places of learning. First, like the coaches from Beaverton, educators need to engage in frequent, positive, useful, and humanizing learning experiences. For that to happen, a second component is essential: schools must focus their efforts. Surrounded by countless barriers, teaching will not improve unless the professional learning resources in schools work in concert, supporting, aligning, and implementing change.

In an Impact School, everyone works together in very specific ways. This involves several forces for change introduced below and described in detail in Chapters 3, 4, 5, and 6 of this book. The main components of focused professional learning are (a) a one-page Instructional Improvement Target, (b) principals, (c) workshops, (d) teams, (e) instructional coaches, and (f) district leaders.

A One-Page Instructional Improvement Target

If a school is going to become an Impact School, a school that is passionately committed to dramatically improving professional learning, everyone in the school must have a clear understanding of the goal and how to get there.

Unfortunately, traditional school improvement plans are often very complex, and because they focus on literacy and mathematics to meet the demands of No Child Left Behind, they frequently overlook core instructional practices. That complexity makes it difficult for everyone in the school to have a shared understanding of the plan, and that lack of understanding leads to a lack of implementation. As Doug Reeves has remarked, "The size and the prettiness of the plan is inversely related to the quality of action and the impact on student learning" (2009, p. 81). Simple plans, with clear goals, make it easier for everyone in a school to work together to dramatically improve teaching.

Principals

The single most important factor in moving schools forward, according to Michael Fullan (2010a), is that the principal is also a learner. In Impact Schools, principals have at least four capabilities:

1. a deep understanding of the teaching practices described in the school improvement plan;

2. a precise understanding of what teaching looks like when teachers use the practices effectively;

3. a complete knowledge of how the school's various professional learning processes (workshops, teams, and coaching) can help each teacher achieve mastery of the practices described in the plan; and

4. the emotional intelligence to guide teachers to use the professional learning supports successfully.

Workshops

The assumption that one-shot workshops can lead to lasting change is naïve and perhaps destructive. Marshall Goldsmith—named by *The London Times* and *Forbes* as one of the 15 most influential business leaders—has studied the impact of his consulting firm's workshops, and he summarizes his findings as follows:

> I [have gone] back to many of my clients and assembled data that answered the question "Does anyone ever really change?" . . . Our database has grown to more than 250,000 respondents. My conclusion is unequivocal. *Very few people achieve positive, lasting change without ongoing follow-up.* (2010, p. 36)

Lasting change does not occur without focus, support, and systemwide accountability. However, this does not mean that workshops should never be used. Workshops, as Michael Fullan (personal communication, July 18, 2010) explained to me in conversation, "introduce ideas into the system. Support is necessary to transfer talk into action, but workshops are efficient ways of starting the conversation."

Workshops chosen intentionally by leaders to inform people about the teaching practices described in the one-page Target can raise awareness and provide administrators and teachers with an overview of the appropriate practices. They can be a useful support for empowering teachers to implement the plan. However, when workshop topics are chosen carelessly, and when workshop topics do not help everyone move toward the goals of the Target, they can actually be destructive, distracting teachers from achieving the desired outcome and reinforcing low expectations for implementation.

Effective workshops focus on the Target *and* they are supported by coaching. Indeed, workshops that do not have coaching support often waste teachers' time because they rarely change the way teachers teach. If a school is offering a workshop, the school's coaches need to be masters at explaining and supporting implementation of whatever is being described during the workshop after it is over. Also, during the workshop, time should be set aside so that teachers can plan how to work with their coaches, setting goals and benchmarks and creating a step-by-step plan that will help teachers implement the practices described in the plan.

Workshops also need to be led in a manner that is consistent with good teaching, with facilitators who "walk the talk" by using learning structures, presentation skills, reflection learning practices, and the communication strategies necessary to promote clear understanding and to develop a positive learning community. Several high-leverage facilitator practices will be described in Chapter 5.

Research conducted at the Kansas Coaching Project, and described in Resource B, suggests that the way a workshop is conducted dramatically impacts (a) how much teachers learn, (b) teachers' expectations about implementing, (c) how engaged teachers are, and (d) how much they enjoy the learning experience.

Teams

In Impact Schools, teams of teachers come together to intentionally plan how to use the high-leverage teaching practices, such as guiding questions, formative assessment, effective questions, or behavioral expectations, described in the Target. Intensive learning teams, described in a later chapter, bring together teachers who teach the same course so that they can conduct a total makeover of their course to ensure that the curriculum is aligned with state standards, that everyone has a plan that they are committed to and that focuses on the most important learning, and to establish a procedure for ongoing focused learning about what works and what doesn't work with the class.

Leaders setting up intensive learning teams employ simple, high-leverage strategies, described in Chapter 6, to ensure that the teams are grounded in meaningful, positive, reflective conversation. They also employ collaboration structures to ensure that everyone has a say in the development of useful products, such as guiding questions, learning maps, and formative assessments that team members can use right away in their classrooms. Like workshops, intensive learning teams also set aside time for teachers and coaches to collaboratively plan how teachers will implement the products created. In Impact Schools, professional learning is structured so that teacher implementation of new practices is a given.

Instructional Coaches

All of the above components of Impact Schools will be useless without coaching to help teachers translate what is being talked about into everyday practice in the classroom. Too often, as Jeffrey Pfeffer and Robert Sutton write in *The Knowing-Doing Gap*, "one of the main barriers to turning knowledge into action is the tendency to treat talking about something as equivalent to actually doing something about it" (2000, p. 29). Instructional coaches (ICs), by providing intensive, focused support for professional learning, do "something" about change.

Following more than a decade of careful study of instructional coaching at the Kansas Coaching Project, we now have a clear picture of the characteristics of effective ICs and the specific activities they need to employ to help translate talk (taking place in workshops and team meetings) into improved teaching (every day in the classroom). Coaches, to borrow Seth Godin's (2010) phrase, are "linchpins" for successful change in school. Without coaches to provide precise instructions, to model in the classroom, to provide positive and motivating honest feedback, few new practices get implemented, and those that get implemented are usually implemented poorly (Cornett & Knight, 2009). One of the most important issues in an Impact School is hiring ICs who demonstrate the characteristics of effective coaches. These characteristics, which we have identified through a rigorous naturalistic study of effective coaches, are also described later in Chapter 4.

District Leaders

At the center of an Impact School are district leaders, led by the superintendent, who put teaching at the heart of school reform efforts. What we expect of principals as they supervise the teachers in their schools should be our expectation for all district leaders—they supportively and positively guide and monitor everyone's progress toward accomplishing the goals in the one-page plan.

Improving instruction is a complex and difficult task at the best of times. That is why we need a simple process to cut through the complexity. When principals, workshops, teams, coaches, and district leaders work together to implement a simple plan, schools can dramatically improve teaching.

Leverage

Systems thinkers such as Peter Senge (1990) have taught us about the importance of identifying the practices that have the greatest impact with the smallest effort. Since organizational improvement on the scale we are discussing here is complex, change leaders (that can include everyone working in a school) must focus on the most important variables related to change. More than two decades ago, Senge summarized this perspective:

> Small, well-focused actions can sometimes produce significant, enduring improvements, if they're in the right place. Systems thinkers refer to this as "leverage" . . . Tackling a difficult problem is often a matter of seeing where the high leverage

lies, a change which—with a minimum of effort—would lead to lasting change. (p. 64)

In their discussion of the strategies of effective change leaders, Kerry Patterson, Joseph Grenny, David Maxfield, Ron McMillan, and Al Switzler make a similar observation: "Enormous influence comes from focusing on just a few *vital behaviors*. Even the most pervasive problems will often yield to changes in a handful of high-leverage behaviors. Find these, and you've found the beginning of influence" (2008, p. 23).

Certain central teaching practices are most likely to have a significant impact on student learning. Those practices, which I'll describe in more detail in my next book, *Unmistakable Impact in the Classroom*, relate to (a) content planning, (b) assessment for learning, (c) instruction, and (d) community building.

In an Impact School, all teachers (a) know and teach according to an instructional plan that is aligned with state standards, (b) know how well each student is performing, (c) use a variety of instructional practices to ensure students master and internalize learning, and (d) implement community-building strategies that create safe, positive, and productive learning communities. In Impact Schools, all teachers are working toward mastering those high-leverage teaching practices to ensure that every student, every day, in every class, receives high-quality instruction.

The concept of leverage also applies to professional learning. In Impact Schools, educators recognize that some forms of professional learning have more impact than others. Thus, Impact Schools do not offer one-shot, stand-alone workshops, but workshops that are tied to other forms of professional learning. Similarly, in Impact Schools, learning that occurs in professional learning communities, workshops, and other learning situations is always supported by instructional coaching.

Simplicity

The challenge of improving instruction in schools is so complex that likely only simple plans will work. However, simple is not synonymous with simplistic. A simplistic plan might be a dummied-down plan, one that removes complexity by removing sophistication. Simple is just the opposite. A simple plan is one that removes distractions so that only what matters remains. A simple plan finds order in complexity. Simplicity is working a problem until the way out becomes clear and never settling for a lack of clarity. As Bill Jensen writes in *Simplicity*, "Our biggest limit is no longer the reach of our imagination. It's now our inability to order, make sense of, and connect everything that demands our attention. We are failing to make the complex clear" (2000, p. 21).

Finding simple solutions for the complex challenges of school improvement is no easy task. Consider, for example, all of the various approaches to instruction that a school might consider implementing. In a typical week, a school leader will receive dozens of e-mails and several catalogues of teaching practices, and over a year will be presented with literally thousands of options for instructional improvement. Consider, too, the complexities of how people experience professional learning. (More on this in Chapter 2.) Further, as we will explore in later chapters, any helping interaction is complicated by issues related to identity, professionalism, status, change, and motivation. Add to that the different, changing needs of the students in each classroom and the complicated and changing desires of the community.

Trying to address all of these factors, and more, is not for the weak of heart, and complex challenges can lead to complex solutions. No wonder many school improvement plans are so elaborate that they look more like government bills than plans for action. Jensen captures the challenge:

> The universal problem seems to be how hard people have to work just to figure out what to do. Task work has been streamlined, but knowledge work had become more cluttered and confusing. Making the right choices-fast, while everything's changing is now the toughest part of getting our work done. (2000, p. 10)

The real truth is that only simple solutions will get the job done. Change leaders need to push for clear goals, clear action plans, and clear methods. This book (focusing on how workshops, professional learning communities, administrators, and coaches can be integrated and aligned for maximum impact) is intended to be a simple solution to complex challenges.

Precision

A concept that is related to simplicity is precision. Teaching, whether we are teaching students, teachers, administrators, or other educators, requires precise explanations. When we explain any new teaching practice, our explanations must be clear and easy to act on or they will not transfer to the classroom. Thus, coaches, professional developers, administrators, and other change leaders must have deep, complete understanding of the practices described in the

Target, *and* they must be able to clearly explain those practices so that everyone can learn, internalize, and use them.

Atul Gawande writes about the importance of precision in his book, *The Checklist Manifesto* (2010), a *New York Times* bestseller written about the power of checklists. Gawande's studies of doctors and medical teams for the World Health Organization offer compelling evidence that precise explanations embodied in checklists can save hundreds of lives and millions of dollars. Checklists provide explicit descriptions of practices to produce a greater likelihood of a widespread, shared understanding of those practices.

Checklists in medicine, and by extension other professions, according to Gawande, are not intended to "dummy down" the sophistication of professional practice. Rather, checklists take care of the simple stuff so that professionals can focus their intellectual efforts on more important aspects of practice. Also, checklists are not created to be followed to the letter by everyone at all times. Professionals need to modify checklists, so they are tailor-made for the unique needs of their own situations. In a school, this means that teachers and coaches must think carefully about whether they need to adapt practices so that they better meet the unique needs of each teacher's students. The goal of precise explanations is, as content coaching expert Lucy West (2009) has said, not "mindless fidelity" but rather "mindful engagement," and teachers need to make adaptations. At the same time, the goal is not "wishy-washy" explanations. Precision that honors teacher professionalism is what we want.

To be precise, change leaders must do what is necessary to fully understand and be able to describe practices. Thus, they need to read instructional manuals inside out, attend workshops on the topics on the Target (to the point of redundancy!), watch multiple examples of teachers implementing practices, and collaborate with others to draft and refine documents, such as checklists, and ensure clear, precise explanations of the practices.

This book explains in simple, practical steps how these core concepts of humanity, focus, leverage, simplicity, and precision can be integrated to dramatically improve student and adult learning. An Impact School provides a humanizing approach to professional learning that focuses on high-leverage teaching, leadership, and professional learning practices that can be precisely implemented using simple methods.

What You Will Find in This Book

The central theme, here, is that if teachers are participating in professional learning activities, those activities (principal observation, coaching, workshops, intensive learning teams, or some other form of professional learning) must have an unmistakable positive impact on how teachers teach and how students learn. For this to occur, professional learning must be designed and delivered for impact. The chapters in the book describe how this might be accomplished.

Chapter 2, Partnership, describes the factors that complicate any helping relationship and introduces the partnership approach, the grounding philosophy behind the Impact School approaches to addressing the complexity of helping.

Chapter 3, Principals, explains why the single, most important factor in an Impact School is a principal who is an instructional leader. The chapter summarizes what principals need to know about instruction, how they should conduct teacher evaluations and brief observations, so they deeply understand how well each teacher is implementing practices in the plan, and what they should do to guide teachers to move toward mastery of the practices in the plan.

Chapter 4, Instructional Coaching, describes how coaches can enroll teachers, collaboratively identify what to work on, explain those practices, mediate so that teachers can fit the practice to their classroom, model the practices so that teachers can see them used in their classrooms with their students, and observe, explore, and question to dig deeper into the implementation of the practices.

Chapter 5, Workshops That Make an Impact, describes how workshops are effective at introducing ideas into a school system and how they can be tied to other components of Impact Schools—in particular, instructional coaching—to produce lasting change. The chapter also introduces best practices that workshop facilitators can adopt to improve the learning experiences of their participants.

Chapter 6, Intensive Learning Teams, describes how to design and lead intensive learning teams—grade-alike teams who work together to makeover a course they teach. The chapter explains how to structure intensive learning teams, so members can develop authentic positive team values, have numerous opportunities to shape the tools being developed, work together efficiently, and create powerful tools—such as formative assessments, learning maps, and guiding questions—that everyone can use in their classrooms to teach children better.

Chapter 7, Partnership Communication, describes five high-leverage strategies that educational leaders can use to shorten the gap between themselves and others, and it provides easy-to-implement tactics people can use to dramatically improve their emotional intelligence. The five strategies are (1) listen, (2) ask good questions, (3) find common ground, (4) control difficult emotions, and (5) love your partners.

Each chapter begins with a mind map that graphically depicts the key concepts in the chapter. Each chapter also contains tools to help make the ideas more accessible. Other elements include a summary of the chapter under the heading To Sum Up and a Going Deeper section that introduces other resources readers can explore to extend their knowledge of the ideas and strategies discussed.

Learning is one of the most motivating, energizing, and humanizing experiences. When we are learning, our world expands, our mind is fully engaged, our emotions are moved and, sometimes, our souls are touched. Learning is an integral part of our humanity, one of the primary ways in which we find joy. When schools embrace authentic professional learning that humanizes, energizes, and motivates, everyone benefits. An Impact School puts authentic learning at its heart. This book tells you what you need to do to create one.

To Sum Up

- A mountain of evidence suggests that our schools are not as effective as they should be, but there is much we can do to improve.
- This book proposes Impact Schools as one way to achieve the goal of every student receiving excellent instruction every day in every class.
- Impact Schools
  - put humanity at the center by recognizing and celebrating the professionalism of teachers;
  - achieve results by focusing principals, coaches, workshops, and teams on achieving the Instructional Improvement Target;
  - seek out and implement high-leverage teaching practices and high-leverage professional learning practices;
  - address the complexity of school improvement by refining plans to be as clear, actionable, and simple as possible; and
  - achieve improvement through precise explanations of practices.

Going Deeper

Bernard Chartres' famous phrase about the pursuit of knowledge, "we stand on the shoulders of giants," is especially true of this book, its core themes, and numerous strategies. Several books provide the foundation for the ideas in this chapter, including the following.

Humanity

Parker Palmer's *The Courage to Teach* (2007) is a beautiful, realistic, celebration of the humanity at the heart of teaching and our own journeys to live authentic lives. Margaret Wheatley's equally beautiful *Turning to One Another* (2009) explains how our conversations with each other, and especially our listening to one another, can lead to more human, respectful, and loving interactions.

Focus

Michael Fullan's work has been the major influence on this book. Fullan's three most recent books, *The Six Secrets of Change* (2008), *All Systems Go* (2010a), and *Motion Leadership* (2010b), provide a theoretical framework for understanding many of the nuts-and-bolts ideas here.

Leverage

I first learned about the concept of leverage from Peter Senge's *The Fifth Discipline*. (1990). Kerry Patterson, Joseph Grenny, David Maxfield, Ron McMillan, and Al Switzler's *Influencer* (2008) introduces the idea of vital behaviors along with a great deal of valuable information about change built around several fascinating case studies.

Simplicity

Bill Jensen's *Simplicity* (2000) offers an outstanding discussion of why simplicity is important and how we can achieve it. John Maeda's *The Laws of Simplicity* (2006) offers eight elegant laws that can help us all create simpler and better tools and solutions. For example, one law is "Reduce: the simplest way to achieve simplicity is through thoughtful reduction."

Precision

Atul Gawande's *Checklist Manifesto* (2010) is a fascinating account of the power of precision. His book details how the lowly checklist can save thousands of lives and billions of dollars. His *Better* (2007) is also a very useful book for anyone leading change.

2

Partnership

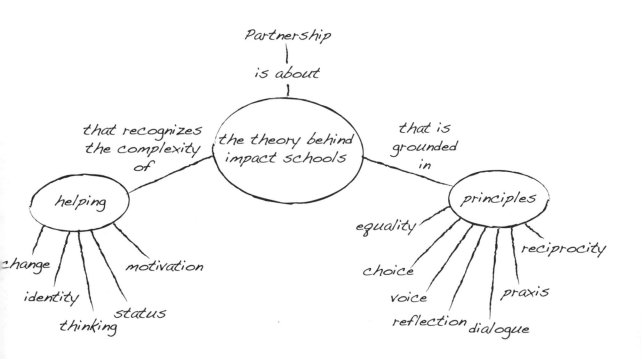

During one of our instructional coaching institutes at the Kansas Coaching Project, a charming, warmhearted leader from a struggling inner-city school said what many people have said to me in one way or another over the years:

> We can't wait. Our kids need to do better today. We can't wait to be nice to teachers. We can't do all this touchy-feely, listening stuff. Our teachers need to get better now. Or they need to be gone. Because our kids deserve better.

I am moved by her passion and her love for the children in her district, and I wholeheartedly agree that every student deserves nothing less than excellent instruction every day in every classroom. I also realize that instructional improvement would be much easier if we could just give teachers a script to follow. But teachers are not workers on assembly lines, and they are not working with inanimate objects. Teachers are living, breathing, complicated professionals, and they work with living, breathing, complicated young human beings. To bring about the improvements we hope to see, we need to recognize—in fact, honor—the complexity of providing support within professional relationships.

Professional learning fails when change leaders underestimate how complicated change can be. Just telling people what to do and expecting them to do it might work for simple tasks like stocking shelves in a grocery store, but such an approach is seldom motivating or effective for professionals. In education, effective professional learning must be grounded in an understanding of how complex helping relationships can be. Failing to understand the nature of helping relationships can doom leaders of change.

This chapter introduces five factors that are at play in almost all helping relationships—change, identity, thinking, status, and motivation. Additionally, the chapter introduces the seven partnership principles, the theoretical framework behind Impact Schools, and a simple response to the complexity of helping.

Helping Others

Change

James Prochaska and his colleagues (Prochaska, Norcross, & DiClemente, 1994) at the University of Rhode Island have conducted more than 55 clinical studies of more than 1,000 people attempting to make major changes in their lives. Their findings have contributed greatly to our understanding of how people experience change. According to the researchers, change involves six stages:

1. Precontemplation, when we are unaware of our need for change

2. Contemplation, when we weigh the advantages and disadvantages of changing to a new way of doing something

3. Preparation, when we prepare to implement a change

4. Action, when we implement a change

5. Maintenance, where we sustain our implementation plan

6. Termination, when we are no longer changing because we have completed the change process

Change leaders are often most troubled by the researchers' findings about precontemplation. According to Prochaska and his colleagues (1994), many people are simply unaware that they need to change. Quoting G. K. Chesteron in their book, the authors highlight the precontemplative's predicament: "It isn't that they can't see the solution. It is that they can't see the problem" (p. 40). Precontemplators, Prochaska and colleagues comment, "love denial . . . Despite all evidence to the contrary, they can't admit to their problems" (p. 83). Most of us, I suspect, are precontemplative about some aspect of our behavior.

In our study of teachers and coaches, we also see plenty of evidence to support the suggestion that teachers can be precontemplative. Educators, like everyone else, can be blissfully unaware of their own need to improve. As a result, when teachers watch video recordings of themselves, they are often shocked to see that the way they teach or coach bears little resemblance to how they imagine it to be. For example, when they watch recordings of themselves teaching, teachers who believe they are very positive can be shocked to discover that they correct students six times as much as they praise them. Similarly, coaches who think they are excellent listeners, realize, after they watch recordings of themselves coaching, that they talk 90 percent of the time.

I have had this experience. When I have watched video recordings of myself interacting during meetings or discussing home renovations with my wife (yes, I really have recorded such a conversations with Jenny!), I have been shocked and, in truth, ashamed to see how frequently I interrupt, how poorly I listen. Watching myself on video feels like hearing my voice on a recording—multiplied to the power of 10. Change leaders need to recognize that the teachers with whom they work often do not see what everyone else sees.

A Simple Truth About Helping: People often do not know that they need help.

Status

When two people come together to discuss professional practice, there is always the possibility that issues of status will arise. Edgar Schein makes this case in his book *Helping: How to Offer, Give, and Receive Help* (2009):

> All human relationships are about status positioning and what sociologists call "situational proprieties." It is human to want to be granted the status and position that we feel we deserve, no matter how high or low it might be, and we want to do what is situationally appropriate. We are either trying to get ahead or stay even, and we measure all interactions by how much we have lost or gained. (p. xi)

According to Schein, we feel a conversation has been successful if we are given the status we think we deserve.

> When a conversation has not been equitable, we sometimes feel offended. That usually means that the value we have claimed for ourselves has not been acknowledged, or that the other person or persons did not realize who we were or how important our communication was. (p. 30)

Schein (2009) cites Thomas Harris, who suggests that when we interact with others, we have the choice to act as a "child," "adult," or a "parent." "In general, if the helper acts parental, the client may feel patronized; if the helper takes on the role of the child, the client is confused and wonders if the roles need to be reversed" (p. 25). Schein suggests that helping is "optimally an adult-to-adult activity" (p. 25). The subtle dance of roles and status is at play whenever a teacher and coach or principal come together to discuss instruction. The very act of helping, Schein (2009) says, puts the helper "one up" in a relationship, and because a teacher most likely does not want to be "one down" in the relationship, he or she may resist a coach's suggestions just to retain equal status. Schein, again, describes this situation well:

Helping situations are intrinsically unbalanced and role-ambiguous. Emotionally and socially, when you ask for help you are putting yourself "one down." It is a temporary loss of status and self-esteem not to know what to do next or to be unable to do it. It is a loss of independence to have someone else advise you, heal you, minister to you, help you up, support you, even serve you. (p. 32)

At the Kansas Coaching Project, we see the impact of status in coaching relationships when we watch video recordings of coaches and teachers interacting. Effective coaches intuitively recognize that they need to, as Schein says, "equalibrate" the relationship, so they are quick to downplay their own status and elevate the teacher, congratulating the teacher on their skill, calling attention to their collaborating teacher's insights during conversation, and downplaying their own skill and success. Skillful coaches use a variety of subtle communication strategies to create equality between themselves and their collaborating teachers.

> **A Simple Truth About Helping:**
> If people feel "one down," they will resist help.

Identity

A third factor complicating helping relationships is the way our understanding of who we are, our identity, is intimately connected with the work we do. As we move through the day-to-day ambiguities of our lives, experiencing the inevitable joys and frustrations, we have to make sense of our experiences. Our days are filled with successes and failures, positive and negative interactions, and over time we create our own story of why life occurs the way it does. Douglas Stone, Bruce Patton, Sheila Heen, and Roger Fisher from the Harvard Negotiation Project, suggest that three identity issues are particularly common: "Am I competent?" "Am I a good person?" and "Am I worthy of love?" (2000, p. 112).

Our understanding of how good and competent we are is frequently tied to our success or failure in our work. In schools, this means that teachers' identities are wrapped up in how they perceive their ability to teach. As Parker Palmer has commented, "No matter how technical my subject may be, the things I teach are things I care about—and what I care about helps define my selfhood" (1998, p. 17).

For many of us, whether in the classroom, in our homes, or in society, our stories about ourselves can be biased slightly in our favor. Consequently, in our minds, we are more often the hero than the villain. We invest a great deal of psychic energy explaining why we are not at fault in a particular situation. In order to protect their self-esteem, their identity, many teachers over time may develop stories that explain why they are not achieving their goals. Of course, some or all of the stories might be true—students lack motivation, the curriculum is impossible to implement, there are too many distractions, the class size is too large, the parents should be more involved in their children's learning—but the most important issue is that the stories we create as we develop our identity become very important in our understanding of who we are in the world. Thus, if we comment on how a person teaches, we are saying something that will likely be taken personally.

A conversation someone has with me about how I teach is much more than a talk about some abstract technical skill—like how to program a DVR. A conversation about how I teach brings me face to face with who I am as person. Stone, Patton, Heen, and Fisher have written about the anxieties we might feel when we participate in conversations that threaten our identity:

> Our anxiety results not just from having to face the other person, but from having to face *ourselves*. The conversation has the potential to disrupt our sense of who we are in the world, or to highlight what we hope we are but fear we are not. The conversation poses a threat to our identity—the story we tell ourselves about ourselves— and having our identity threatened can be profoundly disturbing. (2000, pp. 112–113)

A Simple Truth About Helping:
Criticism is taken personally.

Thinking

Thomas Davenport (2005) has described the attributes of knowledge workers, professionals who use their knowledge, skills, strategies, and brainpower to do their work. Knowledge workers, Davenport tells us, are people who think for a living. Clearly, a teacher teaching 32 children, who is trying to be clear, to keep each student engaged, and to gauge how well each student is learning, is a prime example of a knowledge worker.

In his book *Thinking for a Living,* Davenport (2005) reports on interviews and surveys he has conducted to identify the attributes of knowledge workers. "One important characteristic of knowledge workers," he reports,

> is that they don't like to be told what to do. Thinking for a living engenders thinking for oneself. Knowledge workers are paid for their education, experience, and expertise, so it is not surprising that they take offense when someone else rides roughshod over their intellectual territory. (p. 15)

These findings are not surprising. One of the most rewarding aspects of work is tackling challenging problems. People enjoy the chance to use their brains to invent an elegant solution to a thorny problem. Work that is at an appropriate level of challenge (not so easy as to be boring, not so challenging as to cause frustration) is a central part of a meaningful career (Csikszentmihalyi, 1990), so trying to take the thinking out of teaching runs the risk of removing much of the joy as well.

One way to test out Davenport's (2005) ideas is to consider your own work. What would your response be if you were given a script to follow each day, if you were told exactly what to do hour by hour, and indeed,

> **A Simple Truth About Helping:** If someone else does all the thinking for them, people will resist.

you were watched to ensure that you did what you were supposed to do? My guess is you wouldn't like it; indeed, you might vigorously resist any attempt at reducing the complexity of your work. Of course, today, many teachers are confronted with scripts and pacing guides that they are told to follow to the letter, along with other well-intentioned but problematic models for change. Not surprisingly, when the thinking is taken out of teaching, teachers resist.

Motivation

Imagine that a man, let's call him Rocky, reads an article about a new diet in an airline magazine as he flies home. Concerned about his weight, Rocky becomes engrossed in the article, and by the time the plane lands, he has decided that he will adopt the diet. On the way home, he stops at his local Whole Foods store, picks up all the right foods for the diet, and takes them home, looking forward to his new, healthier way of living.

Now, imagine that a second person, let's call him T-Bone, flies on the same plane and reads the same magazine. T-Bone also becomes engrossed in the writing about the new diet, but he is interested for different reasons. Concerned about his wife's weight, T-Bone decides this diet is exactly what she needs. On the way home, T-Bone stops at the same store, buys the same food, and brings it home to his unsuspecting wife, telling her that he has discovered the perfect diet for her.

Who do you think is more likely to stick with the diet, Rocky or T-Bone's wife? What the research on motivation says is that Rocky has a much better chance of success because he has chosen the goal. I suspect we probably don't need research to figure this one out. Indeed, some of us might worry that T-Bone could be in some trouble for showing up with such a plan. Goals that others choose for us seldom motivate us to change.

In *Drive: The Surprising Truth About What Motivates Us* (2009), Daniel Pink makes the same point. After reviewing hundreds of research articles about motivation and goals, Pink concludes that "Goals that people set for themselves and that are devoted to attaining mastery are usually healthy. But goals imposed by others—sales targets, quarterly reports, standardized test scores, and so on—can sometimes have dangerous side effects" (p. 50).

Pink describes many of the dangerous side effects of simplistic forms of goal setting and motivation. Traditional motivation, he says, "wasn't exactly ennobling. It suggested that, in the end, human beings aren't much different from horses—that the way to get us moving in the right direction is by dangling a crunchier carrot or wielding a sharper stick" (pp. 19–20).

In the research literature, Pink finds ample evidence to show that traditional forms of motivation, using extrinsic rewards, can make things worse. For example, he cites Deci's meta-analysis of 128 research studies showing that rewards decrease intrinsic motivation. He also cites Russian economist Anton Suvorov's conclusions, which, as Pink states, "make sense to any parent who's tried to get her kids to empty the garbage . . . By offering a reward, a principal signals to the agent that the task is undesirable" (p. 54).

The Seven Deadly Flaws of Extrinsic Rewards According to Daniel Pink

1. They can extinguish intrinsic motivation.

2. They can diminish performance.

3. They can crush creativity.

4. They can crowd out good behavior.

5. They can encourage cheating, shortcuts, and unethical behavior.

6. They can become addictive.

7. They can foster short-term thinking. (2009, p. 59)

Pink adds another layer by distinguishing between "algorithmic" and "heuristic" work. Drawing on the findings of behavioral scientists, he explains that "An algorithmic task is one in which you follow a set of established instructions down a single pathway to one conclusion. That is, there's an algorithm for solving it" (p. 29). In contrast, "A heuristic task is the opposite. Precisely because no algorithm exists for it, you have to experiment with possibilities and devise a novel solution" (p. 29).

Researchers, such as Teresa Amabile at Harvard Business School, have found that while rewards work well for algorithmic tasks, they can be, as Pink (2009) notes, "devastating for heuristic ones" (p. 30) since they reduce intrinsic motivation and the value people assign to each task. People need to receive equitable payment for their work, of course, but beyond that, professionals doing non-routine work are usually motivated in other ways.

According to Pink (2009), three factors especially motivate people doing heuristic work: mastery, autonomy, and purpose. First, people doing complex work are motivated by the feeling they get by doing a job well. Indeed, the ongoing pursuit of mastery is an important part of a professional's motivation. Second, to accomplish mastery, people need

> **A Simple Truth About Helping:** People aren't motivated by other people's goals.

to have the freedom to choose their goals and how to achieve them. Autonomy, Pink suggests, "appears to be a human concept rather than a western one . . . Even in high-poverty non-Western locales like Bangladesh, social scientists have found that autonomy is something that people seek and that improves their lives" (p. 90). Finally, people are motivated by doing work that makes a difference. When all is said and done, most of us want to make an impact. Mihalyi Csikszentmihalyi, quoted by Pink, puts it this way: "One cannot lead a life that is truly excellent without feeling that one belongs to something greater and more permanent than oneself" (p. 143).

If we pay no attention to the importance of mastery, autonomy, and purpose for the professionals in our schools, if we assume we simply need to prescribe to teachers what they need to do and then hold them accountable to do it, we trample over much of what we scientists have learned about motivation. We do so, it must be added, at our peril.

Five Simple Truths About Helping

1. People often do not know that they need help.
2. If people feel "one down," they will resist help.
3. Criticism is taken personally.
4. If someone else does all the thinking for them, people will resist.
5. People aren't motivated by other people's goals.

When administrators, coaches, and teachers set out to improve instruction, they are up against a formidable challenge: how to help in a way that makes an impact and still respectfully acknowledge the complexities of helping. I propose a simple solution: we should take the partnership approach and treat adults like adults. The rest of this chapter describes what an adult to adult conversation looks like.

Partnership: The Theory Behind Impact Schools

At its core, the partnership approach is about a simple idea: treat others the way you would like to be treated. You can get an understanding of the partnership approach by considering how you would answer a simple question: "If someone was talking with you about your work, how would you like them to relate to you?" Chances are you would want them to treat you as an equal, to respect your knowledge enough to let you make some decisions about how you do your work. You would probably also want them to ask your opinion and listen to your voice, to talk with you in a way that encouraged thought and dialogue about your real-life experience. If they also demonstrated that they expected to learn from you, it would probably make it all the more likely that you would listen to them.

The partnership approach embodies all of the above ideas expressed in seven simple principles: (1) equality, (2) choice, (3) voice, (4) reflection, (5) dialogue, (6) praxis, and (7) reciprocity. These principles represent the theory that underlies professional learning in Impact Schools. I use the term *theory* here as it is defined in the *Oxford English Dictionary*, a "systematic conception or statement of the principles of something." Further, William Isaacs has described the important role that theory can play in shaping our actions:

> When we undertake any task, like run a meeting, negotiate an agreement, discipline a child—even meditate—we operate from a set of taken-for-granted rules or ideas of how to be effective. Understanding these tacit rules is what I mean by *theory*. The word *theory* comes from the same roots as the word *theater*, which means simply "to see." A theory is a way of seeing ... Without a theory, however—some way to assess what is happening—we shall be forever doomed to operate blindly, subject to chance. (1999, p. 73)

This approach is an extension of ideas first suggested in the fields of education, business, psychology, philosophy of science, and cultural anthropology in the work of authors such as Paulo Freire

(1970); Riane Eisler (1988); Michael Fullan (1993); Peter Block (1993); Edgar Schein (2009); Peter Senge (1990); Richard Bernstein (1983); William Isaacs (1999); Jamie Showkeir, Marin Showkeir, and Margaret Wheatley (2008); Margaret Wheatley (2002); and Jeremy Rifkin (2009). The partnership principles, described below, stand at the heart of professional learning in Impact Schools.

Equality: Professional Learning With Teachers Rather Than Training Done to Teachers

There is a delightful scene in the movie *Il Postino,* a film about Pablo Neruda's stay on the island of Capri while he was politically exiled from Chile. In the film, Neruda has a conversation about poetry with the young man who delivers his mail—the postman who is the focus of the film. It is hard to imagine a more unequal situation: Neruda the great poet—Gabriel Garcia Marquez called him the greatest poet of the 20th century in *any* language—and the postman who barely has basic literacy. However, they have a delightful conversation that embodies the principle of equality.

What strikes me about the scene is the respectful way that the poet interacts with the young man. The postman struggles to find words, stumbling and apologizing his way through the conversation. However, Neruda's every word and action encourage the postman to speak. Despite the profound difference in their knowledge about poetry, Neruda gives all of his attention to the postman. Sitting on a beach, Neruda turns his body toward the postman, listens with great care and empathy, encourages him, and treats him like an equal. Neruda, too, is rewarded because the conversation is joyful, thought provoking, and warmhearted. After their talk, both partners are encouraged, happy, and closer to being friends.

People who embrace the principle of equality see others, as Neruda does in this scene, as having equal value. They listen to everyone with the same care and attention. The superintendent, the experienced teacher, the paraprofessional, the new teacher one day out of college, the principal—all receive the partnership facilitator's full attention.

Equality is central within any partnership. Partners do not decide for each other; they decide together. In a true partnership, one partner does not tell the other what to do; they discuss, dialogue, and then decide together. Partners realize that they are one half of a whole, and in healthy partnerships they find that they are a lot smarter when they listen to their partner . . . when they recognize their partner as an equal.

Peter Block's Four Requirements of Partnership

In his seminal book about partnership relationships in organizations, *Stewardship,* Peter Block (1993) identified four requirements for a partnership.

Exchange of Purpose

Partnership means each of us at every level is responsible for defining vision and values. Purpose gets defined through dialogue. Let people at every level communicate about what they want to create, with each person having to make a declaration. (p. 29)

Right to Say No

Partners each have a right to say no. Saying no is the fundamental way we have of differentiating ourselves. To take away my right to say no is to claim sovereignty over me. For me to believe that I cannot say no is to yield sovereignty. (pp. 29–30)

Joint Accountability

Each person is responsible for outcomes and the current situation. There is no one else to blame . . . if people want the freedom that partnership offers, the price of that freedom is to take personal accountability for the success and failure of our unit and our community. (p. 30)

Absolute Honesty

In a partnership, not telling the truth to each other is an act of betrayal. One of the benefits of redistributing power is that people feel less vulnerable and are more honest. (pp. 30–31)

Close to half a century ago, Paulo Freire (1970) described the importance of equality and partnership in learning, emphasizing that education should be "cointentional." "Authentic education is not carried on by 'A' *for* 'B' or *by* 'A' *about* 'B,' but rather by 'A' *with* 'B'" (p. 82). For Freire, an educator's goals,

> from the outset . . . must coincide with those of the students to engage in critical thinking and the quest for mutual humanization. His effort must be imbued with a profound trust in men and their creative power. To achieve this, he must be a partner of the students in his relations with them. (p. 62)

Educators who embrace the principle of equality recognize that in a partnership, the goal is not to win the other side over to their view. Rather, the goal is to find a match between what they have to offer and what a teacher can use. In the truest sense, if a teacher does not agree with our view of the world or our perspective, in a partnership, the first step is not to argue our point more persuasively, but to try to fully understand the collaborating teacher's view or perspective.

Choice: Teachers Should Have Choice Regarding What and How They Learn

In a partnership, one individual does not make decisions for another. Because partners are equal, they make their own choices and make decisions collaboratively. Indeed, choice is essential for a fully realized life because it is through choices that we make decisions about what we do and who we are. As Freire (1970) states, "freedom . . . is the indispensable condition for the quest for human completion . . . without freedom [we] cannot exist authentically" (p. 31). Similarly Peter Block (1993) emphasizes the primacy of choice: "Partners each have a right to say no. Saying no is the fundamental way we have of differentiating ourselves. To take away my right to say no is to claim sovereignty over me . . . If we cannot say no, then saying yes has no meaning" (pp. 30–31). Without freedom to choose, we are doomed to live someone else's life.

In *The Art of Choosing*, Columbia University professor Sheena Iyengar reviews several studies and concludes that "the desire to choose is . . . a natural drive . . . so great that it becomes not merely a means to an end but something intrinsically valuable and necessary" (2010, p. 10).

Iyengar draws on Eric Fromm to clarify our understanding of choice. In *Escape From Freedom* (1941), Fromm indentifies two important parts of freedom (and by extension, choice). First, freedom is often understood as freedom from something. For example, freedom can be "freedom from the political, economic, and spiritual shackles that have bound men" (cited in Iyengar, 2010, p. 63). There is a second aspect of freedom, however, and that is "freedom to." For Fromm, *freedom* to refers to our own ability to achieve a goal or desired outcome. Iyengar writes of this distinction that

"Freedom from" and "freedom to" don't always go together, but one must be free in both senses to obtain full benefit from choice. A child must be *allowed* to have a cookie, but he won't get it if he can't reach the cookie jar high on a shelf. (p. 36)

Both "freedom from" and "freedom to" are essential conditions for realizing our authentic selves, but such freedom of choice is rarely seen in modern organizations. Peter Block has observed that

> In some ways we are a nation profoundly conflicted about what we believe. We live with political institutions that celebrate the rights of individuals to express themselves, to assemble, to pursue happiness and individual purposes, to pick their own political leaders. We pay enormous attention to the rights and procedures of due process. At times we seem to be on the edge of anarchy and yet we tenaciously cling to our political beliefs and rituals with all their flaws and contradictions. Yet when we enter the factory door or the lobby or the business cathedrals in our major cities, we leave our belief in democratic principles in the car. The halls and chambers of these buildings have flourished on a very different set of beliefs and rituals . . . In the case of most corporations the beginning line is, "I believe in Compliance. . . ." (1993, pp. xii–xiii)

When considering the complexity of helping, there are even more reasons why offering meaningful choices is important. For example, Daniel Pink (2009) explains that people are rarely motivated when they have little choice or autonomy. Similarly, Thomas Davenport (2005) notes that knowledge workers resist change initiatives when they are not offered choices because choice is so central to reflection. This view is echoed in Edgar Schein (2009), who pointed out that people resist various forms of assistance when change leaders put themselves "one up" by telling people what to do without offering choices. Practically speaking, failing to provide real choice in helping relationships is a recipe for disaster.

What does this mean in schools? Is everyone free to choose whatever they wish at all times? Can a teacher choose to just stop learning? Can a teacher choose to have low expectations for students or to treat students with a lack of respect? Aren't there times when an entire school needs to join together to implement practices schoolwide? Is it best if everyone just does what they please at all times?

Clearly, complete freedom is not the solution. Total choice, without structure, would likely lead to total, unproductive chaos. Imagine, for example, what would happen if all the signal lights went dead in New York City. Drivers would be free to drive without restriction since there were no lights signaling them to stop and go. The absence of the restriction of lights signaling stop and go, however, would actually limit each driver's freedom since a snarling traffic jam would likely bring traffic to a stop.

Barry Schwartz, in *The Paradox of Choice*, deepens our understanding of choice, and the need for form to structure choice, by arguing that too much choice is not desirable. "Choice is essential to autonomy," Schwartz writes, "which is absolutely fundamental to well-being" (2004, p. 3). Indeed, according to Schwartz,

> When people have no choice, life is almost unbearable . . . But as the number of choices keeps growing, negative aspects of having a multitude of options begin to appear. As the number of choices grows further, the negatives escalate until we become overloaded. At this point, choice no longer liberates, but debilitates. It might even be said to tyrannize. (p. 2)

Schwartz's (2004) main point is that too many choices can contribute to "bad decisions, to anxiety, stress, and dissatisfaction—even depression" (p. 3). Anyone who has sat through a poorly organized planning session where everyone speaks but nothing is resolved knows that choice without structure or form is not the kind of freedom we want. But form without choice is oppressive. What is needed for choice to flourish is a structure that reconciles freedom and form.

The solution is to create structures that provide focus for human experiences, while respecting the autonomy of each individual. Schwartz (2004) suggests that we should "learn to love constraints . . . to view limits on the possibilities we face as liberating not constraining" (p. 235). Iyengar makes exactly the same point by urging us

> to look to those who have shown how constraints create their own beauty and freedom. Inventors and artists and musicians have long known the value of putting constraints on choice. They work within forms and strictures and rules, many of which they break only to establish new boundaries, sometimes even tighter ones. (2010, p. 213)

Iyengar supports her assertion by including an interview she conducted with the jazz great and Pulitzer Prize–winning composer Wynton Marsalis, who describes how the freedom of jazz exists within form: "You need to have some restrictions in jazz. Anyone can improvise with no restrictions, but that's not jazz. Jazz always has some restrictions. Otherwise, it might sound like noise" (p. 214). The ability to improvise, he said, comes from fundamental knowledge and this knowledge "limits the choices you can make and will make. Knowledge is always important where there's a choice" (p. 214).

Productivity guru Scott Belsky (2010) makes the same point. Form, in the structure of constraints on creativity, he proposes, is essential for getting things done.

> Constraints—whether they are deadlines, budgets, or highly specific creative briefs—help us manage our energy and execute ideas. While our creative side intuitively seeks freedom and openness—the blue sky projects—our productivity desperately requires restrictions. (p. 87)

Choice stands at the heart of Impact Schools, but choice occurs within a structure. Much of the rest of this book articulates how freedom and form co-exist, indeed how meaningful choice can only occur within a structure.

Voice: Professional Learning Should Empower and Respect the Voices of Teachers

If partners are equal, if they choose what they do and do not do, they should be free to say what they think, and their opinions should count. For that reason, those taking the partnership approach recognize that professional learning needs to value the opinions of all participants, not just those of the change leader. In fact, learning is significantly limited unless everyone's voice is encouraged and heard.

When we take the partnership approach, we create opportunities for people to express their own points of view. This means that a primary benefit of partnership is that everyone gets a chance to learn from others because others share what they know. In partnership workshops, for example, all participants have the freedom to express their opinions about the content being covered. Similarly, during partnership coaching conversations, the coach creates a setting where collaborating teachers feel comfortable saying what they think. We hear the real truth when we engage in a real partnership conversation.

To encourage people to share their thoughts honestly, change leaders taking the partnership approach often adopt a method aptly summarized in Stephen Covey's (1989) phrase, "seek first to understand, then be understood" (p. 235). Thus, they enter into conversations by asking questions, and they wait for others to say what they think. By temporarily setting aside their own opinions so they can really hear what others have to say, change leaders powerfully demonstrate that they truly value their colleagues' perspectives. When we empathetically listen to others' ideas, thoughts, and concerns, we communicate that others' lives are important and meaningful.

When leaders do not honor teachers' voices, however, telling them to implement step-by-step programs or practices without asking for their thoughts or suggestions, they communicate the message that they do not trust teachers to think for themselves. To silence the voices of teachers by asking for compliance (just follow the script) rather than ideas and feedback is dehumanizing—treating teachers like objects rather than thinking creative professionals. "Every prescription," Freire explains, "represents the imposition of one man's choice upon another, transforming the consciousness of the man prescribed to into one that conforms with the prescriber's consciousness" (1970, p. 31).

Parker Palmer and Teachers Finding Their Voice

Parker Palmer's *The Courage to Teach* (1998) celebrates the importance of teachers finding their voice. Here are a few of his most important thoughts on the topic.

> The salvation of this human world lies nowhere else than in the human heart, in the human power to reflect, in human meekness and in human responsibility. (p. 20)

> Any authentic call ultimately comes from the voice of the *teacher within*, the voice that invites me to honor the nature of my true self. (p. 29)

> Authority is granted to people who are perceived as authoring their own words, their own actions, their own lives, rather than playing a scripted role at great remove from their own hearts. When teachers depend on the coercive powers of law or technique, they have no authority at all. (p. 33)

Teachers often feel silenced when they are told to implement scripted programs right off the shelf exactly as they are written. However, we do not have to share effective practices that way. Tools that empower teachers to be more organized, to connect with more students, and to prompt thought and mastery can help teachers find their voice in the classroom.

I had this experience when I started out as a teacher at Humber College in Toronto, where I was coached by Dee LaFrance, a wonderful, incredibly kindhearted teacher. Dee, partnering with me, taught me how to implement *The Sentence Writing Strategy* (Schumaker, 1985) a "scripted" program. When coaching me, even though I was a brand-new teacher, Dee always sought my opinions and listened to my thoughts and concerns.

Through our conversations and by watching Dee model lessons in my classroom, I learned about the importance of scaffolded lessons, formative assessment, modeling, constructive feedback, and perhaps most important, the necessity of always holding high expectations for students. With Dee's help, trying out what she shared, I started to find my voice as a teacher, and those early coaching sessions shape my teaching practice today. Indeed, I was so affected by the power of the tools that Dee shared that in 1992, I moved to study with the strategy developers at the University of Kansas Center for Research on Learning, where I continue to work more than two decades later.

Parker Palmer has written beautifully about the importance of teachers finding their voice. "Any authentic call," he writes, "comes from the voice of the teacher within, the voice that invites me to honor the nature of my true self" (1998, p. 29). According to Palmer, silencing teachers and telling them what to do splits their "personhood" from their "practice," cutting them off from what matters most, "the human power to reflect, in human meekness and in human responsibility" (p. 31).

By contrast, to put another person at the heart of the conversation, by asking questions, listening, and respectfully providing powerful tools, provides an opportunity for people to find their voice. Covey (1989) puts it this way: "The more deeply you understand other people, the more you appreciate them, the more reverent you will feel about them. To touch the soul of another human being is to walk on sacred ground" (p. 258).

Reflection: Reflection Is an Integral Part of Professional Learning

When we take the partnership approach, we don't tell others what to believe; we respect our partners' professionalism and provide them with enough information so that they can make their own decisions. Partners don't do the thinking for their partners. Rather, they empower their partners to do the thinking. Reflection stands at the heart of the partnership approach, but it is only possible when people have the freedom to accept or reject what they are learning as they see fit.

Influenced by the writing of Donald Schön (1991) and Joellen Killion (Killion & Todnem, 1991), I have come to see reflection as occurring in three ways: *looking back, looking at,* and *looking ahead.* When we *look back,* we consider an event that has passed and think about how it proceeded and what we might have done differently. When teachers look back at a lesson, for example, they explore what worked and what didn't work, and a look back often prompts them to plan to act differently in the future. Schön refers to this as reflection on action.

When we *look at,* we are thinking about what we are doing in the midst of the act itself. We are monitoring how well an activity is proceeding, considering adjustments that have to be made, and making decisions about what the best method might be for going forward. This form of reflection is a defining characteristic of great teachers. To keep students engaged and learning, teachers need to be watching all the time, making adjustments, and differentiating the way they guide learning every minute of the day. Great teachers are thinking all the time. Schön (1991) refers to this way of thinking as reflection in action.

Looking ahead is thinking about how to use an idea, practice, or plan in the future. When we look ahead, we consider something we have to do in the future and what we can do to ensure success. Change leaders who take the partnership approach make it possible for teachers to experience numerous opportunities to "look ahead" and explore how an idea might be shaped, adapted, or reconstructed so that it fits with their way of teaching and meets the needs of their students. Killion and Todnem (1991) refer to this as reflection for practice. Whether looking back, looking at, or looking ahead, teachers are quintessential "knowledge workers" because so much of their professional practice involves thinking.

As Thomas Davenport (2005), quoted earlier in this chapter, notes, knowledge workers require autonomy. The real joy of being a professional lies in using your accumulated knowledge to tackle a thorny challenge. To reduce the amount teachers reflect on their practice is to reduce the amount teachers enjoy their practice. School leaders who do not create frequent opportunities for teachers to reflect, do so at their peril.

When leaders choose to do the thinking for teachers—by creating scripts, pacing guides, and step-by-step procedures to be followed blindly—they engage in short-term thinking. Pacing guides and similar prescriptions may lead to a quick bump in test scores, but the long-term impact can be disastrous. Schools need to celebrate and retain their star teachers and nourish the development of other outstanding professionals. However, as Rob Goffee and Gareth Jones have written, outstanding employees "will only stay if you can offer them a great place in which to express their cleverness and other clever people to work with" (2009, pp. 15–16).

In schools, this means that prescriptive practices may scare away the best teachers and quite possibly impoverish the thinking of those left behind. Impact Schools, as described in this book, make reflection a part of all forms of professional learning.

Dialogue: Professional Learning Should Enable Authentic Dialogue

We live in an antidialogical age. The people celebrated in the media are the antithesis of dialogical. In politics, media celebrities from the left and the right thrash it out until, it seems, the last shouter is left standing. In sports, many of the most popular shows are debates between journalists and former athletes, everyone intent on talking louder, not wiser. In reality shows, we see manipulation and intimidation celebrated—kindness and respect voted off the island.

To engage in dialogue, then, is a countercultural act. It is, however, also a sign that we truly respect our partners. Dialogue is talking with the goal of digging deeper and exploring ideas together. As David Bohm (1996) has written, dialogue is "thinking together." Since dialogue is a way of communicating where there is equality between speakers, where ideas are shared, and where every partner's ideas are respected, dialogue is the goal of change leaders taking the partnership approach.

Bohm's short book *On Dialogue* (1996) is a concise introduction to this way of interacting. Bohm begins by uncovering the etymology of the word *dialogue*, explaining that the original Greek meaning of *logos* is "meaning" and that the original Greek meaning of *dia* is "through." Thus, dialogue is a form of communication where meaning moves back and forth between and through people. Bohm explains,

> The picture or image that this derivation suggests is of a *stream of meaning* flowing among and through us and between us . . . out of which will emerge some new understanding. It's something new, which may not have been in the starting point at all. It's something creative. And this *shared meaning* is the

"glue" or "cement" that holds people and societies together (p. 1)

Paulo Freire (1970) describes dialogue as a mutually humanizing form of communication. My dialogue partners and I become more thoughtful, creative, and alive when we talk in ways that open up rather than shut down. As Martin Buber (1970) explained close to half a century ago, if I use language to get people to do what I want them to do, if I manipulate, then I treat them like objects, not subjects. In this way, an antidialogical approach is truly dehumanizing. It is only when I encourage and tap into my partner's imagination, creativity, knowledge, and ideas, that I truly respect them as fully human.

Freire (1970) has identified five requirements for dialogue: humility, faith, love, critical thinking, and hope.

Humility

"Men who lack humility (or have lost it) cannot come to the people, cannot be their partners in naming the world . . . Dialogue cannot exist without humility" (Freire, 1970, p. 79). People who take the partnership approach recognize that humility is a prerequisite for dialogue. After all, if I know it all, what could I possibly learn from you?

Humility is manifested in many actions during dialogue. First, we need to go into conversations as learners more than as teachers. When we talk with others with the goal of learning from them rather than teaching them, our way of conversing changes. We begin as listeners and turn the focus onto our partners. During dialogue, the humble communicator is fully present, paraphrasing what is heard, hearing the emotion and meaning of what is said in addition to the actual words.

Humility also means that we are more concerned with getting things right than being right. Therefore, we ask good questions, real questions, to which we don't know the answers, and we listen for the answers. We stop trying to persuade and start trying to learn. As David Bohm has written, "If something is right, you don't need to be persuaded. If somebody has to persuade you, there is probably some doubt" (1996, p. 15).

Too often, our conversations are self-centered rather than learning-centered. When this is the case, we listen for evidence that our conversation partners agree with us, and when they don't agree, we work hard to show them we are right and they are wrong.

Humility in dialogue often means that we simply withhold our opinion so that we can hear others. This may involve a kind of radical honesty. That is, rather than covering up the flaws in our argument or hiding our ignorance, in dialogue we display the gaps in our thinking for everyone to see. If we want to learn, we can't hide behind a dishonest veneer of expertise. Indeed, treating others as equals demands that we tell them truthfully about what we believe, assume, know, and do not know.

In dialogue, we humbly let go of the notion that there is only one right answer—our answer!—and we see conversation as a testing ground for ideas. If the purpose of conversation is learning, the last thing we should be doing is confirming our own misconceptions by solely seeking others who see the world the same as us. As David Bohm has said, "If you are defending a position, you are pushing out what is new" (1996, p. 15).

Humility also lays the foundation for one of the most important practices within dialogical conversations—questioning assumptions. Usually, our assumptions go unquestioned, and we assume that what we assume is the truth. When we take our assumptions for certainties, it leads to many conflicts and failures of understanding when we encounter people whose unquestioned assumptions conflict with ours. Dialogical conversations at their best enable us to explore our assumptions, through conversation, so that we will be better able to learn from others.

Faith

"Faith in man is an *a priori* requirement for dialogue; the 'dialogical man' believes in other men even before he meets them face to face" (Freire, 1970, p. 79). When I engage in dialogue, I recognize that those I speak with are equal to me, and I work from the assumption that they hold within them wisdom, knowledge, ideas, and gifts. When we take an antidialogical approach and tell people what to do without listening, or try to persuade people to do what we think is best for them, without their choice or voice, we show a profound lack of respect for their humanity. Dialogue is never manipulative; it is grounded in free conversation between people who respect each other as equals. If we are equals, I should value your words as much as I value my own.

When we have faith in others, we let go of the notion that we need to control them, tell them what to do, or hold them accountable. We see people as autonomous individuals deserving of our respect. William Isaacs elaborates on respect in his book *Dialogue and the Art of Thinking Together*.

> Respect is not a passive act. To respect someone is look for the spring that feeds the pool of their experience . . . At its core,

the act of respect invites us to see others as *legitimate*. We may not like what they do or say or think, but we cannot deny their *legitimacy* as beings. In Zulu, a South African language, the word *Sawu bona* is spoken when people greet one another and when they depart. It means "I see you." To the Zulus, being seen has more meaning than in Western cultures. It means that the person is in some real way brought more fully into existence by virtue of the fact that they are seen. (1999, p. 111)

When I have faith in my conversation partners, there is a much greater chance that they will trust me, too. Without mutual trust, there is little chance that a conversation will be open enough for true dialogue to occur.

Love

"If I do not love the world—if I do not love life—if I do not love men—I cannot enter into dialogue" (Freire, 1970, p. 78). Dialogue is only possible if we have empathy for others. In dialogue, we start by being empathetic, respectful, and nonjudgmental rather than taking a superior approach, starting by judging others. When we are empathetic toward others, when we move from love rather than control, we recognize our mutual humanity, the great bonds we share with others just because we are all people. This is especially important for people with whom we disagree. William Isaacs also recognizes empathy as a core part of dialogue:

> One lens that can reduce the temptations to blame and increase respect is to listen to others from the vantage point that says, "This, too, is in me." Whatever the behavior we hear in another, whatever struggle we see in them, we can choose to look for how these same dynamics operate in *ourselves*. (1999, p. 124)

Love is necessary for dialogue, but love can also be created by dialogue. As David Bohm writes, "love will go away if we can't communicate and share meaning . . . However, if we can really communicate, then we will have fellowship, participation, friendship, love, growing, and growth" (1996, p. 41).

Critical Thinking

"Only dialogue . . . is . . . capable of generating critical thinking" (Freire, 1970, p. 81). When we go into conversation to confirm our views rather than to learn, we choose to think by ourselves rather than with others. If I only want to hear you tell me that you agree with me, then I don't really want to hear your thoughts at all. If we truly want to learn from a conversation, we are wise to go into it looking for ideas that disprove our way of thinking rather than looking for confirmations that our opinion is correct.

Dialogue is the thinking approach to communication. In the best situation, our ideas flow back and forth so freely that we start to think together—we reach a point where we lose sight of whose ideas are whose. Such conversation is energizing, humanizing, and the most natural way for partners to communicate.

Hope

"Dialogue cannot be carried on in a climate of hopelessness. If the dialoguers expect nothing to come of their efforts, their encounters will be empty, sterile, bureaucratic and tedious" (Freire, 1970, p. 80). Dialogue cannot occur when people are paralyzed by hopelessness. Dialogue can only flourish in situations where there are many possibilities.

In part, this means that a conversation that is dialogical must be open-ended. If I come to you with a plan, and I expect you to implement it, I am not engaging in dialogue. Dialogue occurs when we start by trying to understand together, when we listen and learn rather than tell and resist.

Finally, hope too, for me at least, means that every act of dialogue is a hopeful act, a sign that we believe a better future is possible. When I listen to you, and you listen to me, there is the hope that we can create something new and better, that we can advance thought, and, through dialogue, create a better tomorrow.

Praxis: Teachers Should Apply Their Learning to Their Real-Life Practice as They Are Learning

What do we desire as educational leaders? We surely want the people with whom we work to learn new ways to help students, to reflect on what they do, to change for the better. To encourage such reflective action, we may give teachers many chances to mull over how they might plan to use the new ideas being discussed. For that reason, in a partnership learning workshop, teachers, like children having fun with modeling clay, are able to reshape each new idea until they can see how it might look in their classroom. When we act on the principle of praxis, teachers have opportunities to think about how to apply new ideas to their real-life practices.

Praxis is a rich philosophical term for the creative activity illustrated above. Simply put, praxis describes the act of applying new ideas to our own lives. When we learn about content planning, for example, and spend a great deal of time thinking about and developing guiding questions that focus and reshape our units, we are engaged in praxis. When we learn about telling stories, and then create our own new stories to weave into our lessons, we are engaged in praxis. And when we learn about a new teaching practice or theory, think about it deeply, and decide not to use it in our classes, we are engaged in praxis. When we learn, reflect, and act, we are engaged in praxis.

The concept of praxis has many implications. Most important is the assumption that if we are to apply new knowledge to our lives in some way, we need to have a clear understanding of our current reality. Paulo Freire has suggested that praxis is a profound and important activity because it leads to really analyzing our lives and the world in which we learn. For Freire, praxis is revolutionary: "it is reflection and action upon the world in order to transform it . . . To speak a true word is to transform the world" (1970, p. 75).

In many ways, it is easier to describe what praxis is not, than what it is. Praxis is not memorizing a new routine so that we can teach it in our classes exactly as we memorized it. Praxis is not using cooperative learning activities to ensure that teachers fully understand how to score an assessment tool. Praxis is not running a workshop so that the picture in our mind ends up exactly the same in the minds of all of the other participants. Rather, praxis is enabled when teachers have a chance to explore, prod, stretch, and re-create whatever it is they are studying—to roll up their sleeves, really consider how they teach, really learn a new approach, and then reconsider their teaching practices and reshape the new approach, if necessary, until it can work in their classroom.

Because reflection is central to the partnership approach to learning, praxis is impossible without a partnership relationship. As Richard J. Bernstein observed, "praxis requires choice, deliberation, and decisions about what is to be done in concrete situations" (1983, p. 160). In other words, if participants in our workshop are going to make plans to use what we're explaining, they'll need to feel free to make their own sense of the materials. They will have to be true partners—equal, free to say no, and, we hope, excited by possibilities offered by the new ideas they are learning.

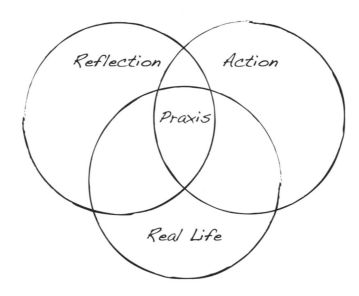

Reciprocity: We Should Expect to Get as Much as We Give

A few years ago, I went to Florida with a group of researchers to study highly effective coaches at their schools. Using the interview methods of anthropologists, we talked with coaches, teachers, principals, and district supervisors of coaches to find out what distinguished these outstanding professionals. We discovered that outstanding coaches love to learn. This did not surprise me because I believe learning leaders cannot succeed unless they live and breathe learning themselves. As the famous symphony director Ben Zander has said, "you cannot be a coach . . . unless you are coach-able" (Liu, 2004, p. 197). The give-and-take of learning, what I call *reciprocity*, is an essential part of the partnership approach.

Reciprocity is the belief that each learning interaction is an opportunity for everyone to learn—an embodiment of the saying, "when one teaches, two learn." People who live out the principle of reciprocity approach others with humility, expecting to learn from them. When we look at everyone else as a teacher and a learner, regardless of their credentials or years of experience, we will be delightfully surprised by new ideas, concepts, strategies, and passions. If we go in to an experience expecting to learn, much more often than not, we will.

When people take the partnership approach and act on the partnership principles, reciprocity takes care of itself; it is the inevitable outcome of a true partnership. Seeing our partners as equals means we come into a conversation respecting and valuing them. Freeing our partners to make choices means they are free to surprise us with ideas that are new and important, and encouraging them to say what they think, to find and express their voice, means we will have an opportunity to hear and learn what it is important for them to share.

Reflection, dialogue, and praxis also increase the chances that we will learn from our colleagues because we are engaged in work focused on real-life situations, and because our mode of communication is designed for sharing ideas. When we think together, when we ensure that reflection is a part of learning, we will be delighted by what others create, imagine, or design. Partnership is about shared learning as much as it is about shared power.

Learning is infectious, energizing, and humanizing. Learning helps us to live fuller, richer lives. When we are engaged in learning, our imagination, brains, and hearts all come alive. If a coach, principal, workshop leader, or intensive learning team facilitator is turned on by learning, his or her enthusiasm breeds energy in others that can be powerful.

When teachers are passionate about learning, their love of growth and development rubs off on students and often infects them with the same passion. Most of us can remember a teacher whose genuine passion for learning drew us in and inspired us to be more than we realized was possible. When coaches are learners, their openness to learning fosters trust and richer communication. When principals are learners, their desire for knowledge and wisdom is a catalyst for everyone else's growth.

Schools, too, can learn. In learning schools, everyone's knowledge matters, and the unavoidable, reciprocal give-and-take of ideas makes everyone smarter. Peter Senge, who popularized the concept of the learning organization, described it this way:

> Learning organizations are possible because, deep down, we are all learners. No one has to teach an infant how to learn. In fact, no one has to teach infants anything. They are intrinsically inquisitive, masterful learners who learn to walk, speak and pretty much run their households all on their own. Learning organizations are possible because not only is it our nature to learn but we love to learn. (1990, p. 4)

Impact Schools are designed to give life to people's innate love of learning through the partnership approach.

To Sum Up

There are at least five simple truths about helping relationships: (1) people often do not know that they need help; (2) if people feel "one down," they will resist help; (3) criticism is taken personally; (4) if someone else does all the thinking for them, people will resist; and (5) people aren't motivated by other people's goals.

The partnership principles provide the theoretical foundation for Impact Schools. The principles are

Equality—professional learning is done with teachers rather than training done to teachers.

Choice—teachers should have choice regarding what and how they learn.

Voice—professional learning should empower and respect the voices of teachers.

Reflection—reflection is an integral part of professional learning.

Dialogue—professional learning should enable authentic dialogue.

Praxis—teachers should apply their learning to their real-life practice as they are learning.

Reciprocity—we should expect to get as much as we give.

Going Deeper

Helping

James Prochaska, John Norcross, and Carlo DiClemente's *Changing for Good* (1994) is an accessible, classic work on how people experience change. Coaches working with the Kansas Coaching Project have used the authors' six-stage model as a way of understanding how to differentiate support to teachers.

Douglas Stone, Bruce Patton, Sheila Heen, and Roger Fisher's *Difficult Conversations* (2000) is one of several outstanding communication and negotiation books developed at the Harvard Negotiation Project.

Thomas Davenport's *Thinking for a Living* (2005) provides an overview of the characteristics of knowledge workers.

Edgar Schein's *Helping* (2009) is a very useful explanation of how status affects and shapes any helping relationship.

Daniel Pink's *Drive* (2009) is an enjoyable and thought-provoking summary of the research on extrinsic motivation.

Partnership

Paulo Freire's *Pedagogy of the Oppressed* (1970) is in many ways the central text behind the partnership approach described in this book. Friere's book is not an easy read, but the effort it takes to understand his ideas is richly rewarded. His book introduced me to the concept of praxis and the power of dialogue to create mutually humanizing conversations.

Peter Block's *Stewardship* (1993) first introduced me to the idea of partnership as a metaphor for human interaction among equals. Block explains why choice and reflection are essential aspects of partnership.

Riane Eisler's books, in particular *The Chalice and the Blade* (1988), provide a feminist, anthropological perspective on partnership relationships.

Sheena Iyengar's *The Art of Choosing* (2010) and Barry Schwartz's *The Paradox of Choice* (2004) both provide great insight into the complexity of choice while also offering fascinating anecdotes about their topic.

David Bohm's *On Dialogue* (1996) is a short book but with clearly explained, simple, and powerful ideas about how to interact respectfully. William Isaac's *Dialogue* (1999) is the definitive book on the topic, and it is packed with powerful, useful ideas.

Parker Palmer's *The Courage to Teach* (1998) is a beautifully written, powerful description of how the head and heart come together in the art of teaching. Palmer has much to say about the role of authentic reflection within the professional work of teaching. Finally, Donald Schön's *The Reflective Practitioner* (1991) is the classic work on the topic of reflection.

3

Principals

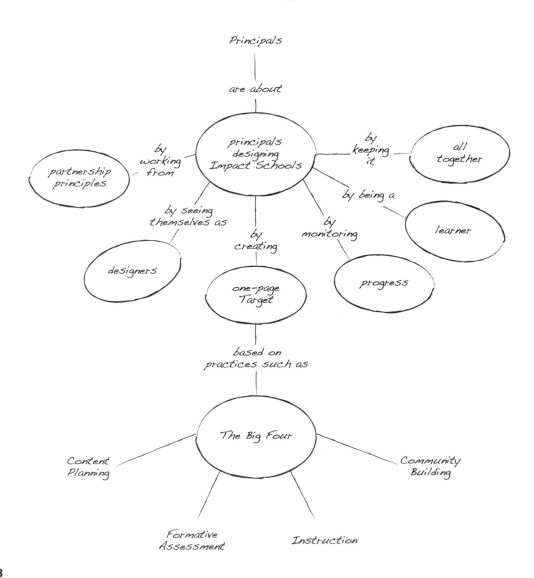

In 1996, I was involved in a fascinating project with Canada's postal service. I was asked to consult with managers across the country to help them become systems thinkers as they approached the retail aspects of the postal service—selling T-shirts, limited-edition stamp sets, postcards, expensive coins, and so forth—which fully made up 25 percent of the post office's business.

The project took me across western and central Canada as I interviewed more than 100 regional managers and directors about the challenges and opportunities they saw for their regions. In the process, I learned a lot of about leadership. A theme repeated in almost every interview: leaders who are respected are the ones who "walk the talk," people who are always willing to do whatever they ask their direct reports to do.

Since then, this concept has gained widespread acceptance. Peter Senge and his colleagues dedicated an entire chapter to the topic in *The Dance of Change: The Challenges to Sustaining Momentum in Learning Organizations* (1999). The authors' research with the Society for Organizational Learning uncovered that "walking the talk" was essential because

> If managers are not authentic in their convictions and sincere in their behavior, there will be little trust, and consequently little safety for the reflection that leads to authentic change. . . . People do expect perfection, but they recognize sincerity and openness—and their absence. (pp. 194–195)

When leaders walk the talk, by employing the partnership communication strategies described in Chapter 7, for example, they communicate that they are committed to the goals of a change initiative, and they are seen as credible, thereby winning their colleagues' respect. Further, leaders who walk the talk have a deep knowledge of the work done by people in the field. In schools, this means that principals understand good instruction and support and lead professional learning that makes an impact.

In Impact Schools, all the forms of professional learning are integrated, so teachers can master and implement the practices on the Target. Thus, instructional coaching, workshops, intensive learning teams, and all other forms of professional learning focus on a small number of high-leverage teaching practices. Additionally, principals' observations and evaluations of teachers similarly focus on the Target. Indeed, the principal plays the central role in translating the Target into the goal of every student receiving excellent instruction every day in every class. When it comes to ensuring that professional learning is focused, effective, integrated, and leading to change, the principal is the hub of a rapidly moving wheel.

There is no way around this: if a school is going to be an Impact School, the principal must roll up her sleeves and be at the heart of the professional learning—co-planning what will happen, observing progress, and keeping the wheel rolling. The reason is simple: the voice of the principal carries more weight than anyone else's in a school. As Jim Collins and Jerry Porras (1994) uncovered when they studied the successful habits of visionary companies, in every work setting, people are most concerned by the person they report to directly. If a principal does not vocally, symbolically, and authentically stress the importance of instructional improvement, then it most likely won't happen.

There are simple but specific actions principals can take to keep professional learning on track and moving forward. Principals can take the partnership approach, modified in a way that accounts for the role principals play in leading change in schools. They can design opportunities for professional learning that make an impact, and they can guide the development of an Instructional Improvement Target that stands at the heart of all professional learning activities. Principals can gain a deep knowledge of effective instruction by exploring comprehensive instructional models such as the Big Four. Principals will be more effective if they walk the talk by being the "first learner" in the school and if they manage projects and themselves effectively. Finally, principals can work with central office to ensure that their initiatives are sustained and supported. All of these practices are described below.

Leading Schools and the Partnership Principles

Equality

Whenever a boss and employee meet, their relationship is structurally unequal. Within the school setting, the same is true. The principal observes and evaluates teachers and makes ultimate decisions about what teachers do in the school, including, in some extreme cases, whether or not a teacher works at a school. In the overall structure of a school, the principal and the teacher are not equal.

However, this inequality is *only* structural. Indeed, if principals confuse structural inequality with true inequality—in other words, if principals start to think they are more valuable or important than others in the school because of the unique role they hold—they will lose the respect of their staff and almost always fail as leaders.

Principals adhering to the partnership approach recognize that although they have different roles than teachers, everyone is equally valuable. Leaders who genuinely win the respect of their staff are those who never miss an opportunity to demonstrate their respect for others. That respect is manifested in the six other partnership principles—choice, voice, reflection, dialogue, praxis, and reciprocity.

Choice

As discussed in Chapter 2, there are limits to choice, and freedom occurs best within form. The principal is the person who designs opportunities for freedom within form. He offers real choices that have real implications, but he recognizes and sometimes creates structures for those choices.

Let's look at an example. Imagine that Charlotte Mason Middle School has identified 90 percent time on task as an Instructional Improvement Target. The goal is written on the one-page Target that everyone helped create and strategies for increasing engagement are shared by coaches, talked about in workshops, and planned during intensive learning teams. The principal, Wendy Bower, conducts weekly observations of all teachers' classrooms, and she notices that Alex Short has on average about 65 percent student engagement. Wendy can handle this situation in a way that honors choice, or not.

When Principal Bower honors choice, she offers Alex lots of options. After explaining to Alex that in the observations she has conducted the average time on task score is 65 percent, she could offer several choices, such as suggesting Alex attend an upcoming workshop, read a book on engaging instruction, review a video program on the topic, or work with the school's instructional coach. Wendy could say something like, "Alex, how you do it is up to you, but we need to reach our goal. You decide what works best for you, and I'll check back to see how things are going." In this way, the principal keeps everyone focused on the Target, while providing real choices that honor the professionalism of teachers.

Voice

To honor voice, principals need to listen to teachers. Indeed, Chapter 7 presents simple strategies everyone can use to listen more effectively. Principals who see teachers as equals embrace the opportunity to hear what others think and feel. Indeed, I recommend principals make a point of having frequent one-to-one conversations with teachers so that (a) teachers have a chance to communicate the joys and frustrations they're experiencing with their work and (b) principals gather an understanding of what teachers think about what is happening in the school.

Here, again, the concept of freedom within form applies. Decisions must be made. Principals must lead team and school meetings that provide an opportunity for everyone to speak, but they also need to use dialogue structures and facilitation skills, such as those described in Chapter 6, to keep conversation focused on action and moving forward. Michael Fullan (2010a) calls this relentless leadership. When it comes to student achievement, principals need to keep the school moving forward.

Reflection

Much of the joy and meaning of professional work involves using knowledge, imagination, wisdom, and ingenuity to wrestle with and resolve challenges through thinking and reflection. If principals or district leaders take this opportunity away from teachers, by doing the thinking for them and telling them what to teach and how, they deny them much of the joy of the job. When administrators honor the principle of reflection, they make sure that, whenever possible, teachers are the ones doing the thinking.

When people come together to really think through challenging issues, by brainstorming, synthesizing, and planning for implementation, when they are really involved in designing and acting on solutions, there is almost always a humane and encouraging positive energy in the room. Furthermore, people who create solutions are more committed to the solutions.

Dialogue

Sharing ideas between two people involves dialogue—two people thinking together. Indeed, I think dialogue is a necessary prerequisite for reflection to occur. Not much thinking occurs when people are told what to do, or at least not much constructive thinking occurs.

Principals can encourage dialogue at both the micro and the macro level. In one-to-one conversations, they can take a listening, rather than a telling, stance. This is not always easy, but by practicing the partnership communication skills described in Chapter 7, leaders can become skillful at entering into conversations as learners rather than teachers—that is, by taking a listening stance. As Safeway's VP of marketing, Diane Dietz, has said, "people love to learn, but hate to be taught" (Liu, 2004, p. 58).

Across the school, principals can foster a culture of dialogue by facilitating group discussions in a manner that opens up conversation rather than shuts it down by using the facilitation skills described in Chapter 6. Principals can also increase the chances of authentic dialogue by setting up workshops and other learning opportunities to increase the communication skills of everyone in the school. Chapter 7, again, provides a starting point for what that learning might entail.

One powerful form of learning is to video record team meetings (assuming everyone accepts the idea) and then having everyone review the recording to see how they interacted. I can attest to the fact that it is a powerful catalyst for change.

Praxis

There are at least two things principals can do to create a setting where praxis is possible. First, they can ensure that all forms of professional learning are meaningful and relevant to teachers. Praxis isn't possible unless what teachers are learning is immediately applicable to real-life issues in the classroom.

Second, principals can ensure that teachers have the freedom to make real decisions about the way they teach. The more opportunity teachers have to creatively think through teaching and learning, the more they are able to think and plan how they are going to teach, and the more committed they will be implementing improvement plans. Praxis involves reflecting on reality so that you can act, and reflection isn't possible unless people are free to choose how to make sense of what they are learning.

Reciprocity

At one level, when principals honor reciprocity, they see themselves as learners in the school. Thus, they approach teachers humbly, expecting to learn from them every day. Indeed, when principals expect to learn from their teachers, in most cases, they are rewarded by learning an enormous about instruction, content, relationship building, students, and so forth. Reciprocity is a way for principals to communicate that they see the talent and expertise of their teachers, but at the same time, it enables principals to expand their understanding of effective teaching practices, thanks to all they learn from staff. Roland Barth made this point back in 1990:

In a school that is a community of learners, the principal occupies a central place, not as the headmaster or "head" teacher, suffering under what has been called the "burden of ascribed omniscience." Rather, the principal occupies a more important position of leadership as the *head learner*, engaging in, displaying, and modeling the behaviors we want teachers and students to adopt. (p. 513)

Beyond a more personal level, reciprocity should also occur at the organizational level, with principals creating structures that enable the school as an organization to learn. Thus, principals can meet one to one or with small groups of teachers, provide teachers with surveys, conduct teaching experiments, establish intensive learning teams, and do many other things to ensure that ideas are being surfaced and widely shared across a school. To create schools where organizational learning is the norm, principals need to constantly look for ways to learn what is happening with the school.

Principals as Designers

One primary task for principals, perhaps the primary task, is to design opportunities for teachers to engage in professional learning that has an unmistakable impact on the way they teach and the way students learn. To accomplish this, principals need to embrace what Tim Brown (2009), CEO of the world-famous design firm IDEO, refers to as *design thinking*.

The idea of the leader as a designer has been raised in different ways by many others. For example, Jim Collins and Jerry Porras (1994), after their study of visionary organizations, concluded that the most effective leaders are "clock-builders":

The builders of visionary companies tend to be clock builders, not time tellers. They concentrate primarily on building an organization . . . The primary output of their efforts is not the tangible implementation of a great idea, the expression of a charismatic personality, the gratification of their ego, or the accumulation of personal wealth. Their greatest creation is the company itself and what it stands for. (p. 23)

Michael Fullan describes leadership similarly in *The Six Secrets of Change* (2008): "Perhaps the best way to view leadership is as a task of architecting organizational systems, teams, and cultures—as establishing the conditions and preconditions for others to succeed" (p. 118).

Peter Senge (2006), too, more than two decades ago, described leaders as optimally being designers:

> If people imagine their organizations as an ocean liner and themselves as the leaders, what is their role? For years, the common answer I received when posting this question to groups of managers was the "captain." Others might say "the navigator, setting the direction," or "the engineer down below stoking the flame, providing energy," or even "the social director making sure everybody's enrolled, involved, and communicating." While these are legitimate leadership roles, there is another, which in many ways, eclipses them all in importance. Yet rarely do people think of it.
>
> The neglected role is that of the designer of the ship. No one has a more sweeping influence on the ship than the designer. . . . It's fruitless to be the leader in an organization that is poorly designed. (p. 321)

Principals as designers are the primary creators of opportunities that enable professional learning to flourish. They ensure that professional learning is aligned to support implementation of the Target, and they use the core questions below as guidelines for effective professional learning. This means, for example, that they ensure workshops focus on the Target and that the workshops are conducted by facilitators who use effective teaching practices.

As designers, principals also ensure that the right people are hired to be instructional coaches and that those people receive extensive support so that they can be successful. Principals also use "design thinking" to find essential resources such as time, money, and expertise. This might involve doubling up classes once a month to free up time for professional learning, as schools do in the Blue Springs District outside of Kansas City, writing proposals for grants such as GEAR-UP or Striving Readers to fund professional learning, or partnering with universities or other school districts to tap into their expertise. All the time, as designers, principals must hold true to the goal of achieving implementation of the Target so that every student receives excellent instruction every day in every class.

Core Questions for Impact Schools

Goal: Students receive excellent instruction every day in every class.

School

- Do we have a one-page instructional improvement plan that clearly describes the critical teaching behaviors that are most important for our students and teachers?

Principal

- Do I know precisely what it looks like when the teaching practices on the instructional improvement plan are used effectively by teachers?
- Do I know exactly how well each teacher is doing in implementing those practices?
- Do I know how to prompt teachers to use the school's professional learning opportunities to master the teaching practices in the Target?
- Do I know how to communicate clearly and positively so that staff are motivated to implement the Target?

Teacher

- Is the content I teach carefully aligned with state standards?
- Do I clearly understand how well my students are learning the content taught?
- Do my students understand how well they are learning the content being taught?
- Do I fully understand and use a variety of teaching practices to ensure my students master the content being taught in my class?
- Do my students behave in a manner that is consistent with our classroom expectations?

Workshops

- Do workshops focus exclusively on the teaching practices in the instructional improvement plan?
- Do workshop facilitators use effective teaching practices?
- Does each workshop conclude with teachers planning how to use their coach to implement the practices learned during the workshop?

Teams

- Do teams and professional learning communities focus exclusively on the teaching practices in the instructional improvement plan?

- Do teachers use coaches to help them implement the methods and materials developed during team meetings?

Coaches

- Do I have a deep understanding of *all* of the teaching practices in the instructional improvement plan?
- Can I provide sufficient support (precise explanations, modeling, observation, feedback, and questioning) so teachers can implement the practices?

The Target

Almost every school in the United States has a school improvement plan. Such plans usually focus on literacy and mathematics goals and include detailed explanations of new practices to be implemented, with objectives to be met, timelines, data, and other information. A great deal of time is spent drafting these plans, often involving multiple staff meetings, and the documents themselves can become quite lengthy statements (sometimes longer than 70 pages) about how schools should improve. Unfortunately, too often, school improvement plans do not make an impact on instruction. As Bill Sommers has said, the plan can become an addition to the wall of binders decorating the principal's office.

There at least two reasons why school improvement plans may fail to accomplish their intended purpose to be catalysts for dramatic improvements. First, if a plan is long, few will fully understand all of the information it contains, and many may not even read it. The human brain generally does not find it easy to understand and use large amounts of information—especially if the information is written in somewhat abstract language. Michael Fullan (2010b) puts this concisely: "Fat plans don't move" (p. 24).

Second, if the plan is too complex, it is also hard for people to understand it fully. The person or people responsible for the program may understand the plan, but there is insufficient knowledge across a school for the coordinated kind of professional learning necessary for unmistakable impact. This means that there are multiple interpretations of the plan, with different teachers implementing it differently, and different administrators and other leaders supporting implementation differently. Thus, the focused collaboration that is essential never occurs.

Finally, school improvement plans often do not address the nuts and bolts of instruction. A plan might include powerful literacy or mathematics programs for improvement, but if those programs are not implemented by teachers using effective teaching practices, they probably won't help students. No program will work until children are engaged. Educational change leaders need to give at least as much attention to instruction as they do to literacy or mathematics programs if they want to see significant improvements and achieve excellent instruction for every student, in every classroom, every day.

At the heart of the improvement plan in an Impact School is the Target, a simple, one-page document that clearly states the school's goals for instructional improvement. The Target can include student learning or behavioral goals or some other form of goal, but what matters is that the document is simple, clear, easily understood, and doable. Further, the Target should be written in such a way that it can be completely understood without any additional explanation.

Writing a one-page Target forces everyone involved to be extremely clear. There is no room for fluff when you only have one page, and there are no extra pages to hide a lack of clarity. This approach to improvement has been utilized by Kent Greens, chief knowledge office for SAIC, a high-tech research and engineering firm:

> We get people focused through one-page tools . . . If you can actually get everything on one page –and not just editing stuff out—that means the tool and the process caused you to reflect on what it is you want to do. If you limit the number of pages people have to explain themselves, it forces them to reflect first and think about what they're trying to do. That's very important. (Jensen, 2000, pp. 52–53)

Instructional Improvement Target

Community Building

- (T) Posts expectations and ensures they are followed by students
- (T) Interacts with at least a 3:1 ratio of interaction
- (S) Are on task at least 90 percent or more
- (S) Keep disruptions to no more than four each 10 minutes

Content Planning

- (T) Creates and shares unit questions with students effectively
- (T) Fully understands the standards for the course being taught

(T) Has created a learning map and shares it with students effectively

(S) Can paraphrase the guiding questions

(S) Can describe the plan for the unit as laid out on the map

(S) Have the questions and map open on their desk before class starts

Instruction

(T) Uses intensive-explicit teaching practices appropriately

(T) Uses constructivist teaching practices appropriately

(T) Uses cooperative learning, stories, effective questions, thinking prompts, challenging assignments, experiential learning, and similar practices appropriately

(S) Maintain a pass rate of 95 percent or higher

(S) Enjoy learning in the classroom

Assessment for Learning

(T) Uses informal assessments effectively

(T) Knows how each student's learning is progressing

(S) Understand the learning targets for all learning

(S) Know how their personal learning is progressing

(T) = Teacher
(S) = Students

The Target does not have to be only written for instruction—although instruction is the focus of this book. Targets can be written for literacy or mathematics goals in school improvement plans. In addition, targets can be longer than one page, if necessary. The one-page limit is somewhat arbitrary. The important thing is that *every* educator in the school fully understands exactly what the Target means and the teaching practices that it embodies.

The Big Four

Student needs, teacher needs, school, district, or state goals may all influence what is included in the Target, but many leaders find it helpful to consider a comprehensive approach to improving instruction, such as Charlotte Danielson's *Enhancing Professional Practice: A Framework for Teaching* (2007).

At the Kansas Coaching Project, we have developed a comprehensive approach to improving instruction based on an exhaustive reading of the research literature and our own experience working with numerous districts across Canada and the United States. We have given our model the nickname the Big Four because it is built around four critical instructional areas of (1) planning content, (2) developing and using formative assessments, (3) delivering instruction, and (4) community building. The teaching practices of the Big Four and tools for coaching and observing those practices are described in detail in *Instruction That Makes an Impact* (Knight, in press). In many of the districts with whom we partner, we use the Big Four as a foundation for developing the Target.

Content Planning

I like to explain the components of the Big Four by describing a course as a journey to be taken by the teacher and students. The goal or destination for the journey is provided by content planning. In the Big Four, this involves unpacking the standards and using them as a foundation for creating guiding questions that guide students to the knowledge, skills, and understandings they need to acquire. Content planning also involves creating learning maps for each unit—every journey needs a map—and sharing the map and questions frequently with students so that they remember the ultimate destination.

Sample Guiding Questions: Paragraph Writing Unit

1. Why is it important to organize our writing?
2. What are several sequencing patterns I can use to organize my writing?
3. What are topic, detail, and clincher sentences?
4. What are the different types of topic, detail, and clincher sentences?
5. What is the best way for *me* to put together the various types of sentences in paragraphs?
6. How can I use my understanding of point of view and verb tense to write better paragraphs?

Sample Learning Map: Paragraph Writing Unit

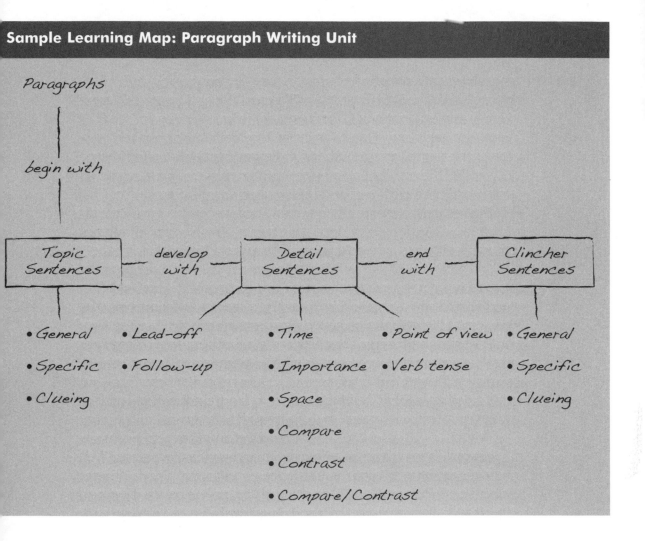

Formative Assessment

Formative assessment is the learner's GPS. When teachers use formative assessment, they answer the guiding questions developed during content planning by clearly stating the answers in discrete statements that describe everything a student needs to know, understand, or do to answer a question—I refer to these statements as specific proficiencies. Following this, teachers identify simple assessments (everything from whiteboards to graphic organizers to quizzes to thumbs-up and thumbs-down) they can use in the moment during teaching to gauge how well students understand what is being taught.

Formative Assessment

1. Identify unit questions.
2. Develop answers (what do my students need to know/need to be able to do to answer this question?).
3. Write specific proficiencies.
4. Identify informal assessments.
5. Use the assessments effectively.
6. Revisit, reflect, revise.

Instruction

The energy that drives the classroom journey is instruction. There are a multitude of practices that an outstanding teacher might use to reach, teach, and inspire students. Out of that multitude, we propose six high-leverage teaching practices that are fairly easy to implement and that can have a powerful, positive impact on student learning:

- *Effective questions* are questions that (a) address knowledge, understanding, or application domains of practice; (b) are open-ended or close-ended; and (c) promote convergent or divergent learning.
- *Thinking prompts* are provocative objects such as cases, vignettes, news articles, short stories, or quotations that teachers use to generate conversation and dialogue in the classroom.
- *Stories* are short anecdotes or narratives that teachers use to generate interest, anchor new knowledge, instill hope, provide a context, offer new perspectives, and build community.
- *Cooperative learning* involves group-learning activities that are mediated by students and in which students have shared goals and specific roles to perform.
- *Experiential learning* involves structured learning activities that simulate the knowledge, understandings, or actions students are learning so that students actually "live out" the content about which they are learning.
- *Quality assignments* involve authentic, appropriately challenging, student-centered activities that engage students and promote deep learning.

Community Building

Community building, the final component of the Big Four, ensures that the journey is a smooth ride. Community building involves developing and teaching clear expectations for all activities and transitions in the classroom, reinforcing those expectations by frequently praising students and calmly, consistently, and fluently correcting them when necessary. Additionally, community building is enhanced when the teacher communicates a deep respect for students and empowers them to communicate a similar respect toward everyone they meet. A focus on community building also involves making the classroom more interactive and engaging.

Mechanical and Metaphorical Learning

A simple distinction lies at the heart of the Big Four. I break learning into two categories: mechanical learning and metaphorical learning.

Mechanical Learning

Mechanical learning refers to learning whose goal is for the student to master content, skills, or information exactly as it is presented. Mechanical learning has right and wrong answers. For example, if a teacher is teaching grammatical concepts, the goal might be to ensure that all students will remember the grammatical concepts in exactly the same way. Thus, all students would know that a subject of a sentence is "a noun that says what a sentence is all about." Similarly, if a teacher is teaching math facts, his goal might be for all students to remember that $4 \times 4 = 16$.

Metaphorical Learning

Metaphorical learning refers to learning where students need to be free to interpret or make sense of learning in their own way. Mechanical learning has no clearly right or wrong answers. For example, if students are learning to interpret poetry, the teacher might want them to come to their own conclusions about what a poem means. Similarly, a teacher might want students to develop their own ways of solving problems. With metaphorical learning, the teacher's goal is to ensure that everyone learns the material in the way that is uniquely appropriate for them.

Both mechanical learning and metaphorical learning occur all the time in the classroom. When a teacher is encouraging mechanical learning, her goal is to ensure that all students have the same picture in their minds as she does. Consequently, when teachers use the Big Four practices for mechanical learning, they use them to confirm understanding and ensure mastery. For example, if during mechanical instruction a teacher is using questioning techniques from the Big Four, she would likely use close-ended, right-or-wrong questions during direct instruction.

When a teacher is encouraging metaphorical learning, on the other hand, their goal is to ensure that all students create their own picture of the content they are learning. Consequently, when teachers use Big Four practices for metaphorical learning, they use it to provide opportunities for students to construct their own knowledge. For example, if a teacher is using questioning techniques from the Big Four, they would likely use open-ended opinion questions during constructivist classroom dialogue.

Whatever approaches to instruction a school embraces, the distinction between these two types of learning is important. Similar distinctions have been referred to, for example, as *convergent* and *divergent thinking* (Guilford, 1967) or *procedural* and *declarative knowledge* (Anderson, 1976). Whatever the term used, the important point is that instructional practices be used in a manner that supports the kind of learning that is aimed at. When educators construct a target, this fundamental distinction must be kept in mind.

The Big Four is only one approach to improving instruction, and in any school, the Target must be tailored to meet teachers' and students' unique needs. It doesn't matter whether a Target utilizes the ideas of Charlotte Danielson (2007) or John Hattie (2009) or the Big Four—or any other instructional approach or a hybrid of practices. What matters is that the approach enables the development of a Target that (a) is easily understood by every teacher, (b) encourages all teachers to be committed to the Target, and (c) helps teachers teach in a way that increases the chances that every student receives excellent instruction every day in every class.

Creating the Target

There are likely as many different ways to draft a Target as there are Targets, but a few simple ideas should be kept in mind. First, every educator should have an opportunity to provide authentic input into the document. Second, the Target should challenge every educator to become a more effective instructor. Third, the Target should describe teaching practices that will genuinely help meet students' needs. Fourth, the Target, when completed, should describe a compelling set of goals that are easily understood and that everyone is committed to achieving.

Guiding the development of the Target is one of the most nuanced challenges facing an instructional leader. If teachers are going to commit to the Target, they must play an active role in its development. As discussed in Chapter 2, people want to be involved in the thinking that leads to initiatives, and they are likely to embrace goals that they help create. However, many teachers do not fully understand how they go about doing their work. Often, we are not the best judges of what we need, simply because we are inside the work, not watching from the outside. Thus, the complexity. Teachers need to co-construct their practices, but they may not fully understand what they need to do.

When guiding the development of the Target, the principal's job, then, is to walk the tight rope between freedom and form. On one hand, they must actively solicit, listen to, and act on the ideas and concerns of teachers. On the other hand, they must ensure that the Target addresses the issues that have highest leverage for improving student learning.

To help with this process, we recommend that principals establish a Target Design Team, a group of teachers and administrators who work with the principal to create a Target that all (or at least almost all) teachers are committed to achieving. This section will cover (a) who should be on the team as well as the (b) inspiration, (c) ideation, and (d) implementation stages of the process.

Who Should Be on the Team?

The Target Design Team is a group of administrators and teachers who will facilitate the development of the target. Although administrators and teachers have very distinct roles, they are both charged with the task of gathering data to support the development of the Target.

My friend Doris Williams, a retired, highly successful high school principal from Harford County, Maryland, advised me that the principal must have the right people on the team if she wants the team to be successful. Doris identified four characteristics that she considers essential for effective team members.

First, team members should be positive, someone whose good humor is infectious and encourages others to be positive. Second, team members should be credible. "You need to have people on the team," Doris said, "that the staff respect and listen to. If your team isn't respected, it will be hard to make progress." Third, team members should be open to new ideas. If Target Design Team members latch onto a plan and are unable to see others' perspectives, they won't create a plan that others feel they own. Finally, since the work of developing the Target must be responsive to everyone's thoughts and concerns, team members should be flexible so that they can change direction whenever that is best for the project.

Tim Brown, in *Change by Design* (2009), describes a three-step process that designers use to create innovative products: (a) inspiration, (b) ideation, and (c) implementation. That process provides a great framework for describing how a team might create a Target.

Inspiration

During the inspiration stage of product development, designers identify the challenge, issue, or opportunity that "motivates the search for solutions" (Brown, 2009, p. 16). To find inspiration, Brown suggests we "go out into the world and observe the actual experience of . . . [people in action, in our case, teachers and students] . . . as they improvise their way through their daily lives" (p. 41). The goal here is get a clear idea of some unmet need, some opportunity that exists in people's lives.

Creating a Target involves a similar goal—to identify teacher and student needs that should be addressed by the Target—and "going out into the world" can be similarly effective. In most cases, however, administrators and teachers "go out into the school" in different ways, with the administrators on the Target Design Team conducting observations of teachers and students, and the teachers on the Target Design Team meeting with their colleagues to hear what they have to say about the design process.

Administrators

Administrators who conduct observations need to explain repeatedly that they are not evaluating teachers; they are gathering information for the development of the Target. Indeed, a primary goal for observations should be to get a picture of which practices are working especially well so that they can be implemented more widely in the school. Since observations are often seen as "evaluative" outside the context of a confidential coaching relationship, we do not recommend that teacher members on the team conduct observations. Design Team teachers have other ways of gathering inspiration, described a few paragraphs below.

Administrators can learn a lot about teaching practices during observations. Thus, administrators might check whether teachers employ guiding questions, whether lessons are aligned with state standards, and whether formative assessments are used. Similarly, they can identify which teaching practices teachers are using (cooperative learning, effective questions, thinking prompts, etc.) by teachers. Finally, observers can note whether behavioral expectations have been taught and whether they are reinforced through sufficient praise and fluent corrections.

Observing students also yields valuable data. Administrators can watch to see if students understand and are following the lesson's plan, and if they understand how well they are progressing in the class. Observers can also watch to see how well students respond to various teaching practices and how many students respond to and correctly answer questions posed during the class. Administrators on a Design Team in Cecil County, Maryland, reported that they learned a lot by asking children a few simple questions, included below, during observations.

Questions to Ask Students

1. What are we learning today?
2. How are you learning it?
3. How will you know when you understand it?
4. What will you do if you need extra help?

Finally, data on student behavior, such as what percentage of students are engaged or on task and how often students disrupt learning, can be very informative. If time permits, administrators can conduct interviews to gather other data. These conversations may not produce an accurate picture of reality because, as my friend Doris Williams has told me, "Whenever a principal talks one to one with a teacher, teachers will always feel they are being evaluated." During one-to-one conversations, administrators might ask how well their curriculum aligns with the state standards or ask teachers for their thoughts on teaching strategies or different approaches to assessment.

So that observation data are consistent, observers from the Design Team must identify what will be observed and practice their observations until they are able to do them reliably. When consultants from the Instructional Coaching Group (ICG) collaborate with school districts, they show video recordings of teachers teaching and provide principals with practice until they are able to gather data reliably. Often, ICG consultants also go into the classroom and conduct observations with administrators until the data gathering is consistent. The Big Four Observation Tool, in the Impact Toolkit in Resource A, is one tool administrators can use to be consistent.

Teachers

While team administrators observe teachers and students, team teachers gather a different kind of valuable data by having one-to-one conversations with colleagues. Again, it is important to point out that these interviews are anonymous and serve to gather information because if teachers feel they are being judged, they are less likely to offer their honest opinions. We suggest that teachers explain to their colleagues that they want to speak for all educators, and, therefore, are trying to learn everything they can during the conversations. Every educator needs to know that everyone has a voice in the creation of the Target.

One-to-one conversations can serve at least three purposes. First, teachers will have a lot of questions about the Target writing process, and no matter how well an e-mail or other written communication is crafted, no form of communication is more effective than one-to-one conversations in these types of situations. Teachers from the Target Design Team should begin by sharing a quick overview of the Target process, emphasizing that (a) each teacher's voice counts and (b) the goal of developing a target and all that follows is to provide meaningful, useful, respectful, focused professional learning done well over a sufficient period of time, with sufficient support so that it can really be implemented. After the brief explanation, teachers should be given ample time to ask questions until all their questions have been answered.

Second, the conversation provides an opportunity for teacher colleagues to strengthen relationships through one-to-one conversations. (Just listening to others does a lot to strengthen relationships, but all of the partnership communication strategies described in Chapter 7 can significantly shorten the gaps between people.) When teachers feel a connection with someone on the team, they are more likely to trust the overall Target development process.

Third, one-to-one conversations will also yield valuable data that can be used to shape the Target. Teachers might start by asking about students' strengths and weaknesses or about the challenges and rewards of teaching. We suggest an overriding question, "What would you like to see on the Target that you think would be a truly worthy goal?" There are a variety of questions that could be used for these interviews in the coaching section of Resource A.

Finally, in addition to information gathered during observations, other student data, such as standardized test scores, tardies, number of students repeating classes, dropout rates, student discipline referrals to the office, and other data, can prove to be very useful. Once observations, interviews, and data are collected, the Target Design Team can begin the process of sharing the data with staff and begin drafting the Target.

Ideation

"Design thinking" expert Tim Brown (2009) explains that during the ideation phase of product development, designers generate, develop, and test ideas. Much the same work occurs when schools are developing their Instructional Target. Administrators and teachers explore, develop, and test possible practices and goals to be included on the Target.

The core activity during this stage is to identify different student and teacher goals (for example, a 90 percent engagement during lessons for students or 100 percent alignment with state standards during instruction) and various teaching practices that can be used to achieve those goals (e.g., thinking prompts and effective questioning to increase engagement and content planning to align lessons with standards).

When possible, and when she is a skilled facilitator, the principal should lead the ideation discussions. If facilitation is not the principal's strength, others, such as the instructional coach, may lead these discussions. While it is more efficient to hold the ideation conversations in large groups, I have found that the gain in efficiency isn't worth what is lost in terms of every teacher having a voice. Therefore, I suggest that ideation meetings be held with small groups of teachers, perhaps grade-level teams or subject-matter teams within a school.

During these meetings, the facilitator will use many of the Partnership Facilitation methods described in Chapter 6. The first goal is to share the data gathered during the inspiration stage and to check with teachers to see if everyone shares the same understanding of the school's student and teacher needs. (The methods described in Chapter 6 for reporting back on interviews during intensive learning teams can be used here.)

The second goal is to introduce practices that might be included in the Target to address student needs. During this part of the conversation, the principal or other facilitators should come prepared to share a variety of best practices, but she should be equally prepared to hear the ideas of teachers about practices to be implemented.

The final goal is to create a draft of goals and practices, a first draft Target. The Target will likely need to go through several revisions until the staff embrace it fully. This will require a number of meetings. (To ensure that those meetings are productive, the facilitator should employ the partnership facilitation skills described in Chapter 6 and the partnership communication skills described in Chapter 7.)

At the end of each Target discussion meeting, the facilitator (most likely the principal) should gather data on (a) whether or not teachers agree with the Target, (b) whether or not teachers are committed to working to achieve the target, and (c) what changes everyone suggests for the Target. One way to do this is to give every participant two differently colored sticky notes and explain that the group will have a chance to cast a secret ballot regarding the Target. Explain that sticky notes of one color should be used to demonstrate the extent to which they agree with the current Target and that the other color should be used to communicate how committed they are to working on the Target. Explain also that each vote is confidential, so everyone should vote and fold their notes so that no one else can see them.

Along with the sticky notes, hand out a piece of paper, or large index cards, and say, "Please let us know what we can do to improve the Target. If you're not voting as an 8, 9, or 10, use this card to communicate what it will take to move you there." If participants do not agree with or are not committed to the Target, use their comments to revise the Target until it is one that everyone, or almost everyone, agrees with and is committed to. Once everyone has voted, gather the cards and sticky notes. Then, put them all on chart paper to show (a) whether or not the team agrees and (b) whether or not they are committed.

Implementation

The third stage of Tim Brown's (2009) three-step process takes up the most time. Implementation is the goal of all professional learning in an Impact School. Indeed, there is little reason to conduct any professional learning that doesn't make a positive impact. Principals create the conditions for implementation by ensuring that all forms of

Photo by Jennifer Ryschon-Knight.

professional learning focus on the Target. At the same time, they see themselves as culture shapers, creating a culture of experimentation, learning, and growth (Killion & Roy, 2009). Much of this book centers on implementation.

This is only one way of creating a Target, and even this method varies each time it is used. What matters is that all teachers have a chance to shape the Target until they are willing to work to achieve the goal. There are quicker ways to create the Target, but unless everyone is actively involved in its creation, the chance of implementation is slim. When everyone is involved, however, the Target can become a clear goal that an entire school is committed to achieving.

Observing and Monitoring Teacher Progress

An essential part of project management is monitoring progress. Someone has to keep track of how well the project is moving forward so that adjustments can be made if things aren't proceeding as expected. In schools, the person who monitors progress is typically the principal. To do this, the principal needs to understand two things. First, she needs to know exactly what it should look like if teachers are effectively implementing the practices in the Target. Second, she needs to know how close every teacher is to achieving the goals in the Target.

If principals are going to observe teachers, they need to have a clear understanding of what to observe and how to observe reliably. This means that they must be the first learners in a school, the first people to deeply understand the practices in the Target. Additionally, all administrators who conduct informal and formal observations need to make reliable observations so that teachers get consistent feedback regardless of who conducts the observation.

Several outstanding books have been written on how to conduct teacher observations. Elizabeth City, Richard Elmore, Sarah Fiarman, and Lee Teitel, for example, in *Instructional Rounds in Education* (2009), describe how networks of educators can "learn to see" and "unlearn to judge" as they observe classrooms. The authors describe observing teachers as follows:

> Classroom observation . . . is a discipline—a *practice,* in the sense that it is a pattern of ways of observing and talking and is designed to create a common understanding among a group of practitioners about the nature of their work. A central part of that practice is deciding in advance *what* to observe, *how* to observe, and, most importantly *how to talk about what is seen.* (p. 86)

Carolyn Downey, Betty Steffy, Fenwick English, Larry Frase, and William Poston in *The Three-Minute Classroom Walk-Through* (2004) propose a five-step walk-through observation structure:

Step 1: Student Orientation to the Work. Do students appear to be attending when you first walk in the room?

Step 2: Curricular Decision Points. What objective or objectives has the teacher chosen to teach at this time, and how aligned are they to the prescribed (district or state) written curriculum?

Step 3: Instructional Decisions Points. What instructional practices is the teacher choosing to use at this time to help students achieve the learning of the curriculum objectives?

Step 4: "Walk-the-Walls"—Curricular and Instructional Decisions. What evidence is there of past objectives taught and/or instruction decisions used to teach the objectives in the classroom?

Step 5: Safety and Health Issues. Are there any noticeable safety or health issues that need to be addressed?

The jury is out for many on whether three minutes is sufficient to gather enough information about teacher and student progress. What matters is that principals take the time needed to accurately observe how close teachers are to the Target. Precise observations are necessary if they are going to yield adequate, useful information. The Impact Toolkit in Resource A includes a sample observation form created for the Big Four.

If a principal is looking for community-building behaviors, for example, he might look for such data as (a) ratio of interactions, the percentage of positive comments made by a teacher compared with the number of corrections; (b) disruptions, the number of times students interrupt the teacher or other students' learning during a set amount of time (often 10 minutes); or (c) time on task, the percentage of students who appear to be engaged during a set amount of time (often 5 minutes).

Classroom Management

- ☐ Time on task: _____ percent
- ☐ Ratio of interactions: Reinforcing _____ : _____ Corrective
- ☐ Disruptions: _____/minute
- ☐ Expectations posted: Yes _____ No _____

Principals can also gather a great deal of data by having one-to-one conversations with teachers about how their year is progressing. In particular, they can often learn a lot more about how close a teacher's lessons are to the state curriculum by talking with the teacher than by observing a lesson since a conversation provides time to discuss the planning for an entire unit.

As principals gather data on what is occurring in each teacher's classroom, they also need to keep track of everyone's progress. We suggest using a teacher progress map, also included in the Impact Toolkit, and depicted in the following figure.

Teacher Progress Map

Date:

Teacher	Behavior	Content	Instruction	Formative Assessment
Teacher				
Teacher				
Teacher				
Teacher				
Teacher				
Teacher				
Teacher				
Teacher				
Teacher				
Teacher				
Teacher				
Teacher				
Teacher				
Teacher				
Teacher				
Teacher				
Teacher				
Teacher				
Teacher				
Teacher				
Teacher				
Teacher				
Teacher				
Teacher				
Teacher				
Teacher				
Teacher				
Teacher				
Teacher				

The teacher progress map enables principals to document how close every teacher is to achieving the Target. For example, a teacher might be observed as having "limited use," "some use," or "mastery" of the community-building practices in the Target. The teacher progress map is used as a planning tool for professional learning. It provides a quick snapshot of where the entire school is as it progresses toward the target. Looking over the map, a principal can quickly see, for example, that professional learning needs to be designed to deepen staff's knowledge of formative assessment.

Community Building

Limited Use

Code your teacher as *limited use* if any of the following factors is observed.
- Time on task is less than 80 percent.
- The teacher has not created and posted expectations.
- The ratio of interaction is less than 1:1.
- Disruptions are more than 10 in 10 minutes.

Some Use

Code your teacher as *some use* if none of the limited use factors is observed and at least one of the following factors is observed.
- Time on task is above 80 percent but less than 90 percent.
- Expectations are posted but are not followed by students.
- The ratio of interaction is more than 1:1 but less than 2:1.
- Disruptions are five to nine each 10 minutes.

Mastery

Code your teacher as *mastery* if the following factors are observed.
- Time on task is 90 percent or more.
- Expectations are posted and followed by students.
- The ratio of interaction is 3:1 or more.
- Disruptions are zero to four each 10 minutes.

Principals as First Learners

Over the years, Gandhi's comment "Be the change you want to see" has become a cliché of the first magnitude. You can buy it printed on postcards, "Gandhi vine-green" T-shirts, and even on "bohemian ceramic latte mugs." The phrase has become a cliché because it touches on a deep truth. People wear it on their T-shirts or send it as a postcard because they know it is true. If we want to see change, we need to do the change, walk the talk. This applies in schools as much as anywhere else. If we want students to be learners, then teachers need to be learners. If we want teachers to be learners, then principals need to be learners.

It can be hard for principals to be the first learner in their school as they already have a very full schedule. Principals are constantly at the mercy of urgent issues, requests for reports, parents with questions, teachers with concerns that need to be addressed right away, and students whose misbehavior has to be addressed immediately. Realistically, if there is a fight in the cafeteria, no responsible principal will ignore the problem and sit in her office fine tuning her slides for an upcoming workshop.

But if principals do not walk the talk by being first learners, there is much less of chance that significant, positive change will occur. If principals don't lead by making their own learning a core priority, teachers, who are also busy dealing with their own urgent issues, will think, "Well, if this isn't important to my principal, why should it be important to me?" Given the realities of their jobs, for principals to find the time to be learners requires that they manage their projects and themselves effectively. At the end of this chapter, several strategies are offered to help accomplish that.

Understanding the Target

One major reason why principals need to be the first learners is that they must have a deep understanding of all of the practices on the Target. If professional learning is to have a positive impact, all leaders of professional learning must have a deep understanding of what everyone is learning. Impact requires deep knowledge.

One place where deep knowledge is necessary is formal and informal observation of teachers to monitor their progress in implementing the Target practices. If principals conduct observations without understanding precisely what the practices should look like, their feedback may be confusing or even counterproductive. Furthermore, if several administrators are conducting observations and provide inconsistent feedback, teachers will likely become frustrated and less motivated to implement recommended practices. "If the admin group doesn't even know what this looks like," a teacher might think, "how am I supposed to do this?"

There are no shortcuts to developing a deep understanding of the Target. Learning about the Target requires reading, attending workshops, talking about the practices, and confirming one's understanding with others who are learning the same practices, including other administrators, coaches, and teachers. Some leaders even contact authors of books they have read to double-check their understanding. Indeed, one reason why the Target is only one page is so that the range of possibilities for professional learning is limited enough so that leaders can have a deep knowledge of everything it describes.

In my experience, too little time is often provided for meaningful professional learning for principals. Sometimes, it is assumed that the principals will understand the practices well enough. Unfortunately, I have found that when it is assumed that principals have a deep understanding of the practices, they usually don't. If administrators are going to have a deep understanding of the Target, they need to have a lot of professional learning in the practices on the Target.

Leaders in Greeley, Colorado, have recognized how important it is that principals have deep knowledge of the practices on the school improvement plan. In order to support a new reading initiative, principals in Greeley attended 12 days of workshops. The knowledge they gained during these workshops significantly deepened their knowledge and had a profound, positive impact on their ability to support teachers as they implemented the reading program. When I interviewed coaches in Greeley, the coaches said there was a night-and-day difference between how effective they were before and how effective they became after the principals had received the training since the principals' observations now were useful and motivating for teachers.

Workshops

A common occurrence during workshops is for the principal to introduce the speaker, stay a few minutes, and then leave the room to work on what is apparently "more important" work. When this happens, there is often a noticeable shift in the way in which everyone in the room approaches the workshop. If you have led a workshop where this occurs, you know that the room just feels different when the principal isn't there.

I suppose that the presence of the principal might encourage some teachers to be more attentive (if the boss is in the room, we need to look like we're working), but I don't think this is the main reason why the room feels different when the principal leaves. By leaving, the principal communicates that he doesn't think the workshop is important, at least not important enough for him to stop doing what else he had planned to do.

Sadly, in many cases, principals are correct. If the workshop is not going to lead to any real change, if it isn't tied to a clearly understood, comprehensive instructional improvement plan, it is not a good use of the principal's time. However, such a workshop is also not a good use of teachers' time. Indeed, one of the reasons why teachers have such a low opinion of workshops is that they do not find them to be useful. If workshops do not make an impact, if the principal doesn't even bother to stay, many teachers rightfully ask, "Why are we here?"

When workshops provide learning on practices on the Target, when they are delivered effectively by people who respect teachers and who use effective teaching practices, and when they are supported by instructional coaches who can help teachers translate learning into practice, then the workshops can make an impact. Workshops that do not meet these criteria should not be held.

As the first learners in schools, principals can do more than attend workshops; they can lead or co-facilitate sessions. Leading workshops is an outstanding way for principals to communicate their commitment to professional learning. Also, few activities can deepen your knowledge more about teaching practices than preparing and delivering a workshop. If the principal is the first leader, leading workshops is a great way to demonstrate that.

Principals can create more opportunities to learn by having one-to-one conversations during which they ask teachers about their experiences in the classroom. Each day offers a new opportunity for learning, and when principals come to teachers with an authentic desire to hear and learn from them, they show that they deeply respect the professionals in their school.

Making It All Happen

All of the ideas presented in this chapter won't do any good if they aren't implemented. And the person who will lead the charge when it comes to implementation within a school is the principal. For that reason, principals must be able to manage projects successfully. Fortunately, many valuable strategies have been developed to help people stay organized and keep projects focused and on track. These strategies generally break into two categories: self-management and project management. Each is described in the following.

MITs

There are simple strategies we can use to control our time rather than letting it control us. The first is to identify what Leo Babauta (2009) refers to as "MITs," that is, Most Important Tasks. If you want to get important work done, you need to be clear on what that work is so that you don't get distracted by other less important tasks.

For many principals, it is often the most important tasks that they do not feel they have time to do, such as conducting drop-in observations, meeting one to one with teachers or students, attending workshops or team meetings, deepening their knowledge, or preparing to lead a workshop.

To ensure that we do what is most important every day, Babauta suggests that we identify no more than three MITs for each day and commit to doing them—no matter what. Babauta writes,

> Here's the beauty of MITs: Usually, the small, unimportant tasks that we need to get done every day (e-mail, phone calls, paperwork, errands, meetings, Internet browsing, etc.) will get in the way of our important longer-term tasks—but if you make your MITs your top priorities each day, the important stuff will get done instead of the unimportant. (2009, p. 58)

Untouchable Time

We can make it easier to ensure that our MITs are completed by employing a second strategy, untouchable time. *Untouchable time* refers to significant periods of the day when you are not to be interrupted. For example, principals may set aside untouchable time every day so that they can spend two periods observing teachers.

To make untouchable time work, principals need to explain to everyone in the school that they need to set aside specific points in the day to do what is necessary to create an impact school. Office staff, in particular, must learn to guard that time. Of course, in the event of an urgent, absolutely essential concern (the president is on the phone to congratulate the principal for winning an award as one of the top schools in the nation, for example), the principal will need to be interrupted.

Principals may want to explain to their superintendent and fellow principals that they will not be available during certain times a day to focus on priorities, such as teacher observation, and that if they must be contacted immediately, then others should phone the school rather than use e-mail so that they can be contacted wherever they might be.

However, everyone needs to know that during untouchable time, the principal should almost always be unreachable.

Managing E-mail

Most principals spend at least 15 to 20 hours a week on e-mail, and they may grow to hate it. They hate the feeling of falling behind and watching their inbox fill up with more and more urgent requests. Then, they find it doubly troubling to never catch up, spending too much time apologizing for late replies. I know the experience. In the past, I've gone several months in a row, many times, never getting to the Zen-like purity of an empty inbox.

Scott Belsky, the author of *Making Ideas Happen* (2010), suggests that the best way to control e-mail (and the single strategy that has had the most positive impact on my personal management skills) is to reply to all e-mail in order from the top to the bottom every day at a certain time. No matter what the e-mail asks, don't skip it. Deal with whatever is in the inbox, in the order it arrives, as quickly as possible. To accomplish this, replies need to be short (four sentences or less), and people need to spend less time thinking about what they have received. Just read it, deal with it, and fire it off.

When I sit down to do e-mail, at specific times, usually at the end of the day, my goal is to clean out the inbox, no matter what. Whenever possible, I forward tasks to others who might be able to respond. When doing so, I ask the person to copy me on the reply, so I know that it has been done.

My short replies are not as detailed and well thought through as they used to be before I adopted Belsky's (2010) approach, but I am still careful to give a prudent response to every e-mail, and I believe people prefer a prompt, even if shorter, response to a more detailed e-mail that arrives too late to be used. Plus, this approach allows me more time to do my MITs, and I love the look of an empty inbox.

Keeping a Physical Inbox

David Allen, in *Making It All Work* (2008), suggests that whenever we receive any request that requires a written response, or some similar task, we put it into an inbox. You can also put notes to yourself in the box, listing tasks that you have to do, such as "Write thank-you note to Alison for October 10 meeting," or "Talk with Alan about the state of the lawn beside the school." Then, twice a week, deal with everything in the box. Just like your e-mail, start at the top and power through until you're done.

This accomplishes at least two things. First, it ensures that you stay on top of tasks, which feels great. Second, by putting tasks in the inbox right when you get them rather than tending to them as they pop up, you can stay focused on your MITs. Then when the time comes to clear the inbox, you can do it with gusto.

Some principals need two inboxes, one for urgent issues and one for issues that can wait. The urgent issues can be addressed each day, at the end of the day, and the issues that can wait can be addressed at the end of the week. As one principal explained to me, having only one inbox means that "too many things will be dropped." The urgent must be addressed, and that won't happen if we wait until the end of the week, especially if we let the inbox fill up and never get to the bottom.

Filing Notes by Month, Not Topic

Scott Belsky (2010) suggests a simple and powerful strategy for staying on top of notes: simply date our notes and put them into a folder labeled with the current month, filing them chronologically. Then, if you need the notes, you can go back to your electronic calendar, find what month you were meeting on the topic for which you need the notes, and pull out the file to get the notes. The method is quick and efficient, and it keeps piles of paper from sprouting up around your office.

You may need to adapt this system by creating a few separate folders for particular types of documents, but the goal, always, is to keep your system simple. If your notes are not confidential, you can place them in your inbox and file them each time you empty your inbox. Confidential files need to be placed in a locked file immediately.

Keep Plans Written Down, Not in Your Head

David Allen (2008) has written persuasively about the power of writing out your plans for all of the projects in your life. Allen points out that we would never plan our days by relying on our brains to remember all our appointments. We write every appointment down, and then we rely on our calendar to ensure we don't miss something important.

Allen suggests that we do the same with all of our projects—for Allen, any activity that consists of more than a few tasks is a project, whether it occurs at home or on the job. Using this approach, we write down each of the projects we need to do, and then we write down all the individual tasks that need to be completed for each project. In this way, we can see everything that has to be completed, and by getting it out of our heads and onto paper, we can do a better job of staying on top of all projects.

Photo by Jennifer Ryschon-Knight.

Getting projects out of your head and onto paper has at least two advantages. First, breaking down step by step all of the actions necessary to complete a project dramatically increases how quickly a project moves from conception to completion simply because it removes all the time wasted trying to figure out what the next step will be.

Second, when I physically lay out all of the projects I plan to complete, I get a clear idea of whether or not I can actually accomplish them. Usually, I have too much to do. After seeing every project, I realize that some things have to be put on the back burner or given up altogether. A critical part of project management is trying to do only what is possible; trying to do more than is possible sets you up for unavoidable failure.

Getting Support From Central Office

Without the support of central office staff, a principal will struggle to make the idea of an Impact School come into fruition. There is much that central office leaders can do to support principals as they go about the hard work of designing an Impact School. In many ways, the degree of support received from the central office can make or break a principal's attempt to lead reform.

Time

Perhaps the most important thing district leaders can do is to find time for principals to do the work of designing Impact Schools. If they want their schools to be Impact Schools, the superintendent, associate superintendents, directors, coordinators, and other central office staff must be intentional about creating time for principals. Here are some suggestions for how to do it.

1. Limit the number of meetings scheduled, so principals are not required to be out of the building too often. Leaders should ask themselves, at all times, if a meeting is really necessary, or if the topic of the meeting can be addressed via e-mail. Before calling a meeting, people should also always ask whether or not the meeting is really necessary. The habit of holding weekly meetings should be reconsidered because it often leads to meetings that really do not have a purpose.

2. Limit the length of meetings. Scott Belsky (2010) recommends that no meeting ever run longer than one hour and that whoever leads the meeting should start promptly and end when the hour is up or the agenda has been addressed.

3. Limit paperwork. Many principals I've collaborated with say that if they could just eliminate paperwork, they would have enough time to do the job they were hired to do.

4. Explore the possibility of hiring administrators to support principals by doing much of the necessary paperwork, so principals can focus on instructional leadership.

Supporting Development of the Target

It is essential that the superintendent, associate superintendents, and central office directors and coordinators support the Targets that are developed by the schools in their district. If schools invest a great deal of time creating a Target only to have new initiatives promoted by district leaders push the Target to the side, teachers' commitment to any new initiative will be significantly eroded. The superintendent or other leaders at central office need to create a unified team working toward the same end. If the central office is organized into silos, or the breeding ground for self-serving political fights, that lack of unity will manifest itself in schools.

To ensure that the district leaders and the schools are on the same page, central office staff must be in frequent communication with principals. Indeed, the associate superintendent responsible for instruction should make frequent visits to schools to discuss how instructional improvement is progressing. By visiting schools, leaders can show everyone in the school that they are committed to the project and that the district intends to stay the course.

Communication between central office and schools also ensures that district leaders are able to share information about programs, practices, or priorities that are considered non-negotiable. If the superintendent, the state, or the board determines that something is essential, for example, content planning that involves guiding questions and learning maps, that practice must be reflected in the Target. Effective communication can ensure that what is created at the school level can be 100 percent supported at the district level.

Perhaps more important, central office must clearly communicate that it is OK for schools to focus on a smaller number of practices so that they can be easily implemented. A major barrier to effective professional learning is the intense pressure everyone in schools feels to respond to every concern at the same time. Here is how one superintendent described it to me in a recent e-mail:

> Principals (via the No Child Left Behind Act [NCLB] and in the near future the reauthorization of the Elementary and Secondary Education Act [ESEA]) are held to stringent accountability standards. The accountability is tied to high-stakes testing, which is tied directly to a school's ability to educate students through a myriad of state standards. When schools fail to meet these standards, schools, school leadership, and school systems are at risk of facing sanctions, including in some cases state takeover.
>
> It is difficult to get everything accomplished and even more difficult to "narrow" the focus for fear that if something is missed, that will be the area of failure. Therefore, many schools develop a plan that takes the approach of attempting to cover *every* area of deficit with 8–10 strategies for addressing

each area. These plans are overwhelming to manage and ineffective; however, they take solace in the fact that they feel that they are comprehensively addressing *everything*.

Federal, state, and district leadership reinforce this type of response. For example, schools receiving Title I funds must submit their school plan, which is reviewed for *all* of the components that are mandated to be in a comprehensive plan . . . the requirement of a *myriad* of data that support the plan (including agendas, sign-in sheets, and minutes for *every* event, including parent nights and back to school events).

District leadership is often guilty of asking school leaders to "show," through some sort of school planning document, the process that they have used to thoroughly review *all* data as well as multiple goals, objectives, and strategies for each area of need. (Personal communication, July 12, 2010)

The pressure brought to bear on principals leads many of them to fear committing what leadership expert Bill Sommers calls a CLM (Career Limit Move). District leaders must fight to make sure that they don't demand that principals do the impossible. They must run interference and clarify with principals that they are expected to identify and focus on key priorities until those priorities are accomplished.

I have been told that bus drivers in a major U.S. city are told that they are free to have three accidents every year, with no negative consequence. The drivers are told this so that they can drive confidently to each stop on time, knowing that they will not suffer consequences for a fender bender even if it is their fault. In other words, the drivers get to do their work in a safety zone, and that safety allows them to in the long run be more successful.

Central office can provide similar support to principals as they venture out to create an Impact School. Leaders can tell principals that the hard work of creating an Impact School will likely lead to some false steps, some mistakes. To decrease the fear principals might have, leaders can tell them they are forgiven in advance so that principals can attack their work with the necessary drive and courage.

Providing Support

Designing a Target may demand that a principal acquire a new set of skills. Principals may need to learn about new instructional practices, methods for gathering data during drop-in observations, partnership facilitation skills, partnership communication skills, and so forth. That is a lot to ask of any one person, especially when that person is also responsible for putting out fires and keeping the school running smoothly. To create an Impact School, principals need support.

One option is for principals to have their own coach or mentor to help them acquire the skills they need. Since the partnership approach to improving instruction may require new skills, traditional support, such as retired principals, will only work if the mentors themselves have the skills. Principals may need to work with someone outside the district until the capacity is developed for support within the district.

An absolutely important form of support is funding. Without a budget for substitute teachers, training, materials, and coaching, the job of leading an Impact School may be next to impossible. Professional learning cannot happen if we continue to try to make it happen without paying for it. New initiatives demand more time and more resources, and money is necessary for that to happen.

District leaders would love to provide significant funding, but they face hard decisions about finances all the time. The important message here is that if professional learning is deemed important, it must be a priority financially, too. When little is expended to support professional learning, little should be expected.

Learning

Perhaps the most important form of support central office staff can offer principals is to be learners along with principals, teachers, and students. Thus, everyone from the superintendent on down should attend workshops, develop deep knowledge of the high-leverage practices described on schools' Targets, and clearly understand the Targets developed at every school.

Given the other demands of their time (Bill Sommers refers to the killer Bs of budgets, busses, and boards), leaders need to apply the management strategies described above, so they can make it their goal to have a deep understanding of every practice on every Target in every school. When leaders are learners, everyone in the school is more likely to get caught up in the infectious joy of learning.

To Sum Up

Partnership

Although a principal's role puts the principal in a structurally unequal position with teachers, the inequality is only structural. Principals working from the partnership perspective see everyone as equal.

Principals as Designers

When principals use "design thinking," they work creatively to ensure that professional learning is aligned, resources are available for professional learning, and the right people are in place to lead various aspects of professional learning, such as coaching.

The Target

In Impact Schools, almost all of the professional learning (teacher evaluations, workshops, intensive learning teams, and coaching) is focused on implementation of the Target—a one-page document that summarizes both the achievement and behavior goals for students and the instructional improvement goals for teachers.

The Big Four

This comprehensive framework, to be described in *Instruction That Makes an Impact* (Knight, in press) involves teaching practices for content planning, formative assessment, powerful instruction (cooperative learning, stories, effective questions, thinking prompts, challenging assignments, and experiential learning), and community building. The Big Four provides a point of departure for developing an instructional improvement target.

Creating the Target

Principals should involve all the staff and the Target Design Team in the development of a Target that everyone considers meaningful.

Observing and Monitoring Teacher Progress

Walk-through tools and teacher evaluations should focus on the practices identified in the Target. Observations must be conducted so that teachers get reliable, frequent feedback on their progress. Principals can use a tool such as the teacher progress map to keep track of implementation of the Target.

Principal as First Learner

Principals must understand the Target, be active participants or leaders of workshops or intensive learning teams, and do everything they can to model the kind of approach to learning they hope to see in their teachers (and students).

Making It All Happen

Principals need to use powerful strategies to ensure they find the time to do all the high-leverage work involved in being instructional leaders.

Getting Support From Central Office Staff

Central office staff, especially the superintendent, must support the Target 100 percent. Leaders must find ways to decrease pressure and increase support for principals in Impact Schools.

Going Deeper

Michael Fullan

Many of the ideas in this chapter and throughout the book are the direct result of my reading of Michael Fullan's work. If instructional leaders have time to read only one book about instructional change and leadership, I highly recommend Fullan's *Motion Leadership: The Skinny on Becoming Change Savvy* (2010b). Fullan's most recent books, *All Systems Go: The Change Imperative for Whole School Reform* (2010a) and *The Six Secrets of Change* (2008), are also extremely informative. Briefly, Fullan provides a theoretical framework for understanding change and leadership and explains how to translate that theory into practice.

Other Leadership Books

Dennis Sparks' *Leading for Results: Transforming Teaching, Learning, and Relationships in Schools* (2006) is a concise and incredibly useful summary of many important ideas of about leadership. Daniel Goleman, Richard Boyatzis, and Annie McKee's *Primal Leadership: Realizing the Power of Emotional Intelligence* (2004) is the definitive work on emotional intelligence and leadership. Stewart D. Friedman's *Total Leadership: Be a Better Leader, Have a Richer Life* (2008) guides readers through self-coaching activities to help balance work and home priorities.

Design

Tim Brown's *Change by Design: How Design Thinking Transforms Organizations and Inspires Innovation* (2009) is a practical introduction to the specifics of "design thinking." Brown explains how the lessons learned by his firm, IDEO, one of the leading design firms in the country, can and should be applied by any change leader. Roger Martin, Dean of the Rotman School of Business at The University of Toronto, in his *Design of Business: Why Design Thinking Is the Next Competitive Advantage* (2009) provides a more theoretical explanation of what design thinking is and why it is important.

The Target

My book, *Instruction That Makes an Impact* (Knight, in press), will offer a detailed explanation of the Big Four teaching practices. Charlotte Danielson's *Enhancing Professional Practice: A Framework for Teaching* (2007) and John Hattie's *Visible Learning* (2009) are two other well-known comprehensive models for improving instruction. Bill Jensen's *Simplicity: The New Competitive Advantage in a World of More, Better, Faster* (2000) is a great book about creating simple plans, such as a Target. Nancy Mooney and Ann Mausbach's *Align the Design: A Blueprint for School Improvement* (2008) is a practical and smart guide to its topic and would help anyone developing a Target.

Monitoring Progress

Elizabeth City, Richard Elmore, Sarah Fiarman, and Lee Teitel's *Instructional Rounds in Education: A Network Approach to Improving Teaching and Learning* (2009) describes how communities of educators can collaborate to conduct rounds similar in structure to doctors' rounds in hospitals. The authors' ideas about instructional core, what to observe when watching teachers, and how to discuss what was observed would be beneficial to anyone charged with the task of monitoring progress toward the Target.

Making It All Happen

Scott Belsky's *Making Ideas Happen: Overcoming the Obstacles Between Vision and Reality* (2010) is hands down the best personal organization and time management book I have read. However, it owes much to David Allen's *Making It All Work* (2008). Allen is the premier productivity guru, and his strategies are widely adopted.

Leo Babauta's *The Power of Less* (2009) is another useful book. Many of Babauta's ideas may also be found on his extremely useful blog, Zen Habits: http://zenhabits.net.

4

Instructional Coaching

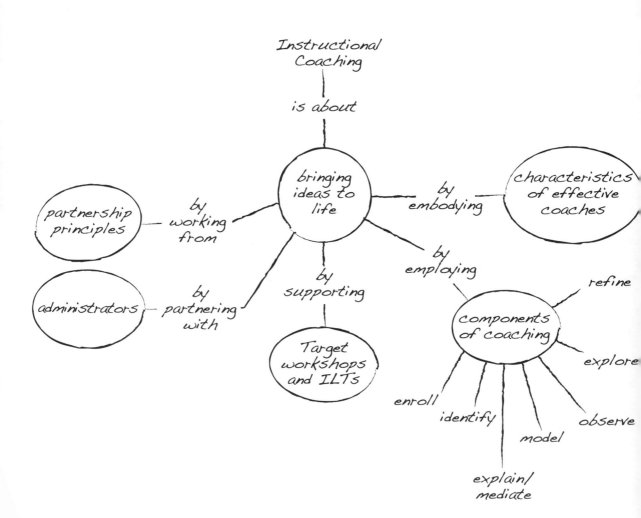

Instructional coaches are essential for professional learning in Impact Schools. Principals provide leadership, guide the development of the Target, and observe and encourage teachers as they grow and move toward the Target. Workshops introduce teachers to the practices that are in the Target. Intensive learning teams provide opportunities for teachers to rethink curriculum in light of the Target. Coaches help teachers take all the ideas and practices they are learning and bring them to life. Without coaching, too often, no significant change occurs (Cornett & Knight, 2009).

Over the past three decades, several approaches to coaching have been created to provide the support and encouragement necessary for professional learning in schools. Among them are cognitive coaching, literacy coaching, peer coaching, data coaching, content coaching, and instructional coaching. Sources for more information on each of these approaches are included in the Going Deeper section at the end of this chapter. This chapter describes how instructional coaches (ICs) can support and stimulate the learning that is at the heart of Impact Schools.

Fundamentally, ICs partner with teachers to help them incorporate research-based instructional practices into their teaching. They are skilled relationship builders who have a repertoire of communication skills that enable them to empathize, listen, and build trusting relationships. ICs also encourage and support teachers' reflection about their classroom practices. Thus, they must be skilled at unpacking collaborating teachers' professional goals so that they can help them create a plan for realizing those goals, all with a focus on improving instruction.

The primary goal of the work of ICs is to support implementation of the Target. They frequently model practices in the classroom, observe teachers, and engage in supportive, dialogical conversations with them about what they observed. An IC, in other words, partners with teachers in respectful humane conversations so teachers can choose and implement research-based teaching practices that will help students learn more effectively.

ICs have the potential to dramatically improve the quality of teaching, and thus student achievement, in any school, but only if the following factors are in place.

Partnership

In my workshops, I often show a video clip of coach Susan Leyden and teacher Sarah Weller as they collaborate to create a graphic organizer to teach the concept of scientific measurement. When I ask people what they notice about the way the two interact, I get a variety of responses. Some note that the conversation is very equal—often people aren't sure who is the coach and who is the teacher. Others observe that there is a genuine give and take between the two and that Susan, the coach, is very responsive to Sarah's suggestions. People also notice that they are both kind to and supportive of each other, and the conversation provides an opportunity for them to encourage each other. But what people notice most frequently is that the two of them are having fun. They laugh and joke with and genuinely enjoy each other's company as they work very productively to create a new lesson plan. At the end of the conversation, both of them walk away better for the time spent together.

When coaches work from the partnership perspective, as Susan Leyden does in this clip, their interactions with teachers embody respect, compassion, optimism, even joy. Their work is focused on supporting teachers as they learn new ways of teaching, but it is through kind, useful conversations between teachers and coaches that much of the humanity of Impact Schools is realized. Instructional coaches can listen to teachers' concerns, see and reflect back the good they see in them, and work in partnership, often in highly enjoyable, exciting conversations, to identify, learn, and implement practices that enable that teacher to reach more students. Effective ICs embody the following partnership principles in all of their actions.

Equality

According to Edgar Schein in *Helping* (2009), mentioned in Chapter 2, helping relationships between adults work best in adult-to-adult conversations. When one adult takes on the role of "parent" while helping other adults, telling them what to do, judging their behavior, holding them accountable, usually the party feeling parented resists.

At the Kansas Coaching Project, we have watched many hours of video recordings of coach-and-teacher interactions. Clearly, talented coaches skillfully and subtly act in ways that communicate that they do not see themselves as having higher status than their collaborating teacher. Indeed, these coaches' authentic recognition that their collaborating teacher is an equal partner permeates everything they do.

Instructional coaches who see their collaborating teachers as equals listen much more than they talk, carefully consider everything teachers say, and position the teachers as judges and decision makers. In doing so, coaches exhibit subtle behaviors such as sitting beside teachers rather than across from them, downplaying their own expertise, and authentically drawing out and celebrating their teachers' expertise. Coaches who act on the principle of equality, as Edgar Schein (2009) suggests, "equalibrate the conversation."

Lynn Barnes, a coach who has worked with me for more than a decade, talks about adopting a "servitude attitude." "We have to care about the people we are serving," Lynn says, "because we cannot go in like the know-it-all expert. Coaches have to find ways to harness the hope and make it work for both teachers and students."

Equality, the core belief that we are partners in learning relationships, runs through the other six partnership principles.

Choice

If a coach and teacher come together as equal partners, the teacher must have choices. Partners don't do the choosing for each other. In coaching, this means, most fundamentally, that teachers have a choice about whether or not they want to work with a coach.

As mentioned throughout this book, choice does not mean that teachers can choose to not participate in professional learning. No professional can choose to be unprofessional. Everyone in the school must be actively engaged in professional growth and development, with the principal as the first learner. My experience has been that most people are interested in, even excited about, learning. But as adults, they just want to have some say in what and how they learn.

The principle of choice is letting go of the notion that we are obligated to control what another person does. Coaches who adopt the partnership approach don't try to get a teacher to do something. Instead, they meet teachers where they are and collaborate with them to help them discover and implement practices that meet their students' and their own needs.

Such a commitment to choice becomes manifest in all aspects of instructional coaching. Thus, teachers decide which practices they would like to implement, drawn from the practices on the Target, and coaches collaborate with them to modify practices so that they meet the unique needs of each teacher's students. Choice is central to the way coaches share knowledge because coaches share information in a way that leaves room for teachers to interpret what they are learning from their perspective. ICs don't tell teachers what to do; they offer precise explanations, ensure that teachers clearly understand those explanations, and then ask teacher what they think about what they've heard.

Voice

When coaches work from the principle of voice, they make it easy for teachers to honestly and openly say what is on their mind. Conversations between teachers and coaches should be as open and candid as the conversations teachers might have with friends they trust.

To encourage teachers to say what they think, coaches must focus on teachers' concerns rather than their own agenda. They can do this by becoming effective listeners, by asking good questions, and by being curious. Coaches need to honor what Susan Scott in *Fierce Leadership* (2009) calls "the sweet purity of silence" so that teachers have an opportunity to explore and communicate their thoughts. Indeed, often the best thing a coach can say is nothing at all.

Reflection

Thinking is an essential part of learning. Much of the pleasure of learning is thinking about what you are learning. Indeed, if you are not thinking about what you are learning, you probably are not learning. When professionals are told what to do and when and how to do it, with no room for their own individual thoughts, that is a spiritual death experience.

Instructional coaches should work as thinking partners for teachers. Coaches offer plenty of options to teachers and ask them, "What do you think?" Coaches explain ideas in a way that leaves room for teacher thought. Rather than saying, "Here's what you need to do," coaches working from the partnership approach say, "Here is something; what do you think of it?"

When coaches and teachers are truly thinking together, both benefit. When we watch video recordings of partnership coaches and teachers co-creating ideas through dialogue, we see two people, like Susan and Sarah at the beginning of this chapter, who are energized, laughing, talking enthusiastically, and simply enjoying themselves in a joyous activity.

Dialogue

Dialogue is the mode of discourse for the partnership relationship. When a coach and teacher engage in dialogue, the coach lets go of the need to push for a particular point of view. The objective of a dialogue is not to have your ideas prevail but to have the best ideas win, and that occurs best when both partners think together through conversation.

Coaches can do much to encourage dialogue. First, they must enter into conversations with a humble openness about what they know and don't know. Coaches need to let go of the notion that they must be the experts and simply and honestly explain what they can and cannot do to respond to a teacher's concerns. A genuine openness and a willingness to be shaped by a collaborating teacher's opinions sets the stage for dialogue.

Second, coaches need to balance advocacy with inquiry. This means that while coaches share suggestions and ideas and explain practices, they do so in a way that encourages the teacher's honest comments about the ideas being shared. Coaches must avoid talking in a way that silences the teacher by pushing for a particular practice, and communicate in a way that encourages the teacher to share his or her thoughts or ideas.

Finally, coaches must ask good questions that prompt both coaches and teachers to think about the assumptions they hold. Simple questions like, "Why do you say that?" or, "What leads you to believe that . . . ?" can be useful, so long as they are questions to which the coach is really curious about hearing answers, not formulaic questions asked to get to a predetermined goal. More on this in Chapter 7.

Praxis

Praxis is all about the goal of this book: impact. Praxis is about dialogue that is embedded in action. To be true to the principle of praxis, a coach's actions are filtered by a focus on teaching. Indeed, everything a coach does or says should be filtered through a central question: what does this mean for the collaborating teacher and their students?

An emphasis on praxis means that the coach, from the start, is intent on helping the teacher explore and plan to implement a practice that is especially meaningful to her particular concerns. That is, conversation is about what the teacher can do, and it is shaped by the coach so that the collaborating teacher is exploring how she will implement the new way of teaching. Although coaching conversations may explore theory, the conversation is always driven by the teacher's real-life concerns and how the teacher can adapt her approach to change her practice, usually be implementing something on the Target, that helps her address her needs.

A major critique of professional development that I have heard from the more than 300 teachers I have interviewed in the past decade is that they find it to be too theoretical and impractical. Coaches who act on the principle of praxis are committed to ensuring that any learning they facilitate is relentlessly practical, responding directly to the real-life experiences of teachers.

Reciprocity

When researchers at the Kansas Coaching Project studied outstanding coaches, one of the characteristics we discovered was that they are learners. Outstanding coaches, we found, are turned on by learning, always seeking new ideas, reading books, and learning from the teachers they observe.

If a coach genuinely respects a teacher, and genuinely sees herself as a partner with a collaborating teacher, she naturally enters into coaching expecting to learn.

Coaches who act on the principle of reciprocity expect to learn new ways to teach every time they observe a teacher and interact with their collaborating partners during all coaching conversations. Further, they expect their collaborating teachers to teach them about the practices on the Target, in part by the way the teachers implement those practices and also by the deep questions they ask that push a coach's thinking. For instructional coaches working from the partnership perspective, much of the joy of coaching is learning new ideas and practices, and learning about themselves, as they explore learning with a collaborating teacher. That joy, too, is often passed on to teachers and their students.

Partnering With Administrators

In Impact Schools, principals and coaches collaborate to support and lead all aspects of professional learning. This partnership is absolutely essential, but at the same time, coaches and principals must structure their relationship carefully so that teachers do not misunderstand the coach's role in schools. If teachers perceive coaches as evaluating or judging them, they may not be receptive to coaching. To ensure that the principal-coach relationships foster rather than hamper effective coaching, here are a few issues that a coach and principal should consider.

The Target

In Impact Schools, professional learning is designed to help teachers implement the Target, so, naturally, coach and principal partnerships are formed around the Target. The principal designs a setting where teachers are able to learn the Target, as explained in Chapter 3, and the coach provides an intensive, respectful support necessary to make it easy for teachers to implement. For that reason, coaches must deeply understand all the practices in the Target, be able to precisely explain and model them, and know what it looks like when those practices are used well in the classroom. Not much will happen unless the coach understands the Target.

Top Down/Bottom Up

Instructional coaching is based on the partnership principles. In projects across the continent, we have found that when coaches take the partnership approach, teachers are more inclined to implement new teaching practices. But, a partnership approach that exclusively relies on bottom-up initiatives has limitations. Bottom up, by itself, does not appear to be enough. The principal has to provide instructional leadership.

When a principal is the instructional leader in absentia, teaching practices may be unsystematically implemented by some and not at all by others, and school improvement may progress in an incoherent manner that is troubling and confusing for teachers and students. A purely bottom-up approach also risks placing teachers significantly out of step with district and state mandates. Finally, if a bottom-up approach offers teachers freedom to choose whether or not to participate, sadly we have found that the teachers who most need to change are sometimes the ones who choose not to participate.

However, a purely top-down approach is not a practical alternative. Years of experience have shown us that when leaders adopt a top-down stance, they run the risk of introducing what counselors refer to as an "ironic process," an approach that "causes the very outcome that it was meant to avert" (Miller & Rollnick, 2002, p. 37). Thus, telling teachers that they must work with an IC actually makes it more difficult for ICs to enroll teachers in instructional coaching. A colleague of mine, IC Ric Palma, told me, "When you tell teachers to do something, they resent it. If they do it, they're going to do it in a half-[baked] . . . manner, and others will just refuse, because they don't like to be told what to do."

What is required is a balance of bottom-up and top-down strategies. ICs should continue to build bottom-up support by positioning themselves as equal partners collaborating with their fellow teachers based on partnership principles. At the same time, the principal clearly is the instructional leader. The principal ensures that new teaching practices reflect the desired direction stated in the Target and works with the Target Design Team to limit the number of interventions to make it easier for the teacher and coach to work together on those few interventions that have the highest possibility of impacting student achievement. The principal builds coherence by ensuring that the Target is authentic and effective and by encouraging schoolwide implementation of strategies. Most important, perhaps, the principal and IC work together to ensure that those who need help get it.

In practical terms, the principal conducts drop-in observations, evaluates teachers, guides the school in designing the Instructional Target, and encourages, monitors, and evaluates to ensure everyone is moving toward the Target. At the same time, the IC provides intensive, respectful support that empowers teachers to implement the practices. In short, the principal focuses everyone's attention on the target; the IC makes it easy for teachers to get there.

Clarifying Roles

Principals can help coaches be more efficient by ensuring that everyone clearly understands the coach's and principal's distinct roles. When Impact Schools adopt a top-down *and* bottom-up approach, the principal conducts drop-in observations, evaluates, and offers teachers choices for involvement on the rare occasion when teachers are not actively implementing new practices. The principal is not only the evaluator, but also the first learner.

The work conducted by ICs must focus on capacity building if it is to have long-term impact. Coaches primarily support teachers as they implement practices (utilizing the coaching components described later in this chapter). In addition, they may lead workshops, facilitate intensive learning teams, and perform other tasks that support and accelerate professional learning.

When coaches focus on capacity building, there are tasks that they do not do. Usually coaches do not sub when teachers are away, do administrivia, or work directly with students except in the service of the larger goal of promoting teacher growth. Certainly, there are occasions when these general guidelines are ignored. Just as a principal may be forced to sub if there is no other alternative, so might a coach. However, this should occur very rarely.

Leaders are often tempted to ask coaches to work directly with students instead of coaching, and no doubt, coaches love the interactions with students. However, this is a quick fix that does not fully exploit a coach's ability to make a lasting impact. When coaches work with students instead of with teachers, they only affect those particular children for that particular year. By contrast, when coaches help teachers reach their students, they help every student teachers will teach for the rest of their lives.

When coaches and principals clarify the coach's roles, the coach is better able to focus attention on helping teachers hit the Target. In my experience working with thousands of coaches across Canada and the United States, their chief complaint is that they are asked to do so many noncoaching tasks that they have little time left for actual coaching. For example, it is not uncommon for coaches to report that they spend less than 25 percent of their time, often less than 10 percent of their time, on coaching. If coaches are essential for professional learning, and coaches aren't coaching, then not much professional learning will take place.

Clarifying a coach's roles also increases the likelihood that he or she will find the job rewarding. According to Marcus Buckingham (1999), who studied data from more than a million surveys about job satisfaction, the most important information employees need to be satisfied with their career is to know what is expected of them. Clearer roles also make it easier for principals to conduct evaluations of teachers because they provide a reference point that principals can use for observing coaches and talking with them about their progress.

Confidentiality

In most types of coaching, whether life coaching (Whitworth, Kimsey-House, Kimsey House, & Sandahl, 2007), executive coaching (Hargrove, 2008), or instructional coaching (Knight, 2007), the practice of coaching occurs within confidential relationships. There are at least three reasons for this.

First, when coaches deal with what matters to teachers, they are privileged to see and hear information most others will not see and hear. To share that private information with others is a violation of a person's privacy. Second, coaching is much more productive when collaborating teachers are open about their ideas, thoughts, and fears. For many teachers, knowing that coaching conversations are confidential makes it easier for them to talk about what really matters. Third, when we ensure that coaching is confidential, we increase the chances that teachers will choose to work with a coach.

However, not everything a coach does, can, or should be confidential. For example, coaches need to keep principals informed of whom they are working with and what they are working on. ICs working with the Kansas Coaching Project discriminate between what should and should not be shared by saying that coaches do not share data or evaluative information. We communicate clearly to teachers that coaching is nonjudgmental. Coaches are partners helping teachers learn new practices, not evaluators. Indeed, in most cases, ICs have no administrative training on how to evaluate teachers, so it would not be appropriate for them to evaluate teachers anyway.

In some schools, confidentiality is not an issue. In especially positive, safe settings, teachers may be more than comfortable having their coach share any information. Indeed, Michael Fullan (2008) identifies transparency as one of his "six secrets of change," stating that "when transparency is consistently evident, it creates an aura of 'positive pressure'—pressure that is experienced as fair and reasonable, pressure that is actionable in that it points to solutions, and pressure that ultimately is inescapable" (p. 14).

To create settings where such transparency is possible may require baby steps. In a culture where there is not a great deal of trust, confidential coaching can be the default mode, but over time, if teachers agree, more information can be shared. The greater the lack of trust initially, the more important confidentiality usually is. What is most important is that principals and coaches clearly delineate what they will and will not discuss, communicate that policy across the school, and act consistently with the policy. Perceived betrayal of trust can severely damage a coaching relationship. For example, when a teacher says something to a coach that she thinks will be kept privately by the coach, and then she discovers that what she said was shared with others, it may be impossible for the coach to ever win back the teacher's trust.

Frequent Meetings

The importance of coach and principal meetings became clear to me while we conducted a qualitative study of outstanding coaches in 2008. Eight researchers and I visited five of the best coaches in Florida, drawn from a pool of 2,600. In each case, we discovered that each effective coach worked in close partnership with his or her principal.

When a principal and coach are serious about achieving the goal of excellent instruction in every classroom, every day, for every student, they will find that they have to meet frequently. I suggest they meet at least once a week.

There are several reasons why this is important. First, the meetings provide an opportunity for the principal and coach to discuss the progress of professional learning in the school. The principal must know who is working with the coach so that she can encourage and support those who are actively involved in learning. Additionally, the principal may need to offer professional learning choices to other teachers who are not collaborating with the coach.

Second, the meetings provide an opportunity for the coach and principal to discuss, explore, problem solve, and plan the general progress of professional learning within the school. In the best case scenario, both the principal and the coach will lead workshops and intensive learning teams (ILTs), so the meetings give them a chance to explore what might be useful to staff. Since the principal conducts walk-throughs and understands exactly how well each teacher is progressing, she will have a good understanding of what is needed. The coach, because he talks with so many staff in school, can bring the teachers' perspective to the meetings to ensure workshops address both the needs identified by the principal and the concerns expressed by teachers.

Third, the meetings also are important because they keep the principal and coach on track. Each week, they share with each other what they have done to move the school closer to the Target. Leading wide-scale change requires relentless focus by leaders, and when the principal and coach meet frequently, the meetings keep both of them on track.

Fourth, the meetings provide a chance for the coach and principal to discuss the teaching practices on the Target. Both need a deep understanding of what each practice is and what it looks like when done well. In the weekly meetings, they can check their understanding of teaching practices with each other. Sometimes the principal will be the expert, especially in cases where a new coach is hired in a school, and in some cases the coach will be the expert. Either way, the meeting provides a chance for coach and principal to discuss practices, confirm their understandings, and work with each other.

Somebody has to lead the meetings to ensure they are efficiently organized and productive. We suggest that the coach should assume this role because most principals are overwhelmed with tasks, but other options are possible. The person who prepares for the meeting should create an agenda that addresses key topics, such as (a) progress since last meeting, (b) successes, (c) problems, (d) questions about practices on the target, and (e) plans of action. Meetings can be short, say 30 minutes, if they are managed well. Both parties should leave the meeting with a clear understanding of next-action steps. I like to use a snazzy Moleskine notebook to take notes and record next

actions, and after a meeting I copy and share my notes with whom-
ever I meet.

These meetings are critical because principal support is necessary
for a coach's success. The coach, therefore, must be well prepared for
the meeting, efficient, and positive. The coach's goal should always
be to make the meeting so valuable that the principal won't want to
go a week without the meeting.

Principal Support

Teachers are inclined to do what the principal emphasizes and to
ignore what the principal ignores. For this reason, it is essential that
the principal communicates support for the coach.

Such support can be communicated both literally, by the principal
speaking up about the importance of the coach and the value the coach
brings to the school, and symbolically, by the principal attending workshops led by the coach, by listening attentively when the coach talks in
meetings, and by taking the time to encourage those who collaborate
with the coach. In dozens of conversations across North America,
coaches have told me that the single most important support they need
to be successful in their jobs is principal support. With it, they can lead
change. Without it, they struggle to make an impact.

Workshops and Intensive Learning Teams

Without coaching, workshops, ILTs, and other forms of professional
learning will have little real impact on the way teachers teach. As
shown in the following, there is a much a coach can do to ensure that
workshops and ILTs move all teachers in the school toward the
Target.

Leading Workshops and ILTs

In many cases, coaches, along with principals, are the perfect
people to lead workshops and ILTs. This is an efficient approach, and
it positions coaches as go-to people for the ideas being learned in the
workshop. Leading workshops also provides another venue for
coaches to synthesize their understanding of the materials they are
sharing within the school. Anyone who has led a workshop knows
how much the act of planning and delivering professional learning
deepens and sharpens one's own understanding of teaching practices.

Coaches must be well prepared to lead workshops and ILTs. First, they need the content knowledge necessary to clearly communicate the practices on the Target. To get this knowledge, which is also required when they coach teachers, ICs need their own extensive professional learning.

Coaches also need to develop the specialized skills of an ILT leader or workshop facilitator, both described in this book. These skills can be learned through partnerships with our Instructional Coaching Group (www.instructionalcoaching.com) or through other organizations. Simply put, at a minimum, coaches need to know what they are talking about, how to talk about it, and how to create opportunities for teachers to talk about it. These skills are difficult to obtain without professional learning for coaches.

Providing Support During Sessions

If coaches are not leading workshops or ILTs, they still perform an important role by helping to facilitate small-group discussions during sessions. Indeed, because coaches usually know a great deal about the practices being discussed, they can provide outstanding support by answering questions when groups hit roadblocks.

Conducting Interviews

Coaches can pave the way for successful workshops and teams by having one-to-one conversations with teachers prior to the session to (a) identify teacher concerns so they can be addressed in the ILT or workshop, (b) clarify the goals of the workshop or ILT, and (c) answer any question teachers might have about the upcoming sessions. The step-by-step process for conducting enrollment interviews like this is described later in this chapter.

Providing Follow-Up

Follow-up is essential for workshops and ILTs to be successful. Before a workshop or ILT ends, time must be set aside for coaches to meet with teachers to organize when follow-up coaching will occur. We suggest coaches and teachers plan exactly what follow-up will occur and when and where it will occur. A form coaches and teachers might use for this purpose is included in the Impact Toolkit in Resource A.

Coaches sometimes conduct brief follow-up interviews immediately after a workshop or session (a) to assess how effective it was,

(b) to determine whether future sessions should be modified to be more effective, and (c) to identify how they might support teachers as they transfer new learning into their own practice. The questions below yield a lot of valuable information during these interviews.

Follow-Up Questions

- In your opinion, what was the most beneficial thing we did in our session?
- How has what you learned changed your thinking about instruction?
- How will what we worked through as a team have an impact on your lessons in the future?
- How do you see the coaches supporting you as you implement the practices we discussed or developed?
- What advice do you have for how we can improve the sessions?
- Is there anything else you'd like to share about how I can be more supportive or about your opinions regarding the session?

Components of Coaching

In *Instructional Coaching: A Partnership Approach to Improving Instruction* (Knight, 2007), I laid out a step-by-step process that coaches can follow when sharing teaching practices with teachers. My colleagues and I have subsequently refined the model based on findings from ongoing research at the University of Kansas. In particular, a design study where we use video recordings to test and evaluate new approaches to coaching led us to significantly refine the way we coach teachers.

Two primary changes have shaped the way we see coaches doing their work. First, we have found video recorders, such as Flip cameras, to be essential tools in a coach's toolkit. Indeed, recording a teacher teaching and sharing that video with a teacher may be the most important activity a coach can do. Second, in watching our own recordings of coaches coaching, it has become apparent how important it is that coaches provide an opportunity for teachers to identify a clear goal that they want to work on during coaching.

In his book *Masterful Coaching* (2008), Robert Hargrove makes a distinction that helps clarify why goal setting is so important. Most coaches, he says, start with a series of ideas (he mentions leadership qualities, but in schools we might refer to instructional practices) and then seek to convince coachees to implement those practices. He calls this "a push approach."

In contrast, Hargrove starts his coaching engagements by asking, "What would be an Impossible Future . . . you are really passionate about?" (an impossible future, he says, "is one that . . . can be only realized by leaders reinventing not just their organizations but also themselves"). Then Hargrove asks, "How are you going to need to develop as a leader to get there?" Starting with what the coachee most desires, he says, is the "pull approach."

These push-and-pull ideas apply directly to instructional coaching. If coaches use the push approach, they try to convince teachers to try strategies that the coach thinks will help teachers be more effective. Sometimes when coaches take the push approach, a collaborating teacher appears to be doing a favor for the coach by learning something new instead of being committed to meeting her own needs in the classroom.

If coaches use the pull approach, they might start by asking, "Today, how close is your class to what you imagine your ideal class to be?" then ask, "What are you going to need to do as a teacher to get your class there?" Pull coaching starts with the teacher's most important goals.

Once goals have been identified, the coach can become what Hargrove refers to as a "thinking partner." Instructional coaches can partner with their collaborating teachers to identify teaching practices that will help teachers achieve their goals. Then, coaches can work to make it easy for teachers to implement the new practices. With pull coaching, when a teacher learns a new teaching practice: learning is not a favor; it is a clear way for the teacher to move from where they are to where they want to be.

These new ideas, the use of video and the distinction between push and pull coaching, are embodied in the following refined steps of instructional coaching: (a) enroll, (b) identify, (c) explain, (d) model, (e) observe, and (f) explore.

Enroll

Not much coaching happens unless coaches are able to enroll teachers in the coaching process. We have found that the partnership approach is a highly effective method for enrolling teachers. Coaches taking the partnership approach to enrolling teachers recognize the importance of the principle of choice and see teachers as professionals who are able to decide for themselves whether or not they could benefit from coaching. Indeed, telling teachers they *must* work with a coach may poison the entire coaching relationship and in the long run decrease the likelihood that coaches will have an impact on the quality of instruction.

Many strategies can be used by coaches and administrators to enroll teachers. Coaches can give brief large- or small-group presentations where they explain coaching to teachers and identify teachers who are interested in collaborating with them. Teachers should also have an opportunity to plan for coaching following any workshop or ILT meeting. Indeed, whenever a workshop or ILT meeting occurs, there should be a form teachers can complete to plan for coaching support for implementing the new practice.

Another approach to enrollment is principals referring teachers to coaches by identifying coaching as one option for targeted professional learning. Thus, a principal might say to a teacher, "I observed your class, and only 60 percent of students were on task. You need to work on that. I have a book you can read, a video series you can watch, some websites you can visit, or you can work with the coach—she's a pro at engaging instruction. You should choose whatever works best for you, but we can't have only 60 percent of the students on task. Our target is 90 percent engagement, and I'll work with you to get us there." In essence, the principal reminds the teacher of the Target, while respecting his professionalism, and provides coaching as one option of many that the teacher can choose to assist with professional growth.

Perhaps the most effective enrollment strategy is for coaches to conduct one-to-one interviews with teachers (Knight, 2007). During enrollment interviews, coaches meet with teachers and ask about teachers' successes, roadblocks, and what the teachers perceive as the strengths and weaknesses of their students. During the conversation, the coach explains the practices he can share with teachers, and the teacher and coach explore whether or not one of the practices might be valuable for the teacher.

We have found that the greater the likelihood that teachers might resist change, the smaller the group the coach should meet with at first, and one-to-one meetings have proved to be especially successful for enrolling teachers.

Each enrollment strategy embodies two important ideas. First, coaches need to communicate their credibility, that is, their realistic understanding of the opportunities and challenges faced by teachers and their authentic respect for the profession of teaching. Coaches who position themselves as experts poised to improve teachers, as opposed to partners, may find themselves with few teachers to coach. Second, coaches should recognize that people are rarely persuaded by talk; people have to experience success to believe a practice will be effective (Patterson, Grenny, Maxfield, McMillan, & Switzler, 2008). Therefore, during the enrollment phase, a coach's job is not to persuade teachers that a new practice will be highly effective. Rather, it is to set up an opportunity for teachers to try out a new practice so that they can decide on their own whether or not it will help them be more effective with their students.

Enroll

Goal: To establish a coaching partnership with a teacher

Actions: Consider using some or all of these practices:

1. One-to-one interviews
2. Large-group presentations
3. Small-group presentations
4. Principal referral
5. Workshops
6. Informal conversations

Time: 5–40 minutes

Identify

Once a teacher agrees to partner with a coach, the coach and teacher need to identify exactly what practice from the Target the teacher will implement. Both partners should look for a practice that has the highest leverage for improving student learning. Often, teachers know where they would like to start with a coach. Since everyone in a school should know the Target, teachers may identify what they want to work on after attending a workshop, participating in an ILT, talking with an administrator after an observation, or simply by reviewing the Target and considering their own students' needs. When a teacher knows what part of the Target they want to address, the coach and teacher can get down to business quickly.

However, some teachers do not have a clear understanding of how they perform when they do their work. As mentioned in Chapter 2, a simple truth about change is that most people do not see the need for change. When teachers are not sure where to begin, ICs should suggest video recording the teacher's class using a camera like a Flip camera. After they record the class, ICs can download the video onto the teacher's computer and suggest the teacher review the video before they get together to discuss what to work on together.

Coaches affiliated with the Kansas Coaching Project also give teachers guidelines on how to get the most out of watching recordings of themselves teaching and two surveys that they can use to focus their attention while watching. The complete surveys are included in the Impact Toolkit in Resource A, and sections of the surveys and the teacher handout are presented below.

How to Get the Most Out of Watching Your Video

Goal: Identify two sections of the video that you like and one or two sections of the video you'd like to further explore.

Getting Ready

Watching yourself on video is one of the most powerful strategies professionals can use to improve. However, it can be a challenge. It takes a little time to get used to seeing yourself on screen, so be prepared for a bit of a shock. After a little time, you will become more comfortable with the process.

- Find a place to watch where you won't be distracted.
- You may find it helpful to read through the teacher and student surveys and/or the big-ticket items to remind yourself of things to keep in mind while watching.
- Set aside a block of time so you can watch the video uninterrupted.
- Make sure you've got a pen and paper ready to take notes.

Watching the Video

- Plan to watch the entire video at one sitting.
- Take notes on anything that is interesting.
- Be certain to write the time from the video beside any note you make so that you can return to it should you wish to.
- People have a tendency to be too hard on themselves, so be sure to really watch for things you like.
- After watching the video, review your notes and circle the items you will discuss with your coach (two you like and one or two you would like to further explore).
- Sit back, relax, and enjoy the experience.

Watch Your Students

Date:

After watching the video of today's class, please rate how close the behavior of your students is to your goal for an ideal class in the following areas:

	Not Close					Right On	
Students were engaged in learning (90 percent engagement is recommended).	1	2	3	4	5	6	7
Students interacted respectfully.	1	2	3	4	5	6	7
Students clearly understand how they are supposed to behave.	1	2	3	4	5	6	7

Date:

After watching the video of today's class, please rate how close your instruction is to your ideal in the following areas:

	Not Close					Right On	
My praise to correction ratio is at least a 3-to-1 ratio.	1	2	3	4	5	6	7
I clearly explained expectations prior to each activity.	1	2	3	4	5	6	7
My corrections are calm, consistent, immediate, and planned in advance.	1	2	3	4	5	6	7

In our studies of coaching, teachers report that initially they find it challenging to watch video recordings of themselves teaching. As one teacher said after watching himself teach, "My first reaction is, 'Who was that man?'" Usually, it takes time for people to get used to watching themselves. However, they do get comfortable with the process, and eventually some very important learning occurs that might not be possible without video feedback.

After teacher and coach have viewed the recording, they meet to identify the goal for their collaboration. We have found that it is usually best to identify a student academic or behavioral goal, such as "increase student engagement to at least 90 percent" rather than a teacher goal such as "implement Venn diagrams." During conversation, the coach must ensure that the teacher is the center of the conversation by asking questions, listening, and respecting what Susan Scott (2009) calls the "sweet purity of silence." First, the coach should ask the teacher what he saw and especially what he liked as he watched the video. Surfacing what went well isn't just a way to create a positive conversation; often when a coach and teacher identify the successes, their work together will focus on extending those successes to other parts of a class.

The coach can move the conversation forward by asking questions that prompt teachers to explore other aspects of the video such as "What surprised you? What did you learn?" Coaches should also clarify their own, and often their collaborating teacher's, understanding by asking probing questions such as "What do you mean when you say . . . ?" "Tell me more about . . . ," and "What will happen if . . . ?"

At an appropriate time, the coach should encourage identification of a goal by asking questions such as "What would you like to see more of?" "What change would you like to see in your students?" and "If things were ideal in your class, what would be different? What would you see and hear?" Teacher and coach also need to identify what data could be gathered to show that the goal has been met. For example, if a teacher wants more students involved in classroom discussion, she might identify that 90 percent of students on average answer questions in a class.

Once the goal and a way to measure progress toward it have been identified, the coach and teacher go on to explore practices on the Target that might be ways to address the teacher's specific concerns. Usually these are practices that the coach was prepared to share based on her own viewing of the video recording, but at other times they arise organically from the conversation. The teacher is then asked what he would like to try.

What matters here is that the teacher picks some practice to learn that she sees as a genuine response to her concerns. This is the essence of "pull coaching." The entire coaching process is pulled along by the teacher's attempt to tackle a challenge that matters to her. In *Switch* (2010), Chip and Dan Heath refer to this as a "destination postcard," "a vivid picture from the near-term future that shows what could be possible" (p. 76). When we are leading change, Heath and Heath suggest that "we're interested in goals that are closer at hand . . . We want a goal that can be tackled in months or years, not decades" (p. 76). A powerful goal simplifies the complexities of the coaching process by showing the coach and teacher where they are working to end up.

Powerful goals are short-term, simple, and precise, but they should also be emotionally motivating, even inspiring. As Jim Collins and Jerry Porras (1994) have written, a good goal should "hit you in the gut." Heath and Heath are suspicious of SMART goals (specific, measureable, achievable, relevant, timely, or some variation). They write,

> in looking for a goal that . . . hits people in the gut—you can't bank on SMART goals. (There are some people whose hearts are set aflutter by goals such as "improving the liquidity ratio by 30 percent over the next 18 months." They're called accountants.) (2010, p. 82)

Powerful goals, Heath and Heath (2010) explain, do double duty: "They show [you] where you're headed, and they show [you] why the journey is worthwhile" (p. 82).

The SMART acronym, in our experience, illustrates some important features of powerful goals: they should be precise, measurable, and achievable. We also agree with Heath and Heath that powerful goals are also simple "destination postcards" that must be emotionally motivating. If a teacher's goal isn't clear and isn't motivating, a lot of time may be wasted during coaching.

Identify a Goal

Goal: The teacher and coach will identify a compelling, specific, measurable goal for coaching interactions

Setting the Goal: Goal setting is a delicate dance, so the process needs to be personalized to each teacher and their students'

(Continued)

(Continued)

unique needs. Therefore, these are guidelines, not a rote process to be followed.

1. Ask questions that prompt teachers to discuss the best aspects of the video, such as "What went well?" Listen. Respect what Susan Scott (2009) calls the "sweet purity of silence."

2. Ask questions that prompt teachers to explore other aspects of the video, such as "What surprised you? What did you learn?" Listen.

3. Probe further (include good probing questions such as "What do you mean when you say . . . ?" "Tell me more about . . ." or "What will happen if . . . ?").

4. Identify a student behavior on which the teacher would like to focus by asking questions such as "What would you like to see more of?" "What change would you like to see in your students?" or "If things were ideal in your class, what would be different? What would you see and hear?"

5. Target data that can be used to measure the desired behavior. This may involve gathering more data, revisiting the data, or meeting again.

6. Collaborate with the teacher to name the compelling, specific goal that will usually be measured by student data (such as time on task or other forms of engagement data, disruptions, correct responses, students responding to questions, student products, teacher's anecdotal data).

Time: 5–30 minutes (excluding preliminary activities)

Explain/Mediate

Once a goal has been set and a practice to be implemented has been identified, the coach must explain the practice. This can be a significant challenge. Often effective practices are complicated and come with extensive explanations. I know of an outstanding paragraph-writing manual, for example, that is more than 400 pages long. For even the most motivated teachers, 400 pages is a lot to read, remember, and implement. The coach's goal, therefore, is to distill the most important aspects of a teaching practice, create simple explanations, and then share those explanations with teachers.

Atul Gawande, in his fascinating *New York Times* best seller *The Checklist Manifesto* (2010), illustrates the coach's challenge and then offers a simple solution:

Here, then, is our situation at the start of the 21st century: we have accumulated stupendous know-how. We have put it in the hands of some of the most highly trained, highly skilled, and hardworking people in our society. And, with it, they have indeed accomplished extraordinary things. Nonetheless, that know-how is often unmanageable. Avoidable failures are common and persistent, not to mention demoralizing and frustrating, across many fields—from medicine to finance, business to government. And the reason is increasingly evident: the volume and complexity of what we know has exceeded our individual ability to deliver its benefits correctly, safely, or reliably. Knowledge has both saved us and burdened us . . .

. . . we need a different strategy for overcoming failure, one that builds on experience and takes advantage of the knowledge people have but somehow also makes up for our inevitable human inadequacies. And there is such a strategy though it will seem almost ridiculous in its simplicity, maybe even crazy to those of us who have spent years carefully developing ever more advanced skills and technologies.

It is a checklist. (p. 13)

Gawande (2010), a Harvard medical professor, studied the impact of checklists on surgery and, in a study with the World Health Organization, found that when surgery teams used simple checklists, they could save thousands of lives and billions of dollars.

Despite Gawande's evidence, for many, building professional learning around checklists is a stretch. As Heath and Heath (2010) wrote, "People fear checklists because they see them as dehumanizing . . . They think if something is simple enough to be put in a checklist a monkey can do it. Well, if that is true, grab a pilot's checklist and try your luck with a 747" (p. 222). Gawande (2010) also writes about people's distrust of checklists:

The fear people have about the idea of adherence to protocol is rigidity. They imagine mindless automatons, heads down in a checklist, incapable of looking out their windshield and coping with the real world in front of them. But what you find, when a checklist is well made, is exactly the opposite. The checklist gets the dumb stuff out of the way. The routines your brain shouldn't have to occupy itself with (Are the elevator controls set? Did the patient get her antibiotics on timer? Did the managers sell all their shares? Is everyone on the same page here?), and lets it rise above to focus on the hard stuff (Where should we land?). (p. 177)

Checklists, Gawande (2010) states, "distill . . . information into its practical essence" (p. 134). Checklists address the major reason why new ideas are not implemented and that is "more often than not that the necessary knowledge has not been translated into a simple, usable, and systematic form" (p. 134). Checklists make knowledge actionable, and this applies in the classroom just as much as it applies to the operating room.

Kerry Patterson and his colleagues (2008) suggest another important reason why checklists can be important: "vital behaviors." According to the authors, who describe several highly successful change leaders in their book *Influencer: The Power to Change Anything* (2008), a critical component of change leadership is to clearly describe a few essential behaviors at the heart of the change being undertaken.

The breakthrough discovery of most influence geniuses is that enormous influence comes from focusing on just a few *vital behaviors*. Even the most pervasive problems will often yield to changes in a handful of high-leverage behaviors. Find these, and you've found the beginning of influence. (p. 23)

Vital behaviors should make up the content of most checklists.

Checklist: Daily Use of Learning Maps

Daily Use	✓	Comments
90 percent of students have their unit map open on their desk when the bell rings to start the unit.		
90 percent of students can locate their unit map without difficulty.		
Teacher begins each class with a review of the content covered up to the current point in the unit.		

Teacher uses the unit map to introduce the day's lesson.		
Teacher prompts students to record new content learned on the expanded unit map.		
Teacher uses the unit map to end each day's lesson with a review of the material covered.		

Additional Comments:

In our work at the Kansas Coaching Project, our experience mirrors Patterson's (Patterson et al., 2008) as well as Gawande's (2010) research. We have found that checklists are essential because they force coaches and other professional developers to be precise about their explanations. Not every teaching practice can or should be described in a simple checklist, but checklist or not, ICs need to fully understand and clearly communicate the vital behaviors of the practices they share (whether we are talking about using guiding questions to plan a lesson, using stories to make a lesson stick, or using checks for understanding to gauge student learning). The less precise a coach's explanation is, the less impact the coach will have on teaching and learning. As the Heath brothers wrote, "clarity dissolves resistance" (2010, p. 72).

Guidelines for Effective Checklists

Gawande (2010) met with Don Boorman, a Boeing employee who has created hundreds of checklists now used by pilots all over the world. Mr. Boorman provided the following guidelines for effective checklists:

1. Keep it short, between five and nine items if possible.

2. Use simple and exact wording.

3. Make it fit on one page.

4. Keep it simple, free from clutter and unnecessary color.

Checklists are tools for precise explanations; however, precision is not enough. Coaches' explanations should be offered in a partnership way; that is, they must be provisional. Coaches need to explain the teaching practice in a manner that recognizes the importance of choice, dialogue, and reflection in the coaching relationship. Thus, coaches taking the partnership approach ask teachers to offer their own suggestions for how the practice being discussed should be adapted or differentiate the practice so it best addresses the needs of all students in the classroom. During explanations, the coach is continually checking with the teacher to see if she would like to adapt the practice in some way. Indeed, the coach should explain the practice in a manner that allows the teacher to think along with the coach as they learn the practice.

Often, when coaches and teachers collaborate, they work on tools or devices that need to be created prior to a lesson. For example, a teacher may be learning how to use a graphic organizer, a learning map, or effective questions to use during a lesson. When this is the case, the coach and teacher will likely spend time together co-constructing the tool that will be used in the classroom.

Coaches adopting the partnership approach do not take a one-size-fits-all approach to professional learning. They recognize that teaching should be differentiated for students and teaching style. They assume that teachers will want to carefully weigh whether or not any aspect of a teaching practice will work for them, and they provide numerous opportunities for teachers to share their thinking about a practice. As Lucy West (2009) has observed, our goal during coaching is not "mindless fidelity" but "mindful engagement." When teachers are given the opportunity to adapt a teacher practice, their first response usually is that they'd like to try the practice without making any changes.

Explain

Goal: To explain and modify how the new teaching practice will be taught so that it is tailor-made for a teacher's students' unique needs

Actions:

1. Meet with the teacher one-to-one.
2. Give the teacher a copy of a checklist (when appropriate) for the teaching practice being learned.

3. Go through the checklist item by item, and explain each one.

4. After discussing each item, ask the teacher whether or not the item is okay with them, or would they like to modify it (95 percent of the time, the teacher will not want to modify it).

5. Modify the form to reflect the teacher's concerns if they wish to change it after discussing the reason why the form is organized in the manner it is organized.

6. Co-construct an observation protocol for additional teaching practices.

7. Confirm already scheduled date for you to model in the classroom.

Time: 15–40 minutes

Modeling

After explaining the teaching practice, ICs ask teachers if they would like to see the practice demonstrated in their classrooms. Terms such as *model demonstration* are a bit off-putting to some, so informal phrases are often preferable, and coaches usually say something less formal such as "Would you like me to try this out in your class with your students so you can see what it might look like?" Again, consistent with the partnership approach, coaches only provide a model lesson if the teacher chooses this option. Usually, if the teacher is interested in learning a given practice and has co-constructed an observation protocol or checklist, she welcomes a chance to see what the practice looks like in the classroom.

Just before the model lesson, the coach provides the teacher with a copy of the observation protocol that was finalized during the explain phase. Then, the coach provides a concise demonstration of the lesson. The model does not need to take up the whole period of the class; indeed, it is often preferable to keep the demonstration short, so long as it is sufficient for the teacher to see the new practice. The partnership principles of reflection and dialogue are emphasized during this stage because, while the coach leads the class, the teacher notes down her thoughts about the lesson on the observation protocol. Soon after the lesson, the coach and teacher engage in a brief dialogue around the teacher's thoughts of the lesson.

There are several simple things a coach may wish to do to increase the effectiveness of the model lesson. First, ICs should clarify with collaborating teachers who will be responsible for classroom management during model lessons. It doesn't matter who is responsible, but it needs to be clarified ahead of time to avoid confusion during the model lesson. Second, ICs should arrive in the classroom before class starts so they can have informal conversations with students to ensure they are at ease with someone else in the classroom. Third, ICs need to make it clear to the students that they are just visiting, and that the collaborating teacher is very much in charge. Indeed, ICs should find opportunities to praise collaborating teachers in front of students, and they should involve the collaborating teacher in the demonstration. Finally, ICs may want to ask students to create name tents so that they can call on each individual student by name.

In most cases, we video record model lessons and download lessons onto a teacher's computer. If they wish, teachers can review the model lesson on their own, and ICs can look back to see how they did. If time permits, the coach and teacher may get together to discuss the video recording and generally explore how the demonstration went.

Model

Goal: To ensure the teacher knows what the new teaching practice looks and sounds like when it is employed effectively

Actions:

1. Arrive in the class well before the lesson is to be given.
2. Give the teacher a copy of the co-constructed checklist (when appropriate) for the teaching practice being learning.
3. Explain how they should use the checklist.
4. Ask the teacher if they would like to record it.
5. Speak to students informally before the class begins.
6. Have the teacher introduce you.
7. Prompt the students to create name tents if you don't know their names.
8. Model the lesson, doing everything on the checklist.
9. Involve the teacher in the lesson, and authentically praise the teacher.
10. Keep your model short by focusing on the practice being learned.
11. Offer to download a copy of the lesson to the teacher's computer.

Time: 15–40 minutes

Observe

After providing a model lesson, coaches offer to observe or video record the teacher implementing the new practice and then have a conversation about how the lesson went. Usually, teachers are very agreeable to having the coach observe the lesson because (a) teachers are working with a coach because they chose to, (b) teachers are learning a practice they chose to learn, (c) teachers helped to construct the observation protocol that they fully understand and had the opportunity to adapt if they wished, and (d) the coach has already modeled the practice. Further, teachers are increasingly comfortable with having their lessons be recorded.

During the observation, coaches use the same observation protocol (or checklist) that the teacher used when observing the coach. ICs need to be attentive to areas where the teacher has skipped over aspects of the teaching practice. Even more important, coaches need to be attentive to what went well during the lesson. When coaches report the effective practices they observe in a class, their comments can be highly encouraging for teachers.

If a teacher agrees to be recorded, as soon as possible after the lesson, the coach should load the video onto the teacher's computer and ask the teacher to review the video to identify three sections he really likes and two others he'd like to discuss further. The coach should explain that she'll do the same thing. The IC and teacher also need to set the next time they will meet.

Observe

Goal: To gather accurate data on the effectiveness of a teaching practice as a method for achieving the goal

Actions:

1. Arrive in the classroom well before the lesson to confirm that the teacher wants you to observe the lesson.

2. Find an inconspicuous spot in the classroom where you can watch the teacher and the students.

3. Position the camera so that you will be able to record the entire lesson.

(Continued)

(Continued)

4. Set up the camera on a tripod so your hands are free to take notes.

5. After the teacher begins to use the new practice, be especially attentive for anything the teacher does well.

6. Write brief descriptions of all the positive aspects of the lesson in the comments column.

7. Put a checkmark in the OBS (observe) column beside each teaching practice you see the teacher do, and leave a blank space in the OBS column beside any teaching practices that you do not see.

8. Before leaving the classroom, confirm that you will meet at your predetermined time to discuss the lesson.

9. Download a copy of the lesson onto the teacher's computer before you leave the classroom.

Time: 15–40 minutes

Explore

As soon as possible after observing a lesson, the IC should meet with the collaborating teacher to discuss the data that were collected. Using the partnership approach to exploring data, the IC and teacher sit side by side as partners and review the data that the IC has gathered. The IC does not withhold her opinion, but offers it in a provisional way, communicating that she is open to other points of view.

If the lesson has been recorded, the coach and teacher can take turns reviewing the video clips and discussing what they see. At this point, the coach must let the teacher do most of the talking, with the IC (a) asking a lot of open-ended questions and (b) practicing effective listening. While every conversation is different, in most cases, the IC should try to set things up so the collaborating teacher is talking at least 70 percent of the time. More on questioning and listening is included in Chapter 7.

During the collaborative exploration of data, it is crucial that the IC communicates clearly the genuinely positive aspects of the lesson that were observed. I am not advocating the use of thoughtless, vague, or empty happy words or phrases. A "language of ongoing regard" (Kegan & Lahey, 2001) has specific characteristics. Kegan and Lahey stress that authentic, appreciative, or admiring feedback must be (a) direct, (b) specific, and (c) nonattributive. By non-attributive, the authors mean that positive comments about others are more effective when we describe our experience of others rather than the attributes of others. Simply put, we share with them what behaviors we saw, and then, like a partner, we let them reach their own conclusions.

Before concluding their conversation, the coach and teacher should clarify how close they are to their goal and identify what steps to take next to move forward together.

Explore

Goal: To identify what went well during the practice attempt and what adjustments need to be made if the goal has not been met

Actions:

1. Prior to meeting, review the recording of the lesson and identify at least three sections that you think are excellent and two sections that you think would be meaningful to discuss.

2. Ask the teacher to also identify three sections that they think are excellent and two sections that they have concerns about.

3. Give the teacher a copy of the observation protocol or protocols.

4. Review the video as well.

5. Identify at least three clips you think are well done and plan direct, specific, non-attributive feedback.

6. Identify sections that you think would be profitable to discuss.

7. Choose questions (review the question sheet) that you think will open up the conversation.

8. Meet with the teacher to review the teacher's and your clips.

9. Pause the recording when you talk.

10. Use open-ended nonjudgmental questions to open up meaningful conversation.

11. Identify a SMART goal for the next step.

Time: 20–60 minutes

Refine

Rarely is a teacher ready to integrate a new practice after one run-through, so coaches must be prepared to provide ongoing support to ensure teachers maintain use of and integrate the new practice into their repertoire of teaching methods. Again, partnership stands at the heart of this model, so during the refine stage, coaches adapt their approach to best meet the needs and concerns of each teacher and to best provide support for the individual practices being learned. Coaches working on unit planning, for example, might spend most of their time in the explain stage of coaching. Coaches sharing a teaching practice that involves a variety of teaching moves, such as reciprocal teaching, might do several model lessons. Coaches working on classroom management might spend the bulk of their time on observation and exploration.

What matters most here is that teachers receive sufficient support to gain a deep understanding of a practice so that they can sustain use of the practice without help of the coach. We have found that such support often takes more time than we might initially assume necessary.

Who Should Be a Coach

Without question, the most important factor relative to the effectiveness of a coaching program is "Who is the coach?" Even in the best circumstances, a poorly skilled coach will struggle to have a meaningful impact on teaching. However, a talented coach can make a real difference in almost any circumstance.

This brief discussion of the attributes of effective coaches is drawn from three main sources. First, my fellow researchers at the Kansas Coaching Project, Tom Skrtic, Jake Cornett, Michael Kennedy, Leslie Novosel, Belinda Mitchell, Mike Hock, and Irma Brasseur-Hock, and I have been involved in two qualitative studies of the attributes and activities of effective coaches. Since this work is ongoing, I will make only occasional references to our findings, but by publication of this book, the research results should be posted at www.instructional coach.org/research.html.

Second, I have observed dozens of coaching programs across Canada and the United States and seen firsthand what works and what doesn't work.

Finally, my reading about leadership, coaching, mentoring, communication, and adult learning has also surfaced several issues. Together, these sources have painted a picture of an effective coach. The key attributes are described below.

Knowledge of Teaching Practices

The IC plays an important role in professional learning because without coaching, little change occurs. The coach is the linchpin for change and, as such, remembers the vital behaviors of a practice, explains it, clarifies and adapts it for teachers, models it, observes teachers, and provides partnership feedback. How effectively a coach provides these kinds of support is directly related to how much he or she knows about the practices being shared.

Coaches can deepen their knowledge of teaching practices by devouring reading material about the teaching practices they share. ICs should read, reread, create mind maps of what they are learning, write notes, and create checklists. Workshops on practices can also be extremely helpful, and since ICs are so essential for professional learning in schools, ICs should be at the top of the list for attending professional learning related to the Target.

ICs can also learn an enormous amount from others. As a result, they should join online professional learning networks via social networking sites such as Twitter, Nings, or Wikis and establish and learn from face-to-face professional learning communities. One valuable activity is to join with other ICs to discuss and review materials related to particular teaching practices and then create checklists that summarize the vital behaviors in those practices.

The best way to learn is through long-term personal experience using practices with students. If a coach has not had this experience, they should establish a learning partnership with an open-minded teacher who will work with them so that both, together, can become experts.

Emotional Intelligence

Knowing what you are talking about is important, but it won't mean much if people do not want to collaborate with you. In almost every interview we have conducted at the Kansas Coaching Project, with coaches, principals, teachers, and others, the overwhelming refrain is that coaches need to be relationship builders. An effective coach is almost always someone whom others enjoy being around. As IC Shelly Bolejack has said, coaches need to have an "infectious personality."

Chapter 7 provides an extended description of the communication skills that especially strengthen our relationships with others, and instructional coaches should strive to master all of those skills. Perhaps more than anything else, ICs need to be good listeners. When coaches really listen, they show teachers that they are focused on supporting them and their students and not pushing a personal agenda. When coaches do most of the talking, on the other hand, teachers may come to believe that coaching is all about the coach, not them, and they may lose interest in the process.

Coaches also need to be positive, optimistic people who are quick to see the good in others. They must be able to read others' facial expressions so that they can better understand what their collaborating teachers are communicating to them. Almost as important as listening is asking good questions. Effective coaches ask questions they are curious to hear the answers to, and they listen carefully to hear others' answers.

Growth Mindset

Carol Dweck, a psychologist at Stanford, has dedicated her career to studying how our own mental models enhance or interfere with our ability to learn. In *Mindset* (2006), Dweck summarizes studies she has conducted that show that people can have either a "growth" or a "fixed" mindset. After 20 years of research, Dweck concludes, "The view you adopt for yourself profoundly affects the way you lead your life" (p. 6).

Dweck (2006) describes the fixed mindset as "believing that your qualities are carved in stone" (p. 7). If you have a fixed mindset, you believe that "you have only a certain amount of intelligence, a certain personality, a certain moral character" (p. 7). To those having a fixed mindset, people are what they are, and there's not much chance of them ever changing.

Dweck describes the growth mindset as believing "that the hand you're dealt is just the starting point for development. This growth mindset is based on the belief that your basic qualities are things that you cultivate through effort" (p. 8). Those who have a growth mindset "believe that a person's true potential is unknown (and unknowable); that it's impossible to foresee what can be accomplished with years of passion, toil, and training" (p. 8). Dweck adds that "the belief that cherished qualities can be developed creates a passion for learning" (p. 8). Everyone, ultimately, has a chance to develop or change their mindset to or from a growth mindset. Dweck reports that she has changed her own mindset from a fixed to a growth perspective.

The implications for instructional coaches should be clear. If an instructional coach has a fixed mindset, she sees teachers as being pretty much the way they are without much chance for improvement. A good teacher is a good teacher; a bad teacher is a bad teacher. An IC with a growth mindset, however, sees every teacher as having unknown potential. As a result, she enters into coaching expecting every collaborating partner to grow, develop, and become a better teacher than perhaps anyone could imagine. Indeed, a coach with a growth mindset inspires teachers to adopt a growth mindset for themselves and, perhaps even more important, for their students.

Humility and Ambition

The unsuccessful experiences of two ICs (whose names have been changed for this book) illustrate why ICs should embody both ambition and humility. John LeClaire began his career as an IC feeling very excited about what he would accomplish. John had had great success teaching writing strategies, and he was enthusiastic about helping teachers use the strategies he knew so well. He gave a passionate presentation at the start of the school year, telling everyone about the power of strategic instruction, and he quickly lined up conferences with teachers in their classrooms, in the staff room, and at team meetings to try to convince them to get on board. John had seen the impact writing strategies could have, and he forcefully explained why teachers should use the strategies to help students.

Unfortunately, the more John pushed his colleagues, the less enthusiastic they became, and the more they put barriers between themselves and John. Furthermore, as teachers turned away from John's overtures, he became more zealous in his attempts at persuasion. Eventually, John was frustrated by what he perceived as his fellow teachers' lack of interest. At first privately, and eventually publicly, he criticized his colleagues for failing to do the right thing for kids. John's criticism alienated staff even more, and at the end of his first year, John felt that his efforts had been a waste of time, blaming the teachers, who, he said, "were too stubborn to change."

Another IC, Lauren Morgan, began with the same optimism as John, and unfortunately, she ended her coaching career just as unsuccessfully. Lauren had a deep respect for teachers, and she felt coaching was a meaningful way in which she could support her colleagues. She was determined not to force herself on teachers and to work with only those who wanted to work with her. Lauren met periodically with teachers, and with admirable humility, she praised their dedication and their commitment to a noble calling.

Lauren was careful to not put herself out in front of the staff; she preferred to stay in the background. Teachers liked her, but they always seemed a little too busy to try out her ideas. As time went by, Lauren found that few teachers were collaborating with her. She waited patiently, but the right time never seemed to come along. Lauren found herself doing more and more busywork within the school and less and less instructional coaching. At the end of the year,

Lauren realized that she had only worked with eight teachers, and most of the eight had only made a superficial attempt at the new practices. Like John, after a year, Lauren was not sure that she had had any positive impact on student learning.

John's and Lauren's cases reveal that too aggressive or too passive an approach to coaching runs the risk of being unsuccessful. Coaches are more successful, in our experience, when they embody a paradoxical mixture of ambition and humility. Effective ICs, we have found, embody attributes very similar to those held by "Level 5 leaders" (the most effective leaders) Jim Collins (2001) describes in his well-known study of great organizations:

> Level 5 leaders channel their ego needs away from themselves and into the larger goal of building a great company. It's not that Level 5 leaders have no ego or self-interest. Indeed, they are incredibly ambitious—but their ambition is for the institution, not themselves. (p. 21)

ICs, like Collins' (2001) Level 5 leaders, "are a study in duality: modest and willful, humble and fearless" (p. 22).

Trustworthiness

One word that comes up again and again as we conduct interviews is *trust*. For ICs to be effective, they need to act in ways that engender trust. Fortunately, David Maister, Charles Green, and Robert Galford (2000) have created a simple equation for breaking down critical factors for engendering relational trust. The equation can be expressed as a simple fraction:

$$\frac{\text{Credibility, Reliability, Intimacy}}{\text{Self-Focus}}$$

As with all fractions, the larger the numerator, the larger the number. Therefore, the more credible, reliable, and easy to talk to coaches are, the more likely it is that they will be able to create trusting relationships.

Coaches can increase their *credibility* by learning their materials inside and out, by reading and rereading materials such as this book, and by practicing until they have a deep knowledge of the teaching practices they share with teachers. Some coaches have benefited greatly by watching and critically analyzing videotape of their model lessons. Since credibility is so important, we believe that when given a choice, coaches are wiser to have a deep knowledge of a few practices rather than a shallow knowledge of a large number of practices.

To engender trust, to be credible, coaches also need to be people of character. This means that coaches act with integrity, are honest, and work hard. Effective ICs recognize the moral purpose inherent in the work they do, and they are driven by a desire to see their teachers grow, their school improve, and their students achieve. When teachers see credibility and integrity in their coaches, they are much more likely to trust them.

Reliability is essential. Indeed, an easy way to damage a relationship with a teacher is to miss an appointment to provide a model lesson. Coaches must be extremely careful to provide materials on time, to meet when they say they'll meet, and to keep their promises.

One way to increase reliability is to be careful not to promise too much. When you are leading change in a school, the temptation is to agree to anything in hopes of moving school improvement along. Although well intended, this is a potentially dangerous practice. Making a promise and not delivering on time can be much more damaging to relationship than explaining that it may take a week or two before you can provide the kind of support a teacher needs.

Intimacy, in the trust equation, refers to the ability of a coach to communicate in a manner that is validating, respectful, and comfortable for teachers. Coaches need to be skillful communicators and use all of the skills described in Chapter 7. When teachers don't feel comfortable about sharing their hopes and fears, the coach's challenge will be much more significant.

Credibility, reliability, and trust are the key concepts on the numerator of the fraction, and the larger they are, the more likely it is that a coach will build trust. Alternatively, self-focus is the concept for the denominator, and as with all fractions, the larger the denominator, in this case the more self-focused a coach is, the less likely it is that teachers will trust the coach. A coach who adopts an attitude that "it's all about me" is likely a coach who struggles to find teachers with whom to work.

Self-focus can be manifested in the simple way in which a coach approaches conversation. Susan Scott (2002) has described how one-to-one conversations can also quickly become "all about me":

A common experience you no doubt have had is the conversation that begins with your telling someone about something you are grappling with and before you've even finished the story, the other person says, "I know exactly what you mean. About three years ago . . ." And he's off and running. In a matter of seconds, this conversation shifted from being about you to being about *him* . . .

This practice of taking the conversation away from other people and making it about ourselves goes on all day, every day, and is a huge relationship killer and a waste of time. Nothing useful happens here. (p. 116)

Coaches must ensure that conversations are not "all about me" but all about the teachers and their students. They need to listen much more than they talk and monitor their thinking and conversation so they don't let their ideas dominate. Taking the time to truly listen to a collaborating teacher is one of the most respectful things a coach can do.

Moving away from a self-focus also ensures that your actions and concerns are about others and not yourself. Thus, coaches should take every opportunity to give credit to others when there are successes. Additionally, coaches should express genuine concern for students, teachers, administrators, and others in the school because it's not "all about me"; it is all about the kids.

Informed and Adaptive Thinking

When I conduct workshops on instructional coaching, I am frequently asked how to respond to particular scenarios. For example, a coach might ask, "What should I do if a teacher has low expectations for students?" Struggling to answer, I usually begin my comments by saying "Of course, the answer is always different depending on the situation."

I have come to believe that giving just one solution to these kinds of questions is wrongheaded even though it might be what people want. So, my response now is that you must do some "informed" and "adaptive" thinking. Let me explain.

By *informed*, I mean in any given situation, the more you know about effective instruction, relationship building, a teacher's personal attributes and preferences, the impact of learning styles, the characteristics of a teacher's students, and so on, the better able you are to respond appropriately. Coaches who know how to align themselves emotionally are able to consider the impact of what they might say in any situation. Similarly, coaches who have a deep understanding of a wide variety of effective teaching strategies are better prepared to meet teachers' needs. The more coaches know, the better able they are to provide support when the teachable moments come along in coaching conversations.

By *adaptive,* I mean that coaches should not take a cookie-cutter approach to responding to teachers' needs. Just the opposite, in fact: in the moment, a coach should consider all of her or his knowledge and then choose a response that is best for the teacher and the students. Ron Heifetz (Heifetz, Grashow, & Linsky, 2009) has similarly described how leaders should adapt what they do to meet each person's unique needs. Thus, sometimes the coach is very direct about what he sees and advocates for a particular course of action. At other times, the coach withholds comment, only asking questions to guide teachers as they go through a process of self-discovery.

Eric Liu (2004), in *Guiding Lights,* his enlightening series of case studies of outstanding mentors, describes the need for adaptability during teaching. His words capture exactly the kind of adaptability coaches should demonstrate.

> We have this notion of the great teacher as the Great Communicator. But the most powerful teachers aren't those who speak, perform, and orate with the most dazzle and force. They are those who listen with full-body intensity, and customize. Teaching is not one-size-fits-all; it's one-size-fits-one. So before we transmit a single thing, we must tune in to the unique and ever-fluctuating frequency of every learner: his particular mix of temperament, skills, intelligence, and motivation. This means, as teachers, putting aside our own egos and preconceptions about what makes this particular lesson so important . . . It means letting go of the idea of control. (p. 47)

To Sum Up

- ICs' actions should embody the partnership principles of equality, choice, voice, reflection, dialogue, praxis, and reciprocity.
- ICs are more successful when principals provide top-down leadership to support coaches' bottom-up support.
- ICs should support and sometimes lead all activities that are shared through workshops and intensive learning teams.
- ICs use the components of coaching, which include enroll, identify, explain, model, observe, explore, and refine.

- Effective ICs understand the practices they are sharing, are emotionally intelligent, have a growth mindset, are both humble and ambitious, and are trustworthy.

Going Deeper

Approaches to Coaching

Many different approaches to coaching are being used in schools today. Six of the most well known are the following:

- *Peer coaching*, first developed by Beverly Showers and Bruce Joyce (1996) in "The Evolution of Peer Coaching," provides structures and procedures to help teachers observe each other and engage in confidential conversations about teaching. The authors describe peer coaching as "a confidential process through which two or more professional colleagues work together to reflect upon certain practices; expand, refine, and build new skills; share ideas; conduct action research; teach one another or problem solve within the workplace" (p. 206).
- *Cognitive coaching*, developed by Art Costa and Robert Garmston (2002), is a process used to improve one's thinking practices. Cognitive coaching is intended to help people help themselves, and as such it prompts them and their coaches to ask what it means to be self-managing, self-monitoring, and self-modifying. According to the proponents of cognitive coaching, if teachers improve their higher-thinking cognitive functioning, they will improve the way they teach, and students, in turn, will have significantly better learning experiences.
- *Content coaching*, developed by Lucy West (2009), began in New York City when Anthony Alvarado was superintendent. West writes, "The *essence* of content coaching is simple: to improve learning, teachers must focus on relevant, important, rich content. Robust lessons center around big ideas in a given domain and give students opportunities to grapple with significant problems or issues using reasoning and discourse particular to that domain" (p. 114). Also see Lucy West and Fritz Staub's *Content-Focused Coaching* (2003).
- *Data coaching*, described primarily by Nancy Love (*Using Data to Improve Learning for All: A Collaborative Inquiry Approach*, 2009), involves coaches developing the capacities of schools to

use data to improve teaching and other factors that impact student achievement. As such, data coaches lead teams and individuals to collect, analyze, and monitor student learning

- *Literacy coaching*, described by multiple authors but especially Cathy Toll (2009, in Jim Knight's *Coaching: Approaches and Perspectives*), surfaces in various approaches discussed in this book. According to Toll, "literacy coaching is a category of instructional coaching that focuses on literacy and related aspects of teaching and learning; various programs of literacy coaching implement a variety of coaching models" (p. 57). Other recommended resources include Jan Miller Burkins' *Practical Literacy Coaching* (2009) and M. C. Moran's *Differentiated Literacy Coaching* (2007). Finally, *Coaching: Approaches and Perspectives* (Knight, 2009a), which I edited, includes chapters by several coaching authors discussing many of the coaching approaches listed here.

- *Instructional coaching* was, to my knowledge, first described in my book *Instructional Coaching: A Partnership Approach to Learning* (Knight, 2007). Recently, Cheryl Jones and Mary Vreeman have published *Instructional Coaches & Classroom Teachers: Sharing the Road to Success* (2008).

Other General Books on Coaching

Many other books have been very helpful to me in my work on coaching—in particular, Joellen Killion and Cindy Harrison's *Taking the Lead: New Roles for Teachers and School-Based Coaches* (2006), Jane Kise's *Differentiated Coaching* (2006), Stephen G. Barkley's *Quality Teaching in a Culture of Coaching* (2010), and Gary Bloom, Claire Castagna, Ellen Moir, and Betsy Warren's *Blended Coaching: Skills and Strategies to Support Principal Development* (2005).

5

Workshops That Make an Impact

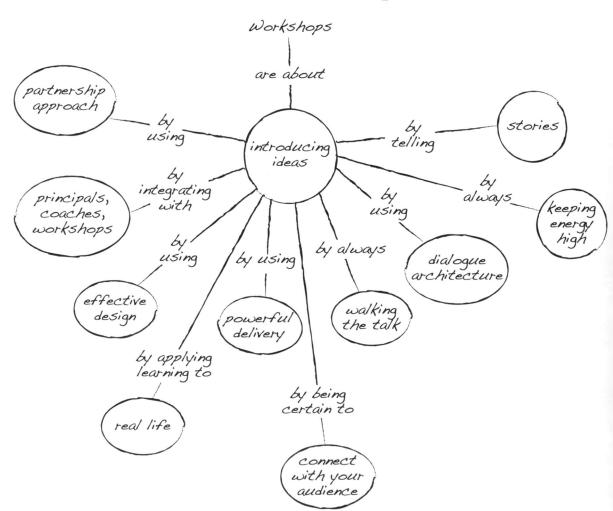

For decades, presentations and workshops have been the mainstay of professional learning in schools. On staff development days, teachers gather in the auditorium or cafeteria to hear someone speak about a certain topic, such as differentiated instruction or cooperative learning. Unfortunately, despite the best intentions of presenters and the value of the content delivered, too often these sessions don't make an impact. After the workshop, overwhelmed by the day-to-day demands of the classroom, teachers return to their students and rarely implement what was discussed in the workshop.

Jake Cornett and I (Cornett & Knight, 2009) looked at over 200 studies of professional development and found that one-shot traditional workshops rarely change professional practice. Worse, in a qualitative study, first described in my book *Instructional Coaching: A Partnership Approach to Improving Instruction* (Knight, 2007), I found that one-shot workshops can actually make things worse rather than better. Strapped for time, having low expectations for a workshop, assuming that they'll never implement what they're hearing about, and, in some cases, feeling defeated by an experience that doesn't recognize their practical and academic expertise, some teachers leave workshops less motivated and less interested in the ideas presented.[1]

Karen Hawley Miles and Matthew Hornbeck (2000) studied professional development expenditures for four urban districts. They found that the districts spent 2.4 to 5.9 percent of the operating budgets, or from $2,010 to $6,628 per teacher, on professional development. U.S. census data estimates indicate that in 2006 there were 6.2 million teachers in America, so the amount spent on professional learning nationally is enormous. If those funds are spent on activities that actually make things worse, this is a tragic waste of money and human potential.

Why, then, include an entire chapter on workshops? Shouldn't schools just eliminate them and focus on other forms of professional learning? The answer is simple: workshops can be highly effective for introducing ideas into a system so long as those ideas are translated into practice through the assistance of instructional coaches and other forms of follow-up. As Michael Fullan put it, "You can't put any kind of precise number on it, but we might say workshops are about 30 percent of professional learning. They introduce ideas into a system, but you need the coaching to really have an impact" (personal communication, 2008).

---

1. You can download this research study at www.instructionalcoach.org/research.html.

This chapter describes how effective workshops should be conducted in Impact Schools by exploring the following factors:

1. Taking the partnership approach

2. Addressing the impact factors

3. Using effective design

4. Applying learning to real life

5. Delivering the message powerfully

6. Connecting with the audience

7. Walking the talk

8. Keeping energy high

9. Using dialogue architectures

10. Telling stories

Take the Partnership Approach

About a decade ago, I conducted a study comparing two approaches to workshops: a partnership approach and an expert approach. The study results suggested that a workshop grounded in the partnership principles can be significantly more engaging, enjoyable, effective, and more likely to lead to implementation than one that is not. A summary of the study is included in Resource B, and you may also download the entire study at www. instructionalcoach.org/research.html.

On the surface, a workshop or presentation does not look like a partnership. After all, workshops usually involve someone leading a group through activities and sharing his or her stories, insights, and knowledge. However, a presenter's impact can be greatly increased if he acts consistent with the partnership principles. How each principle (equality, choice, voice, dialogue, reflection, praxis, and reciprocity) can guide those who design and deliver workshops is described below.

Equality

Leaders, acting on the principle of equality, see themselves as no better than anyone attending their workshops or presentations. If their actions embody authentic respect for others' ideas, gifts, and opinions, if they genuinely listen to and care about what others say, people will usually be open to hearing what they have to say. Equality does not mean that each participant has the same knowledge; instead, it means that each participant's opinion is important, and every point of view is worth hearing. In a workshop based on the partnership approach, all participants should feel that they are truly equal with the facilitator and everyone else.

In the interviews I've conducted with teachers about professional learning, one issue related to workshops has come to the surface: Teachers do not appreciate a presenter who talks down to them or fakes respect or equality. Real respect, however, usually manifested in the six other principles described here, can genuinely open doors.

Choice

The most basic choice, of course, is whether or not to attend a workshop. If we want teachers to get the most out of workshops, we must provide them with choices that allow them to do their best to meet the Targets in the one-page plan. A teacher who has an average of 95 percent engagement in her classroom might not benefit from a workshop on engagement strategies and, if forced to attend, might resent wasting time. Given a choice, she might choose a workshop that would be much more useful for her and, ultimately, more useful for her students.

Choice should also be central to all activities during the workshop. Teachers should be offered choices about who they will work with, what topics they will explore in groups, when they will break, and even when sessions end. Presenters should carefully avoid phrases that are manipulative or that reduce teacher choices. For example, "Can we all agree that . . . ?" is not a real question but a statement that, innocent-looking on the surface, can cause resistance simply because it limits others' choices.

Voice

If partners are equal, if they choose what they do and do not do, they should be free to say what they think, and their opinions should count. Facilitators working from the partnership perspective recognize that professional development must value the opinions of all participants, not just the ideas of the presenter. In fact, most learning is significantly limited unless the voices of more than one person are encouraged and heard.

The simplest way workshop facilitators can encourage people to honestly share their ideas is to listen with every fiber of their being when participants speak. (More on communication strategies is provided in Chapter 7.) If they are going to be heard, participants need many opportunities to speak, sometimes in small groups, sometimes to the entire group, sometimes to partners, and sometimes in solitary writing.

Leaders can also encourage participants to share their ideas and thoughts by using dialogue structures and reflection learning activities—both described below—that create a setting where people feel comfortable sharing ideas. Jim Collins in *Good to Great* (2001) suggests a dialogue structure that simply but powerfully encourages openness:

> When teaching by the case method at Stanford Business School, I issued to each MBA student an 8.5"× 11" bright red sheet of paper, with the following instructions: "This is your red flag for the quarter. If you raise your hand with your red flag, the classroom will stop for you. There are no restrictions on when and how to use your red flag; the decision rests entirely in your hands. You can use it to voice an observation, share a personal experience, present an analysis, disagree with the professor, challenge a CEO guest, respond to a fellow student, ask a question, make a suggestion, or whatever. There will be no penalty whatsoever for any use of a red flag. Your red flag can be used only once during the quarter. Your red flag is nontransferable; you cannot give or sell it to another student. (p. 79)

Reflection

If we are creating a learning partnership, if our partners are equal with us, if they are free to speak their minds and free to make meaningful choices, it follows that one of the most important choices they will make is how to make sense of what we are proposing they learn. Partners don't dictate to each other what to believe; they respect each other's professionalism and provide partners with enough informa tion so that they can make their own decisions.

Offering workshop participants the freedom to consider ideas before adopting them is central to the principle of reflection within the partnership approach to leading workshops. Indeed, reflective thinkers, by definition, have to be free to choose or reject ideas; otherwise, they are not thinkers at all. As John Brubaker, Charles Case, and Timothy Reagan have explained in *Becoming a Reflective Educator*, "The reflective teacher is first and foremost a decision-maker, who must make his or her decisions consciously and rationally" (1994, p. 121). Reflection is only possible when people have the freedom to accept or reject what they are learning as they see fit.

A catchphrase I keep in mind when designing a workshop is "let them do the thinking." By this, I mean that whenever I introduce a case, a thinking prompt, or pose a question, I set out to let everyone process it as they see fit, and I approach our conversations with a sincere desire to hear how my workshop participants see it. I avoid showing a film clip to make a point or asking a question to which I know the answer. Rather, I try to set up each learning opportunity as a prompt to genuine thought. I share ideas in an open way that encourages rather than suppresses thought.

Dialogue

When partners act on the exhilarating belief that they are free to agree, disagree, and reflect on ideas as they choose, something marvelous can happen. When conversation opens up in a workshop, ideas can bounce around a room like balls in a pinball machine. In such a situation, a group can start to communicate so well that it becomes difficult to see where one person's thoughts end and another's begin. An exciting community of thought can arise, and a group can start to think as one big mind, one group of differently talented, unique individuals sharing the joy of muddling over a problem. This kind of communication can be called dialogue, and it is in many ways an honorable goal for any workshop.

Praxis

What do we desire as professional developers? Most likely, we want the people with whom we work to learn new ways to help students, to think about what they do, to change for the better. Praxis becomes possible when teachers have many chances to mull over how they might plan to use the new ideas being discussed. For that reason, in a partnership workshop, teachers have a chance to reshape each new idea until they can see how it might look in their classroom. Furthermore, teachers have many opportunities to think about how to apply new ideas to their real-life practices.

Because reflection is central to this approach to learning, praxis is impossible without a partnership relationship. In *Beyond Objectivism and Relativism* (1983), Richard Bernstein has observed, "praxis requires choice, deliberation, and decisions about what is to be done in concrete situations" (p. 160). In other words, if participants in our workshop are truly to make plans to use what we're explaining, they must feel free to make their own sense of the materials. They have to be real partners, equal, free to say no, and, we hope, excited by possibilities offered by the new ideas being learned.

Reciprocity

When presenters work from a partnership perspective, embodying the principles of equality, choice, voice, reflection, dialogue, and praxis in every action, the final principle, reciprocity, is inevitable. Simply put, when my participants are working on material that matters to them, and they say what they think, chances are they will discover something important, and since, as the facilitator, I'm a part of their experience, I will benefit from their discovery as well.

Reciprocity, then, is going into a workshop expecting to get as much as I give. Reciprocity is seeing learning as a mutually beneficial process. To accomplish this, presenters should ask questions whose answers they really do not know and then wait and listen carefully when people explore answers to the questions. (More on this is given in Chapter 7.)

When I remember to listen as much as I talk during a workshop, what I learn can be very beneficial. Activities that spur new thoughts in my participants spur new thoughts in me. Moreover, the more I learn, the more engaged I am, the better I facilitate, and the more I enjoy the time. Learning along with participants in a partnership-based workshop can be tremendously inspiring, enlightening, and enjoyable.

Address the Impact Factors

For workshops to have a real and lasting positive impact on instruction and student achievement, three additional impact factors (principals, teams, and coaching) must be integrated with the professional learning occurring within workshops.

Principals

Administrators must recognize the value of workshops and communicate that they believe in workshops by attending and frequently leading them. Principals must be the first learners in schools, and if they don't think workshops are worth attending, then teachers will wonder why they are there. Indeed, principals must ensure that workshops are so valuable that they authentically see them as highly valuable.

Each workshop's impact may well hinge on how intentional principals are regarding the planning that occurs for the workshops. Principals must ensure that the topics presented help teachers learn aspects of the specific practices identified in the one-page Instructional Target. This means that they must use the walk-through tools and the teacher progress map to get a clear picture of exactly where instruction is and where it needs to be. If a school identifies 90 percent student engagement as an Instructional Target, for example, and the data show significant room for improvement in that area, workshops should be offered that help teachers achieve those targets.

Principals need to talk with teachers on an ongoing basis about professional learning so that they know what everyone is most interested in learning and understand how teachers perceive the workshops. Principals also must be open-minded and creative, providing professional development time as an opportunity for many different professional learning options. Thus, teachers might engage in curriculum mapping, identifying community behavioral expectations, reviewing Flip camera videos of themselves teaching a lesson, or working in small groups with coaches.

Principals should also fight for the necessary time and a variety of workshop topics so that teachers are able to choose activities that best help them move toward mastery of the Target teaching practices, and principals should encourage coaches and teachers to lead workshop activities so long as they have acquired a deep understanding of the practices being shared and the presentation skills necessary to share those practices effectively. For this reason, everyone in the school should learn effective presentation skills so that many offerings can be available, and funds that might otherwise have been spent on outside presenters can be redirected to supporting other aspects of professional learning, such as coaching. All in all, the principal's chief goal is to ensure that professional learning is ongoing, relevant, and useful as the school moves toward hitting the Target.

Intensive Learning Teams

Both workshops and intensive learning teams (ILTs) should be designed to support the professional learning that occurs in both settings. Thus, teachers might attend workshops to learn teaching practices or approaches, such as content planning or formative assessment, that they will apply during ILTs, or workshops might take the ILT learning deeper by providing more in-depth professional learning on practices that were used during ILTs. Workshops provide opportunities for teachers to go deeper with their learning; indeed, entire ILTs can attend workshops together.

There are many parallels between the learning that takes place in ILTs and learning in workshops. Just like ILT facilitators, workshop facilitators should take the partnership approach—more on this later in this chapter. Facilitators should work to create a learner-friendly environment and consider using enrollment interviews prior to workshops. Facilitators can even begin their workshops with vignettes drawn from information gathered during interviews.

Both ILTs and workshops must be designed carefully to ensure that learning is productive, effective, and fun. Also, the practice of developing team values, introduced during ILTs, can be deepened during workshops, with entire schools working to describe exactly what kind of community they want to be.

Coaches

Workshops do not make an impact unless coaching is a component of the professional learning. Without follow-up, nothing happens, so why offer a workshop on content that no one will actually use? Coaching must be woven into the entire workshop process to ensure results.

Often, workshops can be led by coaches. This makes a great deal of sense because coaches must know well the practices being learned if they are to provide appropriate follow-up. When not leading workshops, coaches should attend them as learners or co-facilitators.

Coaching should be available for every participant following a workshop. Indeed, the fact that coaches will provide follow-up should change the objectives of a workshop leader. That is, teachers can be reassured during a workshop that they don't have to worry about remembering every detail necessary for implementation. Their coach will do that. The coach will remember the key information, help teachers prepare the necessary materials, work with teachers to adjust the new practice so it will fit in the teacher's classroom, and model, observe, and partner with the collaborating teacher until she is fluent in her use of whatever is being learned. Workshops are a bit like window-shopping; teachers look at whatever is being presented from the outside, not really sure how it might work in their classroom. The coach helps the teachers try on something new, makes sure it fits, and helps them take it home for good.

I gained some insight into the necessity of coaching once when I returned home after being away for a few days. When I got to the airport parking lot, I realized that I had forgotten where I had parked the car. What I did remember from parking the car was my certainty that I would not forget where the car was parked. So much for certainty—I had to spend 30 minutes walking through three levels until I finally found my car (I now use my cell phone to photograph the parking space whenever I park).

I learned something important in the airport parking lot that night—our minds can play tricks on us. When we first see or hear something new, we may feel certain we'll never forget it. Unfortunately, a week or two later, we won't remember a thing. I believe that teachers have their own parking lot experience in workshops. During a workshop, the practices being described can seem very clear and easy to understand. But two weeks later, those same practices may be completely forgotten. Coaches can serve as the memory for teachers. When teachers want to implement a practice they learned in a workshop, the coach can take them back through the steps of the process.

For a workshop to make an impact, time must be set aside for teachers to plan how, when, and where they will work with a coach to implement whatever is being described. Indeed, workshops should be all about setting the stage for implementation. There is no point in teachers sitting through explanations of ideas they never plan to use. I would argue there is little point in offering workshops that do not involve some aspect of coaching because without coaching little change will happen.

Use Effective Design

Design is becoming important in almost all aspects of our lives; for example, in Chapter 3 we saw how design thinking is important for principals. As Daniel Pink says in *A Whole New Mind* (2005), "It's no longer sufficient to create a product, a service, an experience or a lifestyle that's merely functional. Today it's economically crucial and personally rewarding to create something that is also beautiful, whimsical, or emotionally engaging" (p. 65).

To understand the importance and potential design holds for presentations and workshops, watch Al Gore's (Guggenheim & Gore, 2006) *An Inconvenient Truth,* a movie that is really a Power-Point presentation.[2] Who would have guessed that a PowerPoint presentation could win you an Oscar and a Nobel Prize, but that is exactly what Gore accomplished with his presentation on climate change, which also has mobilized one of the most powerful move-ments of our time. There are many reasons why the work was suc-cessful, but if you have seen the film, you know that design was one of them.

Nancy Duarte (2008), who helped Gore design the presentation, had this to say about *An Inconvenient Truth:*

> Al Gore has done more than any other individual to legitimize multimedia presentations as one of the most compelling communication vehicles on the planet. He has focused the world's attention on climate change, and it all began with a slide show. He has proven that presentations can tap emotions to incite grass roots change. (p. 86)

Two design factors are especially important when creating work-shops and presentations, (a) developing the content and activities and (b) developing the slides. Both of these are discussed below.

Developing Content and Activities

During a conversation on effective presentations, Nancy Duarte told me that she believes we should spend much more time develop-ing our presentations and workshops if we want them to have an impact. "You can't rush something as creative as a presentation," she told me. "You have to take the time to make it beautiful if you want it to be beautiful."

Duarte (2008) isn't kidding; the following boxed text details her suggestion regarding the way we should use our time if we are devel-oping just a one-hour presentation.

---

2. Actually, Gore appears to use Apple's Keynote slideware.

Duarte's Time Estimate for Developing a Presentation

6–20 hours: Research and collect input from the web, colleagues, and the industry.

1 hour: Build an audience needs map.

2 hours: Generate ideas via sticky notes.

1 hour: Organize the ideas.

1 hour: Have colleagues critique or collaborate around the impact the ideas will have on an audience.

2 hours: Sketch a structure and/or storyboard.

20–60 hours: Build the slides in a presentation application.

3 hours: Rehearse, rehearse, rehearse (in the shower, on the treadmill, or during the commute).

36–90 hours total (p. 13)

I break presentation or workshop development into five stages: (1) preparing, (2) mapping, (3) organizing, (4) integrating activities, and (5) creating slides.

Preparing

I hesitate to call preparing a stage because the truth is that I am always preparing. I read books whenever I have free time. Listen to books when I drive. I rip out articles from papers and magazines. Even when I go to the movie theater, I watch films for clips I might use in my workshops and presentations.

I also take notes daily in a special Moleskine notebook. I keep it in my briefcase so that whenever I have a few moments I can jot down notes or work out a map. If you've been to a workshop that I've facilitated, you've probably seen me writing in my notebook.

Books, though, are my most valuable sources for ideas and inspiration. I believe that after you have read a book, it should look as well used as a lineman's jersey after a football game in a mud bowl. I

Photo by Jennifer Ryschon-Knight.

highlight my books, take notes, and mark passages with sticky notes so important passages are easy to find after I set the book aside.

After I read a book or other document, I type notes, including quotations that I might use in a presentation, workshop, or writing. Once filed, I can go back to my notes whenever I wish to create a presentation. When those typed notes become necessary, I print off a hard copy, and review them from the perspective of the particular workshop I'll be leading. I also keep a copy of the book nearby if I need it. Then I read my notes, highlight key passages, and flag sections that might be relevant to my topic. This review gives me the material I need to map my presentation or workshop.

What matters most to me is that I have a rich array of content knowledge to draw from when it is time to create a presentation.

Mapping

Too often, I think, we move too quickly to our computers when we are designing a presentation. My wired colleagues tell me that they prefer to use digital tools to help them prepare. Thus, they might gather readings in Google Reader, sort through their online library using Evernotes, create their maps using Inspiration, and sort their slides in presentation software. To each their own. Like design expert Garr Reynolds, I find I get the best start by stepping away from the computer. In *Presentation Zen* (2008a), Reynolds puts it this way,

> One of the most important things you can do in the initial stage of preparing for your presentation is to get away from your computer. A fundamental mistake people make is spending almost the entire time thinking about their talk and preparing their content while sitting in front of a computer screen. Before you design your presentation, you must see the big picture and identify your core messages—or the single core message. This can be difficult unless you create a stillness of mind for yourself, something which is hard to do while puttering around in slideware.
>
> Right from the start, most people plan their presentations using software tools. In fact, the software makers encourage this, but I don't recommend it. There's just something about paper and pen and sketching out rough ideas in the "analog world" in the early stages that seems to lead to more clarity and better, more creative results when we finally get down to representing our ideas digitally. Since you will be making your presentation accompanied by PowerPoint or Keynote, you will be spending plenty of time in front of a computer later. I call preparing the presentation away from the computer "going analog," as opposed to "going digital" at the computer. (p. 45)

There are many ways to "go analog," but when I do it, I usually draw a mind map on the whiteboard in my office, or I draw a map in the pages of a notebook that summarizes what I want to present. I take a free-jazz approach to mapping, which means I follow no rules. Sometimes I create a concept map. Sometimes I write lists of ideas on the map. Sometimes I include a word or a short phrase to help me remember activities, stories, or video clips I would like to include in my presentation. I try to be playful and find a way to write down anything that pops into my head.

I might finish my map in an hour and move to the next step, or I might leave it on the whiteboard for a day or a week, so I can keep adding ideas. I have gotten into the habit of photographing my maps

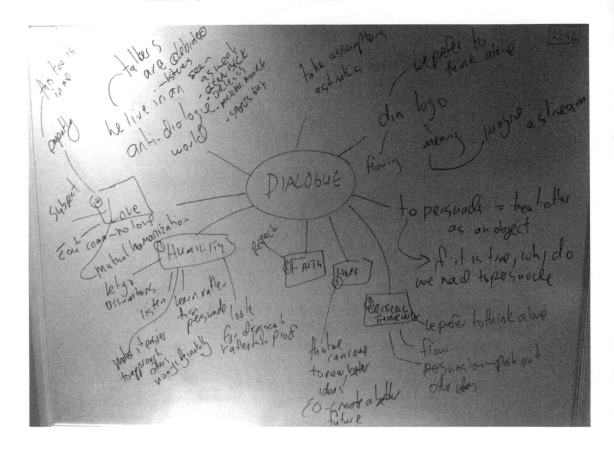

with my iPhone and loading them into my computer, so I have a record after I clean the board. I also have a small whiteboard at my desk, and I use that almost every day—sometimes to flesh out an idea on the bigger map. Throughout the process, I try to come up with as many ideas as possible. More is better, since I will have to cut most of what I have written on the map to create an organized, linear presentation.

Organizing

Once I have finished mapping, I have a lot of ideas to comb through. I begin the organizational process by writing a one-sentence simple statement that totally sums up my presentation's purpose. Garr Reynolds (2008a) writes, "the most fundamental question of all

. . . stripped down to its essential core . . . [is] . . . what is my absolute central point? . . . or . . . If the audience could remember only one thing . . . , what would it be?" (p. 61).

Once I have identified my presentation's purpose, I use a method I learned from Steve Jobs, as described by Carmine Gallo (2009) in *The Presentation Secrets of Steve Jobs.* I create a simple organizing structure, usually built around three big ideas. About Jobs' organizational methods, Gallo writes,

> Jobs draws a verbal road map for his audience, a preview of coming attractions. Typically these road maps are outlined in groups of three—a presentation might be broken into "three acts," a product description into "three features," a demo into "three parts." (p. 50)

For example, I might build a workshop around three simple questions such as "Why do we need coaches? What do they do? What does the research say?" Then I pull out blank index cards or sticky notes and a Sharpie marker. I write a word or two on individual cards (I prefer to use sticky notes that are the size of index cards) for each idea on the map. Sharpie markers are great—I learned this from Nancy Duarte (2008)—because they keep you from writing too many words on a card. If I can't write the words using a Sharpie, I'm probably not clear on the idea or the idea is too complicated.

Once all of the ideas have been marked down on the stickies, I clean off my whiteboard and start attaching all the sticky notes to the board. Across the top of the board I post the three stickies with the big ideas. Then I put the ideas associated with a big idea underneath each. I usually don't worry about order. At this point, I sometimes realize that many of the ideas won't fit, so I toss them or rethink my categories. I may also come up with ideas I hadn't considered; when that happens, I write them on sticky notes and put them on the wall. I might leave these sticky notes on the board for a few days, so I can think about what goes where, what can be removed, and what kind of sequence makes the most sense. I keep rearranging the stickies until I have the right number of ideas and what I think will be the right sequence given the time I have to present. Eventually, I end up with three big categories, with a list of ideas beneath them, organized in the order in which I'll share them during the presentation.

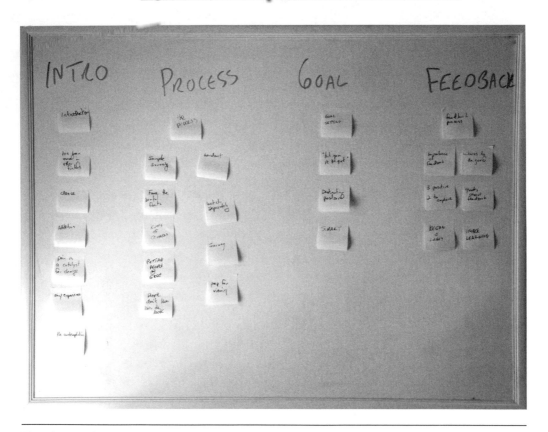

Photo by Jennifer Ryschon-Knight.

Integrating Activities

John Medina, in *Brain Rules* (2008), writes that because of the way we are wired, our brains start to check out after 10 minutes of non-stop talk. He calls this, appropriately enough, the 10-minute rule. Excellent presenters follow the 10-minute rule by providing some sort of change or activity every 10 minutes. Carmine Gallo (2009) explains how Steve Jobs accomplishes this:

> In a 30-minute period, his presentations include demonstrations, a second or even third speaker, and video clips. Jobs is well aware that even his gifts of persuasion are no match for a tired brain constantly seeking new stimuli. (p. 83)

Much of the rest of this chapter describes a variety of learning activities or structures that can be used within workshops, including telling stories; using video clips; setting up cooperative, experiential, or reflection learning; sharing cases; and so forth. All of these activities must be planned into the workshop.

I use a three-step process to integrate activities. First, I review all of the sticky notes with ideas in the order of the presentation. I take a sheet of paper, divide it in half, and on the left-hand column I write all of the major points of my presentation—a kind of outline of the session. Sometimes I need several pages to do this; all of this can be done on a whiteboard or chart paper.

Second, I look over my outline, laid out in the left-hand column, and consider what ideas need to be clarified, emphasized, or enhanced, and where I must provide an alternative learning opportunity for participants to keep them engaged. I also think about activities, stories, film clips, and other learning aids that might be especially effective as part of the presentation, and consider where they might be used. If I identify something I can use within the presentation, I write a note about it in the right-hand column. If I can't think of something, I put a star beside the words in the left-hand column as a reminder or place holder until I come up with a good learning enhancement.

Third, I review my list until I have appropriate activities every 10 minutes, keeping in mind Medina's (2008) 10-minute rule. Eventually, I have a clear step-by-step sequence for my content and powerful activities that will keep my audience engaged and actively learning.

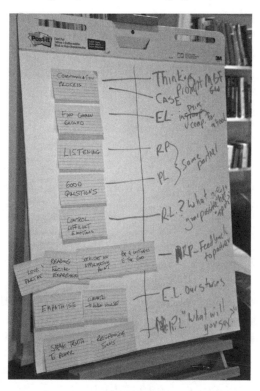

Photo by Jennifer Ryschon-Knight.

Creating Slides

Garr Reynolds (2008a, 2008b) and Nancy Duarte (2008) have started a much-needed revolution in the way we understand and use slides. Thanks to their work, many are now recognizing that slide design is not simply an add-on part of presenting; design is essential. Ignoring slide design for a presentation is like ignoring grammar or style in writing.

What's Wrong With PowerPoint?

Do I really have to answer the question? Everyone has sat through enough PowerPoint presentations to know that the default format for PowerPoint does not lead to clear communication. Nancy Duarte (2008) even reports that the men who created PowerPoint were quoted in the *Wall Street Journal* as saying, "the best way to paralyze an opposing army is to ship them PowerPoint" (p. viii). As Seth Godin in *Really Bad PowerPoint (and How to Avoid It)* (2001) nicely, but pretty directly, puts it, PowerPoint is "a dismal failure. Almost every PowerPoint presentation sucks rotten eggs" (p. 3). (You can watch a Godin PowerPoint presentation at TED.com by searching for Seth Godin on the site.)

There are many reasons why PowerPoint is often less than successful. First, when presenters and workshop leaders cram too much information onto one slide, viewers are overwhelmed. Too many words make our audience check out simply because they cannot take everything in. As Nancy Duarte has written, "at a certain point, the number of words on a slide prevents it from being a visual aid" (2008, p. 6).

Second, when our slides contain too much information, we force our audience to make a choice between reading the slides and listening to us present. Our minds are not wired to do both at once. In her fascinating book on attention, *Rapt* (2009), Winifred Gallagher puts it this way:

> You may *think* you're multi-tasking when you're listening to your boss's report while texting your lunch date, but what you're really doing is switching back and forth between activities. Despite your fond hopes, the extra effort involved actually makes you less rather than more productive. (p. 152)

If our audience can understand what we have to say by just reading our slides, why not just e-mail them the slides? Ideally, we are presenting or leading a workshop because we have something to share that goes beyond what is in PowerPoint or Keynote. In that case, our slides must support, not hinder, communication.

Third, poorly designed slides, often consisting of a mixture of fonts, bullet points, and clipart, interfere with our ability to communicate. Poor design creates "visual vertigo" (Duarte, 2008, p. 10), confuses our audience, and erodes our credibility. What's more, as others become more alert to the impact of effective design, quality slides will soon become the norm, and a poorly designed slide, while somewhat acceptable today, will no longer be accepted.

Source: ©iStockphoto.com/technotr

How Do I Create Effective Slides?

The first step is to recognize that developing slides is a creative act, closer to painting than to filling out a spreadsheet. According to Garr Reynolds, to create good slides you must use your right- and left-brain abilities:

> Once you realize that the preparation of a presentation is an act requiring creativity, not merely the assembling of facts and data in a linear fashion, you'll see that preparing a presentation is a "whole-minded" activity that requires as much right-brain thinking as it does left-brain thinking. In fact, while your research and background work may have required much logical analysis, calculation, and careful evidence gathering or so-called left-brain thinking, the transformation of your content into presentation form will require that you exercise much more of your so-called right brain. (2008a, p. 32)

We can begin by recognizing that slides are not teleprompters; they are more like billboards. In fact, Duarte (2008) suggests that a good slide should be as easy to process as a billboard, and every slide should pass the three-second rule: It shouldn't take more than three seconds to process.

Words. To create better slides, use the smallest number of words possible and avoid bullet points unless they are absolutely necessary. Duarte (2008) has a simple suggestion for breaking the bullet point habit:

> Practice presenting with your slides a few times, then highlight only one keyword per bullet point. Practice delivering those slides again, but focus only on the highlighted word. The other words will still be there, so you can refer to them if needed. Once you can deliver the slides from the keywords, remove all the words on the slides except for the key words, and present them from that. Ideally, replace that word with an image when possible. (p. 221)

Typeface Size. If we reduce the number of words on each slide, we can increase the typeface size. My simple rule is go for the smallest number of words and the largest font possible. Guy Kawasaki (visit his website at www.guykawasaki.com), talking about presenting to potential investors, offers another way to determine font size. Estimate the age of the oldest investor in your audience. Divide that number by two; make that your font size. Duarte (2008) shares the following rule of thumb: If you view your slides at 66 percent size, you'll be able to determine whether or not your audience will be able to read them.

Most designers agree that the secret of good design is that it is "more about subtraction than addition" (Reynolds, 2008a, p. 120). Effective slides are restrained, simple, and exploit white space. Often effective slides are built upon a single image.

Images. I have created a library of images, organized in iPhoto, that I use in various ways. Some of these images I have purchased from websites (e.g., www.istockphoto.com) or downloaded from free sites (e.g., www.fickr.com/creativecommons.com). Others are photographs taken by wife, Jenny, who happens to be an accomplished photographer and designer. I also own a high-quality scanner that allows me to scan photos, drawings, or hand-drawn images onto my hard drive to use in presentations.

Backgrounds. So that the message of each slide is prominent, the background of the slide should remain "in the background." I never use the default background but choose extremely simple backgrounds, most frequently white. Duarte nicely sums up the purpose of the background: "Backgrounds are intended as a surface on which to place elements. They are not in themselves a work of art . . . the background should never compete with the content" (2008, pp. 118, 120).

Handouts. The habit of printing off slides and sharing them as handouts is not particularly effective. Reynolds (2008a) calls these slide printouts slideuments:

> Slides are slides. Documents are documents. They aren't the same thing. Attempts to merge them result in what I call the "slideument" . . . The slideument isn't effective, and it isn't efficient, and it isn't pretty. Attempting to have slides serve both as projected visuals and as a stand-alone handout makes for bad visuals and bad documentation. (p. 68)

If your slides are primarily made up of single words, images, and brief statements, as recommended for effective slides, printing out these slideuments would not help your audience. A better idea is to create a separate document containing a summary of the ideas you presented, a bibliography, and other information that participants might find useful. If you are leading a workshop, you may choose to create a workbook for participants. All in all, when workshop leaders recognize the importance of design as a part of leading a workshop, they can do a lot to make their workshops more effective.

Apply Learning to Real Life

When I ask teachers about professional development, they almost always say they are most interested in ideas that they can take back and use in their classrooms. Thus, workshop facilitators would be wise to create learning experiences that explicitly make the connection between content being presented and life in the classroom. This can involve posing a work or personal problem and then structuring a small-group discussion so people can explore how content being covered can help solve the proposed problem. Workshop facilitators can also use thinking prompts (video clips, cases, or other prompts to dialogue) or experiential learning (role-playing or learning simulations) that stimulate conversations about real-life issues. Each of these is described in more detail below.

Reflection Learning

Reflection learning provides opportunities to explore immediately how content being covered can be generalized and implemented. It allows learners to consider realistically how content being covered might be translated into new behaviors or strategies and to problem solve from new perspectives. Most important, perhaps, reflection learning enables praxis by offering concrete opportunities for learners to reflect, invent, and act on knowledge.

My colleague Susan FitzRandolph has developed a simple but powerful reflection learning activity to teach motivation theories to business leaders in her organizational behavior classes. She asks her students to identify someone they manage whom they believe could be more motivated about their work. Each manager then picks one real employee with a motivation "issue" and discusses that employee with their group. Each group subsequently chooses to help one of the managers develop strategies to increase their employee's motivation.

Once all groups have chosen a challenge for which they are going to invent solutions, Susan proceeds to explain, one at a time, various theories of motivation, and each group discusses how the theory might provide possible strategies for motivating the chosen employees. Each time she introduces a new theory, the groups explore whether or not the theory illuminates why the particular person is not motivated. In this way, learners immediately see how to apply knowledge to real challenges in their lives.

Reflection learning activities create energy because they prompt participants to address real issues that matter to them. When we are working on topics that count, we usually stay interested and engaged.

Thinking Prompts

Any object that facilitators can share to stimulate conversation and dialogue can function as a thinking device. Film clips, digital video recordings, photographs, cases, student work, paintings, literary works, and songs are some examples. Thinking prompts provide learners with an opportunity to consider the content being introduced, to discuss prior knowledge, and to explore the "real-world" positive and negative implications of the material being covered.

I learned about thinking prompts from Paulo Freire (he calls them cognizable objects). In *Pedagogy of the Oppressed* (1970), Freire explains how use of a thinking prompt allowed participants in an adult learning group to express their real thoughts and feelings authentically:

> In one of the thematic investigations carried out in Santiago, a group of tenement residents discussed a scene showing a drunken man walking on the street and three young men conversing on the corner. The group participants commented that "the only one there who is productive and useful to his country is the souse who is returning home after working all day for low wages and who is worried about his family because he can't take care of their needs. He is the only worker. He is a decent worker and a souse like us."
>
> The investigator had intended to study aspects of alcoholism. He probably would not have elicited the above responses if he had presented the participants with a questionnaire he had elaborated himself. If asked directly, they might even have denied ever taking a drink themselves. But in their comments on the codification of an existential situation they could recognize, and in which they could recognize themselves, they said what they really felt. (p. 111)

What counts with thinking prompts is not participants' immediate interaction with them but the dialogue that occurs after the prompt has been experienced. To provide opportunities for authentic

dialogue, facilitators should begin discussion with open-ended opinion questions such as "What do you make of this?" or "What do you
think and feel about this?"

Once discussion begins, facilitators should suspend their own
views to avoid the risk of dominating the discussion and silencing
other learners. Facilitators should try to accept every person's view as
valid to encourage and model openness and genuine desire to learn
from others. Our openness significantly affects the openness of the
overall conversation. Our actions communicate our commitment to
partnership, to learning with participants as opposed to teaching to
participants.

Experiential Learning

I use the term *experiential learning* to refer to any learning activity that lets learners experience what they are learning about during a workshop. This type of learning creates experiences that
enable learners to act out the behaviors, strategies, or other content
being learned. It can allow learners to see how well they can use
new concepts they are learning, remind learners of the concrete
attributes of a particular phenomenon being studied, or enable
learners to gain new insights into their thoughts, assumptions, and
behaviors. Experiential learning can be fun, challenging, engaging,
and provocative.

Effective experiential learning provides learners with a simula-
tion of some or all elements of content being covered during a learning session. Thus, learners engage in experiences that simulate reality.
Experiential learning can be manifested in a variety of ways, including teachers' practicing visual imagery reading strategies, coaches'
role-playing providing feedback, or other activities that simulate
more complex situations related to teams, culture, or leadership.

What matters in experiential learning is that learners experience
content in a way that simulates the real-life cognitive, emotional, and
sensual elements of the content being covered.

Deliver the Message Powerfully

A presenter's delivery can make or break a session. If the presenter
does a poor job of speaking, no matter how great the content,
audience members are less inclined to implement the presenter's
ideas. Even the most knowledgeable presenters can lose their

audiences if they don't deliver their message in a way that is engaging and clear. Fortunately, there is a lot we can do to deliver our message powerfully.

Simple, Precise Language

Although the following may sound obvious, I will point it out anyway because it is a very important part of delivery: presenters must be clear about exactly what they want to say. If presenters are not clear in their own minds, their language won't be clear. Once they know what they want to say, they need to find the simplest and clearest way to express the ideas. Presenters should shy away from buzzwords and acronyms and use simple, clear language that listeners will immediately understand.

However, simple language should not be a dummied-down version of content. Just the opposite, simple language is what is created when presenters take the time to find the clearest, most direct, easiest-to-understand way to express their ideas. John Maeda, the director of the Rhode Island Institute of Design and author of the helpful book *The Laws of Simplicity* (2006), puts it this way:

> The process of reaching an ideal state of simplicity can be truly complex, so allow me to simplify it for you. *The simplest way to achieve simplicity is through thoughtful reduction.* When in doubt, just remove. But be careful of what you remove. (p. 1)

Simple language is not easy to find, but it is essential if you want your audience to act on what you are saying.

Atul Gawande (2010) points out that precise, simple language is necessary if we want people to implement the practices we are sharing. Indeed, the absence of simple, precise language is a major reason why new ideas do not get implemented.

> One study in medicine . . . examined the aftermath of nine different major treatment discoveries such as the finding, that the pneumococcus vaccine protects not only children but also adults from respiratory infections, one of our most common killers. On average, the study reported, it took doctors 17 years to adopt the new treatments for at least half of American patients.
>
> What experts . . . have recognized is that the reason for the delay is not usually laziness or unwillingness. The reason is

more often that the necessary knowledge has not been translated into a simple, usable, and systematic form. (p. 133)

Sound Bites

One way to make your message clearer and more accessible to your audience is to create short, powerful phrases that concisely capture a key idea or concept—sound bites. Steve Jobs is a master at this technique. When he first introduced the iPod, for example, Jobs described it as "1,000 songs in your pocket." And, when he introduced the iPhone, he said, "Today, Apple re-invents the phone." Carmine Gallo (2009) describes Jobs' sound bites as "Twitter-like headlines":

> Jobs takes the guesswork out of a new product by creating a one-line description or headline that best reflects the product. The headlines work so well that the media will often run with them word for word. You see, reporters (and your audience) are looking for a category in which to place your product and a way of describing the product in one sentence. Take the work out of it and write the headline yourself. (p. 39)

Sound bites are as effective during a workshop as they are during a MacWorld keynote. Lynn Barnes, an IC from Topeka, Kansas, who leads instructional coaching workshops, talks about a "servitude attitude" as her way of describing servant leadership. Lynn repeats the phrase during her workshop, and her participants always remember the phrase after the workshop is over.

Similarly, instruction expert Anita Archer has popularized the phrase "I do it, we do it, you do it," to summarize a method of instruction that involves (a) teacher modeling, (b) teacher-guided student practice, and (c) independent student practice. The phrase has become well known in schools around the world, in part because the methods are effective, but also, I believe, because the simple, catchy phrase is easy to remember. In fact, I'm certain that if Anita was talking about "metacognitive modeling," "scaffolded-guided practices," and "student-guided practice to mastery," her methodology would not be nearly as well known. Learning from these examples, workshop leaders should work to find simple phrases that concisely communicate critical information they want their audiences to learn.

Pacing, Passion, Authenticity

One of the most important aspects of delivery is, as Anita Archer likes to say, "keeping a perky pace." Carmine Gallo (2006), who has studied many of the world's best presenters, offers this comment on pacing:

> The world's best communicators speak a little faster than average. . . . The average American speaks at a rate of 125 words per minute (wpm). Peter Jennings, by comparison, speaks at a rate closer to 200 wpm . . . I find that very few people in my seminars speak too fast. Most of them have the opposite problem—they talk way too slow. It's like watching sap drip from a tree. The last thing you want to be is a sap. If your listeners are tuning out, or looking at their watch during your presentation, it's quite possibly your rate of speech is too slow. (p. 153)

Pacing is not just important for broadcasters. Gallo (2006) notes that Steve Jobs and Cisco CEO John Chambers both speak at about 195 wpm. To improve our effectiveness, most of us should record and improve our pace. One way to accomplish this is to ensure that we talk about ideas with passion. Presenters should think a great deal about the teaching practices they are sharing and about what they love about the information they're sharing. Then they must let their audiences in on the love affair.

Trying to fake passion is a recipe for disaster. If an audience senses that you are just pretending to be enthusiastic about what you are explaining, they will likely dismiss what you are saying as untrustworthy or useless.

In summary, remember that PowerPoint or Keynote is not delivering the presentation, you are. Don't feel that you have to address each slide. It is much more important to connect with your audience and provide them with a variety of learning opportunities (about one every 10 minutes).

Connect With the Audience

In Chapter 7, I describe several communication strategies that workshop leaders can use to connect with participants, including emotionally intelligent practices, such as authentically listening, asking good questions, finding common ground, and building emotional connections.

Other simple things can also have a big impact on how effectively a presenter is able to connect with an audience, such as position in the room and eye contact. Where a presenter stands can put a barrier between them and the audience. To better connect, presenters should step away from the podium (or step out from a behind table) so nothing stands between them and their audience.

Perhaps the most important way of connecting with an audience is to make eye contact. I try to increase eye contact by thinking of a workshop or presentation as a series of very short one-to-one conversations with participants. Thus, I look at one participant for a few seconds, talking with them before looking at another participant, moving my line of vision around the room so that everyone feels I have had an individual conversation with them.

Effective eye contact doesn't mean staring down every audience member. We shouldn't stare into the eyes of our audience like a boxer at the start of a boxing match or like a star-crossed lover lost in his partner's eyes. That could be seen as insulting or possibly even a little creepy. Communication expert Bert Decker, in *You've Got to Be Believed to Be Heard* (2008), suggests we use eye contact to create connection but not overdo it. "A feeling of involvement requires about five seconds of steady eye contact. That's about the time we take to complete a thought or a sentence" (p. 114).

Another simple way for presenters to connect with audiences is to use a remote control device with their laptops so that they can move through their slides without having to go over to the computer, look at it, and push a key to move a slide. Also, when possible, presenters can increase eye contact by keeping their bodies facing the audience, not facing the screen. For this reason, it is helpful to set up the computer in a location that allows presenters to see the computer screen so that they can see what slide the audience is seeing without having to turn their back to audience. Apple's Keynote software allows you to see the slide you are on, the upcoming slide, a timer for your presentation, and your note slides on your monitor if you wish.

Walk the Talk

If we talk about the power of particular teaching practices, but then fail to use them during our presentations, participants will be a lot less inclined to use them. A presenter who lectures about cooperative learning, for example, might have a hard time convincing his audience that they should use cooperative learning simply because his audience will be asking, "If cooperative learning is so good, why isn't he using it?" Consequently, when presenters embody the Big Four teaching practices in their presentations about those practices, for example, audiences get a chance to see exactly how they might be used and are much more likely to adopt and implement them.

In a conversation with me about workshops a few years ago, Anita Archer made this point clearly:

> When I go to teach [a particular teaching practice], there should be no dissonance between how I present it and what I want teachers to do. So if I want teachers to use active participation, we say answers together, we say answers to partners, we write things down, we use hand signals. Then I will do that as I teach. If I want teachers to monitor, I will monitor. If I want teachers to use I do it, we do it, you do it, then they see that all day long, even before we've talked about it, I do it, we do it, you do it.

The Big Four teaching practices, discussed in Chapter 3 and described in detail in *Instruction That Makes an Impact* (Knight, in press), can easily be used to conduct workshops, including learning maps, guiding questions, thinking prompts, appropriate high-level questions, and experiential learning. Presenters should vary their use of the various practices. For example, a presenter might use think-pair-share, jigsaw, gallery walk, and open-space dialogue as forms of cooperative learning during the same workshop, and similarly use video clips, cases, and newspaper articles for thinking prompts.

Adopting the partnership approach has implications for how presenters use the various teaching practices. For example, they need to give participants frequent opportunities to choose the topic they want to discuss and to give voice to their opinion, and offer activities that are clearly relevant to participants' interests and needs. To act on the principle of praxis, presenters should encourage teachers to bring their curriculum materials so that they can develop real-life teaching tools they can use in their classrooms. Indeed, when teachers see the relevance of what they are learning and have ample opportunities to plan how to use the materials, they are highly engaged in activities.

By adopting the partnership principles, presenters also adopt an open stance as they share information. That is, just like ICs, while they are precise in their descriptions of all practices, they are provisional, by communicating to teachers that they are free to adapt a given strategy to make it work for students. To be precise and provisional, presenters often share checklists and offer a turn-to-your-neighbor activity so teachers can consider whether or not they would like to make adaptations to a given approach.

Keep the Energy High

During any workshop, facilitators need to keep participants engaged and energized. As Jim Loehr and Tony Schwartz have written in *The Power of Full Engagement* (2003), "without the right quality, quantity, focus, and force of energy, we are compromised in any activity we undertake" (p. 30). For that reason, presenters must artfully structure their workshop so a mixture of learning activities and content delivery encourages as high an energy level as possible. An admirable goal for a presenter should be that the conversation during the workshop is just as engaging as the conversation during breaks. Fortunately, there is a lot a presenter can do to keep participant energy level high.

Movement

Participants will be more energized if they move around periodically during a workshop. Movement also provides opportunities for them to meet others and share and learn with them. If participants work with the same four people all day during a workshop, they only hear the ideas of those four. However, if they move about the room and work with many different people, they have opportunities to tap into the collective wisdom of the entire group.

A simple way to structure movement during a workshop is to ask everyone to identify a number of partners at the start so that they know in advance who they can collaborate with at various times throughout the day. Workshop leaders I've worked with in Connecticut ask people to find spring, summer, fall, and winter partners at the start of their workshop. I have adopted this strategy. Whenever I ask people to find their spring, summer, fall, and winter partners, I explain why I'm doing this—so that everyone can tap into the collective wisdom of the group—and I always add, "If you'd prefer not to move; don't feel you have to. This is your choice." I want participants to know that the activity is for their benefit, but I respect their choice if it is not an activity they would like to do.

Photo by Jennifer Ryschon-Knight.

Learning Environment

The right learning environment is an important starting point. Strapped for cash, educators may want to save a few dollars by holding presentations in crowded, stuffy, run-down rooms. If possible, I think it is wiser to spend the money to find a more learner-friendly setting.

The ideal setting has natural sunlight, sufficient space for participants and the presenter to move around freely, and a tidy and organized appearance. Participants also appreciate healthy (and sometimes unhealthy!) snacks and drinks, including caffeine, chocolate, and other stimulants. Providing sufficient break time makes it easier for teachers to stay fresh and energized.

Reading Nonverbals

In the 1990s, I interviewed 80 university students to learn what was working and wasn't working for them as learners. One response that surfaced again and again was that the best professors seemed to have a sixth sense about students' understanding of materials. When they were struggling in class, students told me, the best educators seemed always to know and either consulted one-to-one with students during the class or adjusted their teaching style to ensure understanding.

To ensure participants are engaged, presenters must continually monitor their behavior. If they are not engaged, certain kinds of behaviors occur over and over. A good presenter pays attention to the brutal facts, so to speak, and adjusts presenting to be more engaging.

What are the signs of lack of engagement? When I studied video recordings of adult learners who were watching a long lecture and demonstrated a lack of engagement, certain signs became obvious: participants nodded off or engaged in side conversations. Also, unengaged participants took more trips to the restroom, had more sips of water, and spent more time resting their heads on their hands while listening.

A good presenter has to develop a sixth sense about whether or not participants are engaged. When participants are engaged, they laugh at the humorous video clips, ask questions, and engage in the activities. When participants aren't engaged, the room feels different. There is a deadness to the room.

If a presenter wants participants to be energetic, he has to be energetic too. That means that presenters must make sure they are well rested before their presentation.

Use Dialogue Architectures

Using careful planning and various tools to maintain a structured workshop may seem antithetical to a partnership approach, but nothing could be further from the truth. Structure provides the framework that allows for reflection, dialogue, and meaningful conversations about learning. As mentioned at different points throughout this book, freedom occurs best within form. Knowing the form of language and of a poem provides a structure for poetic communication. Similarly, structure provides the framework that allows for reflection, dialogue, and meaningful conversations about learning during workshops.

Dialogue architecture is a way of structuring workshops so that participants are free to express ideas, learn from each other, and reflect on the material they are learning. Many forms of dialogue architecture can be used to keep a workshop moving and productive. I prefer dialogue architecture that provides participants a lot of freedom while maintaining structure so that the session moves along smoothly.

Guidelines for Activities

The simplest, but perhaps most important, dialogue architecture presenters can use is to make sure that they are clear and explain exactly how all activities will work. An easy way to accomplish this is to write down explanations for all activities and share them with participants. Most people appreciate it if the guidelines for activities are also either included in handouts or displayed on an overhead while they do the activity.

Stop and Go

Presenters can use a variety of signals and tools to guide participants through a session. For example, I use a timer on my computer, which my participants can see, so that they know how long they have to complete an activity. Also, I frequently use music to signal a transition within an activity. For example, during a gallery walk, when several groups of participants are looking at different posters that have been created by participants, I use music to let groups know it is time to move to the next poster. There's nothing like Aretha singing "Respect" to get groups moving along.

Getting People's Attention

There are also simple ways to get a group's attention. The easiest to use is an attention signal such as teaching participants that when you raise your hand and say, "May I have your attention, please?" they should also raise one hand and stop talking, as soon as possible.

Bringing People Back From the Break

When presenting to large groups, it is important to have a structured way of bringing the group back from the break. Without structure, breaks can take a lot of time. Some participants may become frustrated because they are experiencing too much downtime, and presenters find valuable time slipping away.

There are many ways to bring people back. Some presenters use nice-sounding chimes or other sounds to signal that the break is over. My preference is a simpler way, an approach that I learned from classroom management expert Jim Fay. Right before a break, I tell participants that we are about to take a break and that although the break is 15 minutes long, they may take as long as they'd like, "one hour, two hours, whatever they wish." Then I add, "However, you must know that in 15 minutes I will show an absolutely hilarious film clip, so if you are not back in 15 minutes, you'll miss it."

This approach provides participants with the freedom to come back when they can, but at the same time it ensures that almost everyone will be back on time. I have seen superintendents running down the halls of a hotel because they wanted to make sure they were back for the funny film clip. Of course, if you use this method, you'd better deliver on your promise and have a truly hilarious clip to show when participants return.

Getting Feedback From Participants

I also like to use structures that allow me to get feedback from participants. For example, I frequently use response cards to gauge whether or not participants understand the content we are learning. Thus, after explaining the difference between mechanical and metaphorical learning, for example, I might ask participants to hold up a card to represent their level of understanding with 1 equaling "I'm lost," 2 equaling "I've got questions," and 3 equaling "I understand. Let's move on."

Spokespeople Hosts

One way to structure groups is to ask people to volunteer to be responsible for reporting back on their group's actions (spokespeople) or to guide a discussion about a particular topic (hosts).

One fun way to identify speakers is to ask everyone in your audience to close their eyes. Ask them to point at the person whom they want to be the spokesperson. Then ask them to open their eyes. The person who is pointed at the most becomes the spokesperson. Usually, this activity leads to a lot of laughter, and it also identifies the spokesperson. A spokesperson's job is quite simple. After a small group performs a task, the spokesperson tells the larger group what transpired. For example, if a group is working on developing guiding questions, a spokesperson tells the larger group what questions were created and what they learned while developing the questions.

Photo by Jennifer Ryschon-Knight.

Tell Stories

I may have learned more from stories than anything else in my life. Stories told by my mother and father shaped who I am and who I want to become. My love of education, my distrust of slick salespeople, my enthusiasm for hockey, and my distaste for power-hungry people all are based on the stories I heard my parents tell over and again. In fact, much of my own development as a person has been learning to tell the story of my own life.

Not surprisingly, stories have come to play a central role in the workshops and sessions that I conduct. On the surface, stories might not appear to involve a partnership. Stories, after all, are most often one-directional, with one person talking and another individual or group listening. During story time, talker and listener have clearly defined roles, and the talker appears to be the main actor. If we drew a picture of a story, we might show a talker with an arrow pointing in one direction—out to an audience.

However, in reality, storytelling is a quintessential partnership activity. Although a story does begin with one teller, it only becomes real when a listener hears it and makes it something that is personally meaningful. That is why stories involve partnership. A person creates and tells a story, and listeners, in partnership, re-create the story in their minds. As Richard Stone (1995) commented, listening to a story can be as creative an act as telling.

> When you hear my story it is transformed into a tale that feels intimately like your own, even palpably real and personal, especially if you repeat it to another . . . After a few tellings, it no longer matters from where these anecdotes and tales originated. They take on a life of their own, permeating our experiences. (p. 57)

Stories serve numerous functions. They enable us to shape or structure the general chaos of personal experience; they convey truths too simple or too complex to be stated in logical sentences; they help us make sense and meaning of memories and experiences; they prompt us to wrestle with problems and create our own meanings; and they connect us with larger ideas and, perhaps most importantly, to each other. As Russian historian William Ralston has stated, "one touch of storytelling may, in some instances, make the whole world kin."

Creating Stories

Each of us carries within us an encyclopedia of moving, humorous, and profound stories. The trick is to remember them and then retell them in a way that others recognize as storytelling. This is much easier than it appears, and a few suggestions on how to create stories are included below.

To begin, a simple exercise might help speakers create stories that draw from the raw material of their personal experience. By developing a personal timeline that summarizes the events that take place in their lives, or a portion of their lives, moving from birth to the present, presenters can open up the rich reservoir of stories that lies buried in their memories.

Start by drawing a horizontal line across a page to represent the chronology of your life. Include on the timeline the critical incidents you have experienced, memorable people you have worked with, and so on. Your timeline should be a kind of graphic autobiography. Following this, identify the points on the timeline where interesting or illustrative events occurred. These points will become your stories.

Next, pick one event from your life that you think would make an excellent story. Once you have chosen a story to work on, write down the main elements of the story. You might want to brainstorm ideas by jotting them down on a piece of paper or developing a mind map; the important thing is to tell the whole story. In story writing workshops, I have used tape recorders to help participants get the goods from the initial story and then refined the raw materials into a story that will touch the hearts of any audience.

Once you have recorded the details, embellish the story. For example, describe the feelings you felt when you experienced the event that makes up the story. What feelings do you think an audience should feel? Similarly, what sensual details are important to the story? What are the sights, scents, sounds, touches, and tastes you experienced or that your story should invoke?

Finally, consider all the characters in the story. Does your story contain heroes or villains, and if so, who are they? Who are other important people in the story whom you might have overlooked? Once you have recorded all the events, details, and characters, develop a structure that audiences will easily recognize as a story.

Perhaps the single attribute that separates a story from other forms of communication is its structure. In essence, a story consists of events placed in a sequence to delineate a process of change, the transformation of one event into another. This sequence of events represents a kind of grammar, a structure that audiences recognize as a story. Frequently, that story grammar moves from order, to chaos, and back to order.

Whatever structure you choose for your story is up to you. Nonetheless, the following suggestions provide a generic structure: begin by describing the setting, then the problem, then the disruption, and finally the solution. List the events leading to the problem, list events leading to the solution. If there is a moral, explain it.

Integrating Stories Into Workshops

A research study I did interviewing 80 working college students about how they learned in college hammered home to me how important stories are. I spent over an hour with each student, asking all kinds of questions about their experiences in colleges and university. Those conversations eventually turned to everyone's ideas about great teachers, and again and again the people I interviewed emphasized that what separated the great teachers from the rest was stories.

Presenters who wish to incorporate stories into their learning experiences might wish to consider the following suggestions:

1. Develop your personal library of stories. When you keep your eyes and ears open, stories will pop up.

2. Integrate stories into your sessions at their most effective points.

3. Frame stories with introductory and summative comments.

4. Use stories that are truly illustrative of your topic.

5. Keep stories short.

6. Don't be the hero in your own stories.

7. Give participants clear guidelines if they are asked to share their stories.

Stories achieve a lot when they are used to educate. Most important, stories enable a partnership between speaker and listener that communicates in ways that differ from other forms of communication. A story, at its best, provides insight into tacit dimensions of whatever is being discussed. A story provides a context for understanding. To hear an effective story is to be reminded that we are alive, sharing the world with other people who know and have experienced events that are similar to those that make up our lives. Good stories, like all aspects of good presentations, remind us of our humanity—an important component of the partnership approach.

To Sum Up

For maximum impact, effective workshops . . .

- focus on the teaching practices identified in the one-page Target;
- provide coaching support for any teaching practice described during a workshop;
- are built around and embody the partnership principles of equality, choice, voice, reflection, dialogue, praxis, and reciprocity;
- provide numerous ways for teachers to apply learning to their work in and out of the classroom;

- are designed to deliver messages clearly and powerfully;
- involve slides and other aspects of design to ensure that messages are simply and beautifully delivered; and
- are led by facilitators who
  - o use many strategies to connect with their audiences;
  - o walk the talk by using the practices they are describing during their workshops;
  - o keep energy high;
  - o use dialogue architectures to maintain a structure that respects the individual choices of teachers; and
  - o tell stories.

Going Deeper

A few years ago, I had the pleasure of driving internationally recognized researcher, author, and presenter Tom Guskey to and from the airport when he came to present at a conference at the Center for Research on Learning at the University of Kansas. Guskey is a dynamic presenter, and at our conference, he gave a fantastic presentation that ended with an enthusiastic standing ovation. During the drive back to the airport, I asked him how he came to be such an outstanding presenter. His response was simple: "I've read every book I could ever read on how to give presentations."

Since that talk, I've read a large number of books on presenting. Whatever success I've had as a presenter and workshop leader, I credit to the authors of these books. In the following I've included some of the books in this area that I have found most helpful.

Design

Garr Reynolds and Nancy Duarte have started a revolution in the way people use PowerPoint, Keynote, and other slide share software. Reynold's *Presentation Zen: Simple Ideas on Presentation Design, and Delivery* (2008a) and *Presentation Zen Design: Simple Design Principles and Techniques to Enhance Your Presentations* (2008b) and Nancy Duarte's *slide:ology: The Art and Science of Great Presentations* (2008) are practical books that illustrate by their design as much as by their words why design thinking is an important part of creating a workshop or presentation. Reynolds makes the case for better design in the use of PowerPoint, and Duarte, who collaborated with Al Gore to develop the slides for his presentation An Inconvenient Truth, provides multiple design suggestions that can help anyone improve the look of their slides.

Reynolds' blog is at www.presentationzen.com; you can also follow him on Twitter: @PresentationZen. Duarte's design company website is at www.duarte.com. Her blog is http://blog.duarte.com; you can also follow her on Twitter: @nancyduarte.

Delivery

Bert Decker is internationally recognized as an expert in presenting, and in *You've Got to Be Believed to Be Heard* (2008), he provides outstanding advice on topics such as maintaining energy and eye contact, being persuasive, and making an emotional connection. He also has a great approach to planning a presentation, and some unique ideas related to the power of video to serve as a reflection tool for presenters.

Carmine Gallo has written two books that I've learned a lot from. *The Presentation Secrets of Steve Jobs* (2009) holds a magnifying glass up to Steve Jobs and describes how he meticulously prepares for presentations, the Zen-like simplicity of Jobs' slides, his posture, verbal delivery, use of video, props, and guest speakers, and his "twitter-ready" simple and precise language.

In *10 Simple Secrets of the World's Greatest Business Communicators* (2006), Gallo proposes, a bit tongue in cheek, the following 11 secrets:

1. Be passionate, use your head to reach their heart.

2. Inspire your audience by getting them to care about your message.

3. Prepare, then toss the script.

4. Start strong but don't bury the lead.

5. Clarity, lose the jargon or lose your audience.

6. Brevity, keep it short.

7. Say it with style.

8. Command presence through body language.

9. Wear it well, the way you dress speaks volumes.

10. Reinvent yourself, continually improving your speaking skills.

11. Believe you belong; the success of your presentation will be direct result of the vision you hold of yourself as a speaker.

Decker's blog is at http://decker.com/blog; you can also follow him on Twitter: @BertDecker. Carmine Gallo's blog is at http://carminegallo.com; you can also follow him on Twitter: @carminegallo.

Stories

There are many great books on the age-old art of storytelling, but Stephen Denning's *The Leader's Guide to Storytelling* (2005) has been most helpful to me. Denning makes a powerful argument for the importance of stories: storytelling "is an equal partner with abstractions and analysis as a key leadership discipline" (p. xv). He also offers great suggestions for how to craft and tell the right story for a given situation. For example, a story designed to encourage change is most effective when told using a minimalist style, so that "it leaves plenty of room for the audience to imagine a new story in their context" (p. 62).

Among the other great books on stories, I've found Annette Simmons' *The Story Factor* (2006) and Nancy Mellon's *The Art of Storytelling* (2006) to be especially helpful. Chip and Dan Heath's *Made to Stick: Why Some Ideas Survive and Others Die* (2007) and Daniel Pink's *A Whole New Mind* (2005) provide great insights into why stories are important and how to craft and deliver them. Interestingly, Pink identifies story as one of the essential six senses necessary for a right-brained approach to life, necessary for success in a future he refers to as the *conceptual age.*

Daniel Pink's blog is at www.danpink.com; you can also follow him on Twitter: @DanielPink. The Heath brothers' blog is at http://heathbrothers.com; they also write an excellent online column for www.fastcompany.com.

The following are online resources I have found both useful and inspirational.

- *Storycorps.net*—www.storycorp.net provides a venue for people to interview loved ones and then post their stories on the site. The hundreds, perhaps thousands, of stories on this site are profound, humorous, heartbreaking, and inspirational. I've learned a lot about stories by listening to stories on this site.
- *Slideshare.net*—www.slideshare.net is like YouTube for slides. You can find thousands of ideas for presentations here just by reviewing others' slides. You can also search for people like

Garr Reynolds, Daniel Pink, and Seth Godin and see examples of their slides. Some of our own presentations are posted on this site.

- *TED*—one of the best ways to improve as a presenter is to watch many of the world's best presenters on the www.ted.com website. TED, which stands for technology, entertainment, and design, is an annual conference attracting hundreds of the world's most creative and articulate people. Their presentations, usually no more than 20 minutes each, make for riveting watching, and, for me at least, TED might be the best site on the web.

6

Intensive Learning Teams

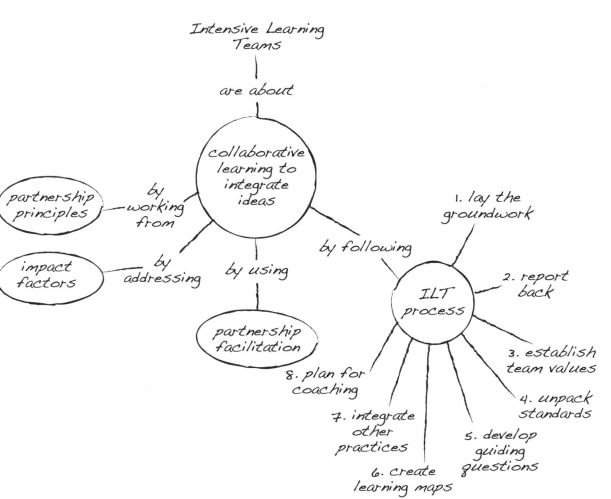

Intensive Learning Teams

|
are about

collaborative learning to integrate ideas

partnership principles — by working from

impact factors — by addressing

by using — partnership facilitation

by following — ILT process

1. lay the groundwork
2. report back
3. establish team values
4. unpack standards
5. develop guiding questions
6. create learning maps
7. integrate other practices
8. plan for coaching

In the past two decades, much has been written about the power and potential of teams and collaborative learning. In his seminal work *The Fifth Discipline* (1990), Peter Senge celebrated the concept of learning organizations where "people continually expand their capacity to create the results they truly desire, where new and expansive patterns of thinking are nurtured, where collective aspiration is set free, and where people are continually learning how to learn together" (p. 3). Since *The Fifth Discipline*, other powerful approaches for group conversation have emerged (for example, Harrison Owen, 2008, and Juanita Brown & David Isaacs, 2005).

James Surowiecki has especially made the case for the power of group learning. His *Wisdom of Crowds* (2004) elaborates on his central thesis that "on average [a group] will consistently come up with a better answer than any individual could provide" (p. 235). Surowiecki's book is filled with case studies that show that collective intelligence is usually superior to individual intelligence. He writes,

> Ask a hundred people to answer a question or solve a problem, and the average answer will often be at least as good as the answer of the smartest member. With most things, the average is mediocrity. With decision making, it's often excellence. You could say it's as if we've been programmed to be collectively smart. (p. 11)

In education, collective intelligence is celebrated through several approaches to collaborative learning already being implemented successfully in schools, including data teams, professional learning communities, and positive behavior supports.

Data teams (Love, 2009) are structured so that teachers can analyze student achievement and behavior data by (a) identifying a student learning problem, (b) verifying causes of the problem, (c) generating solutions, and (d) implementing the solutions and monitoring results. Professional learning communities (DuFour, DuFour, Eaker, & Karhanek, 2010; Dufour & Eaker, 1998; Hord & Sommers, 2008) are results-oriented collaborative teams of teachers who concentrate on improving teaching and learning. Finally, positive behavior supports (Sprick, Garrison, & Howard, 2002; Sugai et al., 1999) involve educators who collaborate to gather and analyze behavioral data and identify and evaluate interventions designed to create more positive and effective learning climates in schools.

Excellent descriptions already exist for these forms of collaborative inquiry, and more information is included in the Going Deeper section at the end of this chapter, so I will not be describing them here. This chapter, instead, lays out the practical step-by-step procedures of intensive learning teams (ILTs), another form of collaborative professional learning that I first implemented with Dr. Ethel Edwards of the Topeka School District around 2005 along with a broader discussion of the partnership approach to collaborative learning.

ILTs bring together groups of teachers from across a district for short, intensive collaborative meetings to refine or reinvent the course or grade that they share responsibility for teaching. For example, an ILT might bring together all mathematics teachers teaching Grade 6 for five full days across an academic year to rewrite sixth-grade mathematics curriculum. While ILTs usually bring teachers together to write a new curriculum, they may also provide an opportunity for teachers to create formative or summative assessments, explore and integrate new teaching practices, develop behavioral expectations, identify other high-leverage ways of improving what or how they teach, or consider how to implement other curriculum, teaching, or resource materials or practices.

ILTs consist of several components. First, the facilitator (often an instructional coach) meets one to one with every participant prior to the first meeting to (a) ensure that everyone understands what the goals and procedures of an ILT are, (b) gather data about teachers' assessment of students' strengths and needs, and (c) invite teachers to participate in an upcoming ILT. Next, at the beginning of the first session, the ILT facilitator reports back on what she heard during the interviews. Then, team members, working in small groups facilitated by instructional coaches (ICs), discuss and articulate the values they choose for the team.

Once the foundations for the ILT have been established, the group turns to the work of curriculum development. This usually involves unpacking the state standards, developing guiding questions, and creating learning maps. ILTs then explore and plan other teaching practices that can be integrated into the new curriculum. At the conclusion of each session, time is set aside for teachers and instructional coaches to discuss how ICs can best support implementation of the new practices in classrooms. The nuts and bolts of this process are described in greater detail later in this chapter.

The Challenge

Most of us would agree that Surowiecki's (2004) concept of collective intelligence makes sense. Unfortunately, most of our own experiences suggest that meetings and group work can be unpleasant time wasters—too often boring, dehumanizing, and unproductive. As Patrick Lencioni (2002) says, "the fact remains that teams, because they are made up of imperfect human beings, are inherently dysfunctional" (p. vii).

To create the setting for successful team learning, leaders must consider specific factors when designing the structure for team interactions and keep an eye on those factors during the minute-by-minute motions of the team. This chapter addresses some of those factors, describing how teams can (a) be grounded in the partnership principles; (b) address the other impact factors of workshops, principal observations, and coaching focused on the Target; (c) be led through use of partnership facilitation skills; and (d) be structured as intensive learning teams.

Partnership Principles

Equality

Teams founded on the partnership principles are structured so that each member has a chance to shape and refine whatever the team creates. As an equal member on a team, my voice counts as much as anyone's, and no one else's voice should silence mine or anyone else's.

Team facilitators acting on the principle of equality see themselves as equals facilitating, not supervisors pushing a process. They recognize that their role is to establish processes that enable the teams to be productive and not to lead a team to a predetermined outcome. They have faith that the team can come up with good outcomes without constant direction from them, and they focus their efforts on creating an optimal setting for group learning.

Choice

As emphasized throughout this book, choice is essential within partnerships. Telling professionals exactly what to do and giving them little choice is a sure-fire way to decrease motivation and increase resistance. Teachers, like all knowledge workers, want to be a part of the thinking behind the work they do (Davenport, 2005), and they want to have some say in the goals they pursue (Pink, 2009). Therefore, providing teachers with choices is essential for any team or learning community to be productive and effective.

But choice without structure is not the answer. Too much choice can be counterproductive (Schwartz, 2004). A balance of structure and choice (freedom within form) is an essential attribute of any community of learners. To be productive and to respect the voices of teachers, teams must employ structures that move the collaborative work ahead efficiently while also honoring the choices of teachers. Several of these structures are described in the partnership facilitation section later in this chapter.

Voice

A learning community won't feel authentic and meaningful for people unless their ideas are heard and they have real input into the process and outcomes. The way teams are facilitated and led, in large measure, determines whether or not teachers feel they have a voice.

First, facilitators, like all instructional leaders, must be fully present during conversations. They must listen carefully to each participant, paraphrase what they have heard, and build bridges, where possible, between different perspectives. At times, this may mean intervening to ensure tensions between participants don't get out of hand and interfere with group learning. Additionally, they may have to mix up activities to ensure energy levels stay high. Often the most important thing a facilitator can do is silence her own voice so that everyone else can speak. Partnership facilitators must make it their constant goal to acknowledge, even celebrate, the voices of all participants.

The way group collaboration is structured is also important for creating a setting where everyone is heard and productive. The dialogue structures described later in this chapter are essential for keeping things moving and for authentically involving everyone in creating and deciding what to do. The critical word here is *authentic*. If teachers are to have a say, it must be real. When teams make decisions only to have them overturned later by someone higher up in the system, their commitment to the initiative and their overall openness to change will be damaged.

Reflection

More than anything else, a team or learning community is a setting where people can think together. Unfortunately, under intense pressure to deliver improved achievement scores, teachers find it hard to pause and think when they feel as if everyone is watching what they are doing. Jennifer York-Barr, William Sommers, Gail

Ghere, and Joanne Montie describe this challenge in *Reflective Practices to Improve Schools* (2005):

> The demand for accountability and the steady flow of curricular and instructional initiatives add to the pressured context of teaching . . . To change our practices, to change our beliefs, and to alter our own theories of change, we must slow down and have reflective conversations that allow us to think through possible changes . . . Shifting from a culture of doing to a culture of learning and doing, however, is not easily accomplished. (p. 3)

Teams such as ILTs are one way to foster the shift to a "culture of learning and doing" by providing ample opportunities for educators to think with others about how they will teach. Thus, partnership facilitators recognize that their primary duty is to create activities that allow for participants to explore and reflect with others as they create tools or products that can be used in the classroom.

Dialogue

One of the challenges of creating an effective team is to structure conversations so participants move away from interactions that are confrontational and polarizing to conversations that are dialogical and unifying. Confrontational conversations are those where one person offers an opinion, whereupon others talk about why they agree or disagree. These kinds of conversations are often competitive—where people win if their opinion is accepted and lose if their opinion is rejected. This means that interactions tend to be driven by those who are loudest and most persuasive, rather than by what is right or best in a given situation.

Confrontational conversations do not foster learning. First, rather than tapping into the wisdom of everyone in a group by exploring all options, confrontational conversations tend to be explorations of one or two people's ideas—we consider whether or not we agree with Tom or Tammy, and then we make our arguments. Second, confrontational conversations have negative emotional side effects. If conversation is about winning and losing, and you lose, you may feel bad about that. Finally, confrontational conversations often silence participants who don't want to enter into the battle. Thus, good ideas are lost, and good people end up being alienated by the process.

Dialogical conversations move away from confrontation to mutual pursuit of the truth. The goal is for everyone to think together, not for everyone to accept or reject one person's ideas. Thus, during dialogue, the group's goal is to get to a point where they lose sight of who said or proposed what, and everyone collaborates to explore together whatever is being explored. William Isaacs in *Dialogue and the Art of Thinking Together* (1999) puts it this way:

> Dialogue is about a shared inquiry, a way of thinking and reflecting together. It is not something you do to another person. It is something you do with people. Indeed, a large part of learning this has to do with learning to shift your attitudes about relationships with others, so that we gradually give up the effort to make them understand us, and come to a greater understanding of ourselves and each other. (p. 9)

To create a learning community where dialogue thrives, facilitators must employ partnership facilitation skills, described later in this chapter, and partnership communication skills, described in Chapter 7. Creating a setting where dialogue is the mode of discourse is not easy, but every step closer to dialogue is a step closer to the kind of mutually humanizing conversation that should be a central goal of any community of learners.

Praxis

In large measure, a team or learning community lives or dies based on whether or not praxis is honored. When sessions are designed with praxis in mind, real-life application is always a part of the conversation. People are not talking about ideas that they might use some day. With praxis, there is no gap between knowing and doing because people are learning and making plans to use ideas right away in the classroom.

For this kind of conversation to occur, learning must be personally relevant. If teachers are provided with opportunities to explore their content, for example, by developing unit plans they can implement in their classes right away, the group's facilitator may simply need to get out of the group's way so that they can do the work. However, if the teachers don't see the relevance of the work they are doing, they may feel that the sessions are a waste of time and find it hard to be engaged. Relevance leads to engagement; irrelevance wastes time.

Reciprocity

Margaret Wheatley, author of *Turning to One Another* (2002) is our generation's apologist for the power of conversation. She reminds us that sharing ideas and stories is not simply a utilitarian process we go through to achieve a goal; conversation is something fundamental to our humanity. We are more human when we share ideas, listen, laugh, and work with others on what matters to us. Wheatley writes,

> Human conversation is the most ancient and easiest way to cultivate the conditions for change–personal change, community and organizational change, planetary change. If we can sit together and talk about what's important to us, we begin to come alive. We share what we see, what we feel, and we listen to what other see and feel. (p. 3)

Reciprocity leads to the kind of mutually humanizing conversation Wheatley (2002) describes. When give-and-take, sharing, and learning are all wrapped up in one experience, we feel energized, valued, connected, and alive. Unfortunately, positive, meaningful conversation is not always common in an organization, including schools. That makes ILTs all the more important because they provide a setting where reciprocal dialogue can become the norm. Indeed, when effectively facilitated and structured, ILTs can be springboards for re-culturing schools. However, if ILTs are to have real impact on instruction and student achievement, the three additional impact factors (principals, workshops, and coaching) must be integrated with the professional learning occurring within teams, as discussed in the following.

Address Impact Factors

Principals

As with other forms of professional learning, principals must understand and support the work that teams are doing. Most important, this means that the principal must lead change so that what occurs in teams, like ILTs, is designed to address the Target.

The Target provides clarity and focus to everyone's efforts in schools. Without that clarity, time is wasted, energy is depleted, and entropy rules the day. But with focus, significant change can occur. Patrick Lencioni, in his highly practical business fable *The Four Obsessions of an Extraordinary Executive* (2000) describes the importance of focus as follows:

> An organization that has achieved clarity has a sense of unity around everything it does. It aligns its resources, especially

the human ones, around common concepts, values, definitions, goals, and strategies, thereby realizing the synergies that all great companies must achieve.

Principals, therefore, must be in constant communication with central office staff so they fully understand district initiatives and ensure that they are built into the Target. Additionally, central office staff must understand each school's Target and ensure that they do not place additional, unreasonable demands on schools. Most often, this can be easily worked out. Most districtwide teams like ILTs are primarily concerned with creating a curriculum that is aligned with state and national standards, and since this is a high-leverage way to improve test scores, most schools address standards in their Target. When there is a gap between the needs identified by a school and district goals, both central office staff and principals must negotiate a solution that honors each school's needs while also reflecting the district's broader goals.

Principals also must support the professional learning that occurs in teams by monitoring teachers' progress toward implementing practices. This means that they observe teachers to see how well implementation of practices, such as learning maps and guiding questions, is progressing and check with teachers to see how effective the practices are for helping students succeed. Principals play a critical role not only in monitoring progress but also in listening to teachers to see whether or not the Target needs to be modified.

Instructional Coaches

ICs, too, are essential for the success of any team in a school. As part of any team meeting, participants should plan with a coach how to implement whatever practice is being adopted. This accomplishes several things. First, it makes it easier for teachers to implement what is being discussed and learned because the IC will help them organize materials, remember how to implement the practices, and generally make it easier for them to implement.

Second, planning for implementation, right away, changes the nature of conversations during team meetings. Everyone realizes that what he or she is discussing is going to be implemented. Indeed, conversation that is focused on implementation should be a signature characteristic of any Impact School.

Third, coaches can gather data on the effectiveness of the practices developed during the collaborative learning. Following ILTS, for example, we suggest ICs immediately meet with teachers to hear what they think about what has been created. Coaches provide the support that makes it easy for teachers to implement practices, but they also gather data that enables revisions to be made if necessary.

Finally, coaches can play a major role in running teams. For example, they can facilitate discussion and planning, or facilitate small-group discussions. In short, ICs play a major role in all aspects of collaborative learning.

Workshops

Workshops support professional learning in at least three ways. First, through workshops teachers can learn about practices that they will employ for planning during teams such as ILTs. Teachers might learn about developing guiding questions during a workshop and then apply that knowledge during ILTs.

Second, workshops can deepen teachers' knowledge of practices after professional learning, such as ILTs. For example, teachers who have been developing checks for understanding to use in their classrooms might attend a workshop to deepen their knowledge about developing rubrics. Of course, planning for coaching would be a part of the workshop to make it easier for teachers to implement what they are learning.

Finally, workshops can reinforce what is learned or developed during a workshop. From time to time, it can help any learner to revisit what she has learned and rethink how she is implementing a given practice. Workshops can provide this kind of reinforcement for professional learning.

Partnership Facilitation

Leading collaborative learning is exciting but can sometimes be daunting. On one hand, like a referee at a sporting event, when facilitators do their job well, no one even notices that they are there. On the other hand, creating learning opportunities that appear to run on their own takes a lot of planning and skill. Much must be done to ensure that a learning community is productive and moves ahead effortlessly.

Productivity guru David Allen, in *Getting Things Done* (2001), employs a metaphor for the state of "perfect readiness" when he writes about how people should manage themselves. I think his metaphor is an apt one for partnership facilitation. "Perfect readiness," Allen says, involves a "mind like water":

> Imagine throwing a pebble into a still pond. How does the water respond? The answer is totally appropriately to the force and mass of the input; then it returns to calm. It doesn't overreact or under react." (pp. 10–11)

Partnership facilitators must have minds like water. They must be ready to process whatever comes their way, be quick to intervene as much or as little as is necessary to keep the ball rolling, and retreat from intervening as soon as possible. In the best scenarios, teachers should be so consumed by the activities they are in engaged in within a team that they barely notice the facilitator's input.

A large part of partnership facilitation involves skillful application of the partnership communication strategies described in Chapter 7. In addition to partnership communication, there is much a facilitator can do to design and support a positive, productive learning community, including the following.

Reducing Friction

A primary goal of partnership facilitation is to design learning experiences that run smoothly, or, to put it another way, partnership facilitators must reduce friction during collaborative learning. "Friction," the authors of fearofphysics.com (n.d) tell us,

> is the "evil" of all motion. No matter which direction something moves in, friction pulls it the other way. Move something left, friction pulls right. Move something up, friction pulls down. It appears as if nature has given us friction to stop us from moving anything. (para. 1)

Friction isn't all bad. As the authors point out, without friction, "we wouldn't be able to walk, sit in a chair, climb stairs, or use a mouse to surf the web. Everything would just keep slipping and falling all over the place" (fearofphysics.com, n.d., para. 4). But in collaborative learning such as ILTs or data teams, friction, which I will loosely describe as resistance to motion, can make or break team learning experiences. To paraphrase, friction can be the evil of group learning. Therefore, an important but often overlooked goal for partnership facilitators is to do everything possible to remove anything that slows down the team learning process.

Champion rower Craig Lambert, in his book *Mind Over Water* (1998), describes what a frictionless team, in his case a rowing team, feels like:

> Suddenly the boat gets quiet; we hear only eight oars grabbing the water together, finishing as one. Some energy flow grips us like a river current, synchronizing our motions; we row as one body . . . The boat is perfectly level. Set up beautifully, we skim the surface on an invisible laser beam running from horizon to horizon. There is no friction; we ride the natural cadence of our strokes, a continuous cycle. The crew breathes as one. (pp. 124–125)

The kind of frictionless teamwork Lambert (1998) has experienced on a rowing team is less common on learning teams in schools. Fortunately, however, there are many strategies facilitators can use to reduce friction. The most important are listed below.

Thorough Planning

Facilitators can significantly decrease friction by ensuring that every activity is clearly explained and every task easy to do when adults come together to collaborate. If people are unclear about how they are to act or the outcome they are aiming for, they easily lose focus or become anxious. Simple directions, and simple activities, go a long way toward reducing this type of friction. Indeed, when facilitators carefully think through all activities, participants will not need to waste their brainpower trying to understand what they are doing and can focus their energy on the learning task itself.

To ensure that their instructions, activities, and the overall flow of the team's work are clear and simple, facilitators should take time to plan *everything* that will happen during a session. Facilitators should also take the time to debug activities so that they can be ready if something doesn't work out exactly as planned.

The purpose of the plan is not to create a sequence that must be slavishly followed minute by minute. Indeed, my experience has been that once the team starts working, the plan is often set aside to accommodate real creativity and learning. Respecting teacher choice means facilitators must be willing to change direction when that is the desire of the team. However, creating a detailed plan forces facilitators to understand deeply what every activity involves before the activity is employed, and that understanding will help facilitators create clear explanations and increase their own comfort level with the process. I like to create plans that include all directions, laid out in five-minute increments. (An example ILT plan is included in the Impact Toolkit in Resource A.)

Coaches Facilitating Small Groups

Frequently, learning teams include large numbers of participants. For example, if a large district brings together all of the eighth-grade mathematics teachers and all of the eighth-grade special education mathematics teachers into one team, there could be more than 30 team members. In such instances, smaller working groups will be necessary, such as groups containing four to seven teachers.

Coaches can reduce friction in the smaller groups by serving as small-group facilitators, ensuring that every activity moves forward smoothly. As such, the IC absorbs any anxiety so participants don't have to worry about how to do whatever they do.

To ensure that coaches can artfully lead small groups, the team facilitator must prepare them in advance, explaining all activities and checking that each coach fully understands everything. The facilitator should emphasize to ICs that they are to shape a positive learning culture within their small groups, and thus must communicate confidence in the procedure and demonstrate a positive attitude throughout the process. Every interaction is an opportunity for ICs to foster the development and growth of a learner-friendly culture, described below.

Attending to Creature Comforts. Attention to a few simple things can go a long way toward reducing friction. When budgets allow, team facilitators should make available simple snacks and stimulants like coffee, pastries, fresh fruit, water, and, perhaps most important, chocolate. In my experience, participants see such attention to their comfort as an unnecessary but very welcome sign of respect.

Additionally, facilitators should try to hold their sessions in a learner-friendly setting where there is natural light, incandescent lighting, ample space, and the ability to adjust the temperature. For ILTs, I prefer rooms that are too large to rooms that are too small. Issues such as heat, space, and light are small concerns, but they add up, and if facilitators are careless about them, they can significantly increase the friction during team learning.

Parker Palmer, in *A Hidden Wholeness* (2004), summarizes some of the small touches that can yield significant results when setting up a room:

Let the room be neither cramped nor cavernous . . . Let there be eye-level windows to provide visual relief and allow the outside world to come in. Let the decor be warm and inviting, with simple grace notes such as fresh flowers. Let there be carpet on the floor so the sound does not bounce around, and acoustics that permit soft voices to be heard by all. Let the lighting be incandescent and warm, not fluorescent and cold. (p. 85)

By taking the time to address creature comforts, facilitators communicate that they genuinely care about their team members' comfort.

Clearly Organized Handouts. If team members find themselves lost in a mountain of poorly organized handouts, there is a good chance they will become frustrated, stop being engaged, or both. To decrease this type of friction, team facilitators must make sure that handouts (if they are used) are clearly labeled and easy to find. This might be accomplished by putting all handouts together in a binder or notebook, ordered in the sequence in which they will be needed during the session. Another method is to color code handouts so that team members can quickly find them and get down to business.

High-Quality Materials. School districts have a duty to be frugal with the public's funds, so facilitators often feel they must cut corners. Whenever possible, however, facilitators should use materials that work well and are appropriate for a given situation. This means that new materials sometimes have to be purchased. New markers that work well, sticky chart paper, new pencils, and fresh notepads all create a positive setting. Simple frustrations, like markers that don't work, probably won't make or break a session, but when you have the chance to reduce friction, do so.

I had the pleasure of attending a one-day workshop at Nancy Duarte's design studio in Mountain View, California. At our tables at the workshop, someone had neatly placed inexpensive silver-colored pails with new markers and pencils, and white baskets filled with elegantly printed and designed handouts. There were also a whiteboard and beautiful notepaper on every table. These little touches made a big difference, and they made me just a little bit more excited about the session since such cool stuff was laid out for us to use.

Doing the Dirty Work. When people come together to work, there will be many menial tasks (typing up notes, reviewing data, designing and printing out graphic organizers, creating slides, moving chairs and tables, cleaning up after meeting, and so on). Facilitators can reduce friction simply by doing a lot of this work. As Patrick Lencioni (2010) wrote, "There is something so powerful about a person who in one moment can be confident enough to confront a client about a sensitive personal issue, and then in the next moment humble themselves and take a position of servitude" (p. 174).

When facilitators are careful to remove friction every chance they get, they may find that their efforts go unnoticed. Little touches, like candy or nicely arranged group workspaces, might be mentioned, but I do not believe I've ever read an evaluation that said, "Room temperature was perfect." Don't be deterred by this, however, because removing friction isn't actually something that should be noticed. When ILTs are well planned and progress without a hitch, the smoothly progressing learning activities are clear evidence of a job well done.

Often, the reason why learning teams progress smoothly is because facilitators recognize the importance of (a) participants having freedom to choose what and how they will learn and (b) activities being carefully structured to ensure the collaborative work is productive. Partnership facilitators accomplish this by attending to a key theme of this book, freedom within form.

Freedom Within Form. Throughout this book, we have explored the implications of the idea that freedom occurs best with a form. Thus, principals ensure that teachers have an authentic voice and real choice with respect to the creation of the Target, but they also monitor progress and intervene when progress is not being made. Similarly, ICs provide precise and clear explanations, often guided by checklists, but they ask teachers for input on how to modify those practices, so they are tailor made for each student and teacher. As for workshop facilitators, they share information about effective practices, but they do so using teaching techniques such as thinking prompts that empower teachers to do the thinking during sessions.

In the same way, partnership facilitators also utilize freedom within form. Keith Sawyer's study of the creative power of collaboration, *Group Genius* (2007), highlights this seeming paradox at the heart of creative teams:

> The key to improvised innovation is managing a paradox: establishing a goal that provides a focus for the team—just enough of one so that team members can tell when they move

closer to a solution—but one that's open-ended enough for problem-finding creativity to emerge. (p. 45)

Sawyer builds on Mihaly Csikszentmihalyi's (1994) research on optimal experience, the way people experience life when they are at their best, what Csikszentmihalyi refers to as "flow" experiences. Sawyer (2007) concludes that the most effective teams have "group flow," which he describes as "a peak experience, a group performing at its top level of ability" (p. 43). Sawyer describes many examples of group flow in groups of musicians, basketball players, comedy writers, and designers. When discussing group flow, Sawyer quotes basketball great Bill Russell talking about his peak experiences playing with the Boston Celtics:

Every so often a Celtic game would heat up so that it became more than a physical or even a mental game, and would be magical. That feeling is difficult to describe, and I certainly never talked about it when playing. When it happened, I could feel my play rise to a new level . . . The game would just take off, and there'd be a natural ebb and flow that reminded you of how rhythmical and musical basketball is supposed to be . . . It was almost as if we were playing in slow motion. (pp. 41–42)

Group flow is not limited to musicians, athletes, and writers, however. Sawyer (2007) suggests 10 conditions for group flow, which I have summarized below.

1. *A Goal.* "One study of more than 500 professionals and managers . . . found that unclear objectives became the biggest barrier to effective team performance" (p. 44).

2. *Close Listening.* "Innovation is blocked when one (or more) of the participants already has a preconceived idea of how to reach the goal" (pp. 46–47).

3. *Complete Concentration.* "Flow is more likely to occur when attention is centered on a task . . . the challenges that inspire flow are those that are intrinsic to the task itself" (p. 48).

4. *Being in Control.* "People get into flow when they're in control of their actions and their environment" (p. 49).

5. *Blending Egos.* "In group flow, each person's idea builds on those just contributed by his or her colleagues. The improvisation

appears to be guided by an invisible hand . . . small ideas build and an innovation emerges" (p. 50).

6. *Equal Participation.* "Group flow is more likely to occur when all participants play an equal role in the collective creation of the final performance" (p. 50).

7. *Familiarity.* "When members of a group have been together for a while, they share a common language and a common set of unspoken understandings" (p. 51).

8. *Communication.* "The kind of communication that leads to group flow often doesn't happen in the conference room. Instead it's more likely to happen in freewheeling, spontaneous conversations in the hallway, or social settings after work or at lunch" (p. 53).

9. *Moving It Forward.* "Group flow flourishes when people follow the first rule of improvisational acting: 'Yes, and . . . ' Listen closely to what's being said; accept it fully; and then extend and build on it" (p. 54).

10. *The Potential for Failure.* "Most businesses are designed to minimize risk, and most punish failure. But research shows us over and over again that the twin sibling of innovation is frequent failure. There's no creativity without failure, and there's no group flow without the risk of failure" (p. 55).

Partnership facilitators can reconcile the paradox of freedom and form and at the same time move closer to group flow by employing dialogue structures for collaborative learning. Dialogue structures are activities that are propelled by the free choices of participants but organized such that outcomes are reached effectively. Four dialogue structures are described here, and several more are described in the Impact Toolkit in Resource A.

Modified Open Space. Harrison Owen's *Open Space Technology* (2008) describes a group conversation process that is driven entirely by the interests and choices of participants. During Open Space, participants list topics they would like to discuss, and then they organize themselves by joining with others who are interested in the identified topics. Whoever proposes a topic that is discussed serves as a host for the conversation and generally keeps the conversation moving. Also, if people don't feel they are contributing to or learning from a group, they move to another group. Owen calls this the law of two feet, suggesting that if a conversation isn't working, you use your two feet to find another one.

I have used many Open Space techniques during less "open" collaborative learning opportunities. For example, I often ask participants to choose the topics they would like to host, or to choose a suggested topic they would like to address. This is a simple way to organize participants into groups that are most relevant to them. I also ask those who propose a topic to be hosts of conversations, and then ask them to make sure someone is willing to report out at the end of the conversation. Finally, I also subscribe to the Law of Two Feet. If people realize they are in the wrong group, I suggest they move to one where they can learn or contribute more significantly.

Structured Choices. Inevitably, teachers in ILTs arrive at points where it becomes necessary to make decisions before the group can move on. For example, during an ILT session I was facilitating with sixth-grade mathematics teachers in Cecil County, Maryland, it became

Photo by Jennifer Ryschon-Knight.

obvious that we would not be able to map the units we were discussing until the group decided whether to organize the curriculum into 9 or 10 units.

As our time together progressed, and each person offered his or her perspective on the issue, I sensed that the group was getting restless, and we were on the verge of wasting a lot of time without a decision. I also knew that no one could make a single decision that would satisfy everyone. This had to be a group decision.

I suggested a structured choice, which I hoped would provide an opportunity for everyone to have a say. I put three pieces of chart paper on the wall and wrote 9 Units across the top of one piece of chart paper, 10 Units across the top of the second chart paper, and 10 Units With Modifications across the top of the third. I invited everyone to write their thoughts on sticky notes and affix them to the chart paper that represented their view.

During breaks, during lunch, or whenever participants felt like taking a break, they were to review what others had written and consider either changing their vote, changing what they'd written, or leaving things as they were. At the end of the day, almost all of the sticky notes were on the 9 Units chart paper. When I asked the group if they were satisfied with the decision, they were happy to accept it. They accepted the decision because it was one that they made freely. Without the simple structure for their choices, however, they might never have arrived at the agreed-upon decision.

Affinity Diagrams. First developed by Japanese anthropologist Jiro Kawakita, affinity diagrams are frequently used in collaborative group activities. First, all participants pick a topic to be discussed and write down their ideas on sticky notes. Second, they affix all their sticky notes to the wall. Then, usually without talking, they sort the stickies into groups that are related. Affinity diagrams allow a large amount of information to be generated and organized very quickly.

Dynamic Planning. A simple process that I developed with colleagues from Canada Post, dynamic planning provides a way for groups to develop implementation plans. It involves six steps.

1. Everyone in a group lists on index cards all of the tasks that must be completed in order for the group to reach a goal. This

Photo by Jennifer Ryschon-Knight.

usually happens with everyone standing around a table, writing cards, and laying them on a table.

2. The group organizes the tasks listed on the cards into the sequence that makes most sense.

3. They estimate how much time each task will take.

4. They write on the card when each event will be completed.

5. They decide who is responsible for completing each task and record those names on a card.

6. Finally, they create a spreadsheet that lists all the tasks, when they will be started and completed, and who is responsible for completing the task, and everyone gets a copy of the spreadsheet.

There are many other dialogue structures included in the Impact Toolkit in Resource A. While each of them may be used in any collaborative learning situation, they have proven to be especially useful during ILTs.

Intensive Learning Teams

Almost every school district allots times for some teachers to work together to create curriculum guides. Usually this involves small groups of teachers working together to create a curriculum that teachers across the district will be expected to implement. For teachers on the curriculum team, these are great learning opportunities as they share and learn with others and work their way through the state standards to develop the curriculum. Teachers on these committees leave the sessions with deeper knowledge of the material, and they often feel fired up about teaching a class that they now have a deeper knowledge of.

Unfortunately, the enthusiasm and knowledge of the curriculum development team does not always flow down to the rest of the teachers. For many, a curriculum that they did not create is just another "thing" the district is making them do. Furthermore, if they were not on the curriculum team, teachers miss out on the learning that occurred when the guide was developed. Not surprisingly, curriculum that is created for teachers, not with teachers, is often implemented poorly—if at all.

ILTs involve everyone who will be expected to teach a curriculum. By bringing together all relevant teachers, ILTs ensure that everyone has a voice in the curriculum and that an entire grade-level of teachers shares their knowledge with each. One important kind of professional learning is that which increases teachers' knowledge of the content they teach. ILTs are a quick and powerful way to accomplish this.

Intensive Learning Teams

1. Lay the groundwork: preliminary one-to-one conversations
2. Report back
3. Establish team values
4. Unpack standards
5. Develop guiding questions
6. Create learning maps
7. Integrate other practices
8. Plan for coaching support

Laying the Groundwork: Preliminary One-to-One Conversations

ILT facilitators must ensure that the first words teachers hear about ILTs prepare them to successfully experience the team. First impressions profoundly affect how teachers perceive and experience an ILT. I have found that brief, one-to-one conversations between facilitators and potential team members are an effective way to introduce ILTs. In cases when facilitators are unable to meet all teachers, ICs can conduct these conversations.

The one-to-one conversations prior to an ILT are like the one-to-one conversations prior to workshops or coaching. They usually begin with the facilitator explaining the ILT process and asking the potential team member if he or she has any questions about the goals and processes of the team. The coach or facilitator should explain to teachers that the ILT is meant to be a useful, positive conversation about a course they teach and a chance to learn and share with other teachers.

The facilitator may need to emphasize that the ILT provides an opportunity for genuine, useful conversation that is driven by teachers' choices, ideas, and concerns. Thus, during the conversation, facilitators must put the teacher at the heart of the conversation by being outstanding listeners, using the strategies described in Chapter 7, and asking questions so the teacher does the majority of the talking. In this way, the facilitator's actions communicate that the ILT is about the teacher and not about the facilitator. Facilitators should begin by asking, "What questions do you have about ILTs?" Guidelines for conducting these conversations are summarized below.

Guidelines for ILT Introductory Conversations

1. Explain why you're meeting.
   - To explain the ILT process
   - To answer any questions teachers might have
   - To gather information about (a) what kind of learning community would work best for everyone, (b) teachers' most pressing concerns right now, (c) and students' strengths and needs
   - To see if the teachers want to participate in the project
2. Ask, "What questions do you have about ILTs?"
3. Ask questions.

- Questions to get input about what team interactions should be like include
  - Do you have any questions about the ILT process?
  - For this learning project to be a good use of your time, what would you like to see happen or not happen?
  - What do you think are the important and necessary characteristics of an effective learning team?
  - What else can you tell me about how the session can be shaped so that you find it worthwhile?

- Questions about current reality include
  - What have been your successes and roadblocks this year?
  - What are the strengths and weaknesses of your students?
  - What do you like about being a teacher?
  - What else can you tell me about your students' greatest needs?

- Final questions include
  - Do you have any more questions for me?
  - Do you want to participate in the ILT?

Reporting Back

Listening may be the simplest, most powerful way to communicate respect. As Margaret Wheatley writes,

> Listening moves us closer. When we listen with less judgment, we always develop better relationships with each other. It's not differences that divide us. It's our judgments about each other that do. Curiosity and good listening bring us back together. (2002, p. 36)

Facilitators who want to foster a learner-friendly culture can do so during the one-to-one interviews as described above, and they can further shape the team's culture by beginning the ILT by letting teachers know that they have been heard. I like to do this by beginning with some form of authentic exploration of the information I gathered from teachers during the interviews. This group discussion should be accurate, and thus it has to honestly deal with important issues. I have found, though, that when teachers talk about why they love to teach, why they care about students and learning, the conversation is always positive, even celebratory.

I like to report what I heard in interviews by creating vignettes, short soliloquies of a sort, that I write based on my notes from the one-to-one conversations. The vignettes capture a major theme that came up again and again in interviews. Two examples of vignettes are included below, and several more are included in the Impact Toolkit in Resource A. Although it may appear that these vignettes are the words of one person, they actually combine the comments of many people I met with prior to an intensive learning team.

Proud of Her and Me

My first two months of teaching were two months of terror. I questioned whether I ever wanted to teach again. And today, still, when I have a bad day, it's awful. It used to get to me. I can feel awful, stressed, and anxious, wondering what I did wrong. I can feel defeated, and I wonder what's the point of teaching. I feel like I'm wasting my time. I have left school in tears.

I have to learn that it's all about helping kids; it's not personal. I have to think about how to fix it—think about ways to improve. On bad days, I can't let it show. Kids watch your every move. My simple smile might make a kid's day a million times better.

But about 95 percent of my days are good days. You cannot put a price on how it feels to know that you're making a difference. It's the best feeling, a great feeling, wonderful! When lessons go well, when kids get what I want them to get, I feel like I'm on top of the world, like I'm successful. I love watching the light bulb go on. I love seeing the kids come back after they go to high school. It's exciting when you see a kid go a long time without losing it in class. I love it when a little girl in my math class says she doesn't need the calculator. I feel thrilled, ecstatic, and proud of her and me. Yes, the hardship was worth it. Yes, my work in college to become a teacher is paying off. Yes, I am supposed to be at my school. I love it; there are no other words for it.

They Have a Right to Be in Music

I think everybody has a right to their dignity. And, if you pay attention, with even the kids with the most severe disabilities, if you're patient and you pay attention, they can communicate with you.

What upsets me is when teachers don't even seem to try . . . like this one little guy I had last year. He was very capable of doing what they were doing in his teacher's class. They even did some projects like Lego activities. But the teacher wouldn't let him be with the other kids. She put him with the children with behavior disorders over in the corner with just two or three blocks. And, she made it a point with every activity to make him different and separate and not let him in. And that makes me real angry.

You have to advocate for the kids all the time. I mean, the kids can't do that. So, you have to go out, and I suppose it's like being a salesman, but you have to go out and convince all these people that the kids can do this, and they can fit in, and they can do the Lego activity, and they do have the right to be in music. It should just be accepted—I mean, everybody should have a chance, but they don't. They're just intimidated. They see the handicap; they don't see the child. And once they get to know them . . . some of the people, the ones I've had the greatest problems with, once they get to know them, they've ended up being the greatest advocates for these kids. They just needed some education.

Early on in the first ILT session, I report back on my one-to-one conversations by reading the vignettes and then asking participants to discuss whether the vignettes are accurate, whether something significant has been left out, and what they think and feel about them. I usually read one vignette, we discuss it, and then I read a second one, and so forth, and I usually create three or four vignettes. The vignettes should accurately summarize themes that arise in most teachers' one-to-one conversations. In the best situations, the group of teachers should feel a connection with others in the room as they recognize that their own fear, joy, triumph, or frustration is shared by many other teachers. Many teachers report that this is the first time they have recognized the common ground they share with their colleagues. That common ground, and the honest conversations about current reality, can make the first hour of an ILT an important starting point for creating a learner-friendly culture.

Establishing Team Values

Much has been written about mission, vision, and values statements. These kinds of documents have great potential so long as they are authentic and represent the true opinions of the collective. If activities to create mission or value statements become meaningless rituals, however, they lose their punch and can even be counterproductive. As a friend of mine is fond of saying, "Lemmings have shared vision!"

Nevertheless, authentically created and revised team values—and the critical word there is authentic—can have a profound, positive impact on an ILT's culture. Richard DuFour and Robert Eaker (1998) write,

> The most effective strategy for influencing and changing an organization's culture is simply to identify, articulate, model, promote, and protect shared values. When school personnel make a commitment to demonstrating certain attitudes and behaviors in order to advance the collective vision of what their schools might become, they are, in effect, describing what they hope will be the visible manifestation of their school's cultures. Furthermore, shared values provide personnel with guidelines for modeling their day-to-day decisions and actions. (p. 134)

Early in the ILT process, therefore, I set aside time so that all participants can discuss the kind of team they would like to create. The discussion of these ideas begins during one-to-one conversations, starts to bloom during the dialogue around the vignettes, and fully flowers when participants discuss the kind of community they would like to create.

Most of the time in ILTs, teachers work in groups of five to seven. To start discussion of possible values, I usually ask a simple question: "What kind of team do you want to be?" Each group discusses the topic, records all ideas on chart paper, and then reports back their ideas. At that point, I usually recognize the group's good start, leave the chart paper posted, and move to the next ILT activity. The simple act of discussing the values, which often address such concerns as respect, listening, productivity, and encouraging diverse points of view, gives all participants a chance to have input into the kind of culture they want to create and experience. Further, the activity reinforces the importance of a learner-friendly culture.

At the end of the first ILT session, before leaving the room where we have been meeting, I review the chart paper with participants' comments about team values and type them in bullet form on my laptop. If a comment is repeated, I don't type it, but each new item is listed as a separate bullet. At the start of the second session, I share the list of bullets and ask each group to edit what I have written by adding, removing, or modifying.

I repeat the process of typing everyone's notes and providing time for teachers to review the document in every meeting of an ILT. Once we have a fairly static document, I share it with the group and ask, "Do we still agree with these values or should we change anything?" This activity gives each team member a chance to shape their team's culture, and the values remind all of us that we must act in a manner consistent with those values.

Sample Team Values

Purpose: To develop and integrate a course sequence, teaching strategies, formative assessments, and lesson plans that help kids learn and enjoy mathematics

Values:

Respect. We are honest; we listen carefully to each other; we demonstrate the courage to confront each other; and we resolve our conflicts constructively.

Efficiency. We don't waste time.

Productivity. We produce useful materials and tools that are teacher friendly and that help kids learn.

Supportiveness. We support each other and have fun together.

Validation. We value the expertise of everyone on the team.

Positive Thinking. We work together until we find solutions.

Consistency. We teach the same things, at the same time, in classrooms across the district.

Risk Taking. We are committed to implementing the materials developed by this group.

A learner-friendly culture and smoothly flowing activities can make a big difference on how well an ILT proceeds, but even the friendliest, smoothest running group won't mean much unless the teachers create products that they can use to reach more students. In short, ILTs succeed or fail based on whether or not team members become better teachers.

Although an ILT could focus on any practices facilitators and teachers identify as important, all the ILTs I have facilitated over the years have begun by writing a new curriculum, and writing a new curriculum begins with exploring the standards.

Unpacking Standards

Perhaps the easiest way to improve test scores in a district is to empower teachers to teach lessons that are aligned with the state standards. If students are to do well on state assessments, teachers must address what is on those assessments. One of the first activities in most ILTs, then, is to go through the state standards and identify where each standard's key indicator is found in the curriculum.

In *Unwrapping the Standards,* Larry Ainsworth (2003) provides a process for conducting a deep analysis of standards. Ainsworth suggests going carefully through standards to identify the specific skills and content that all students must learn. This can be done by circling all nouns, which usually refer to content knowledge, and all verbs, which usually refer to skills.

Developing Guiding Questions

Once all standards have been located in the curriculum (if the course is built around a textbook, this might mean identifying where each standard is addressed in the text), teachers can move forward with their redesign of the curriculum by developing guiding questions for each unit. Effective guiding questions (a) address the state standards; (b) are mostly open-ended; (c) prompt students, in some cases, to use technology tools or learning strategies; (d) prompt students to think about how the content is meaningful, important, or related to their lives or other learning; (e) prompt students to identify important concepts, ideas, or content structures to be learned; and (f) are written in easy-to-understand (kid-friendly) language.

Lynn Erickson (2007) provides additional advice, suggesting that effective questions address not just the content (what students need to know) and skills (what students need to be able to do) but also understanding (the bigger ideas about content and knowledge). Effective questions, therefore, Erickson suggests, point to the conceptual level of learning, so that students learn why something is important and how ideas fit together. If students don't appreciate why they are learning something, the learning experience will lack relevance and be little more than a meaningless, unpleasant task. By addressing understanding, teachers can increase student interest and motivation and also increase the likelihood that learning will stick.

Creating Learning Maps

Once questions have been identified, a logical next step is for teachers to map out their units. Learning maps can be organized as flow diagrams, concept maps, or webs, whatever pattern seems most appropriate for the content. Effective maps address all the important knowledge, skills, and understandings to be learned while also depicting the connections between different information on the maps.

Integrating Other Practices

Even the most productive ILTs will need several days to write all the guiding questions and learning maps for a course. Once that work is done, teams often move to identifying the specific proficiencies that students are to acquire or master and the informal assessments that can be used to monitor learning. If an ILT's curriculum is fully developed before the team meets, the members might begin with formative assessment.

Formative Assessment

Several authors have tackled the job of breaking down what is to be learned and uncovering how to assess that learning (Chapuis, 2009; Popham, 2008; Stiggins, Arter, Chappuis, & Chappuis, 2009). Typically, the process begins with creating general answers to each guiding question (what students need to know, understand, and do) and creating specific proficiencies, short sentences that describe each discrete component of what students need to learn. Effective specific proficiencies are

1. targeted, providing a partial answer to a question;

2. focused, containing only one idea;

3. complete, written as a complete sentence;

4. short, as concise as possible;

5. accessible, easily understood by students; and

6. comprehensive, providing, in combination with the other specific proficiencies, a complete answer to a guiding question.

Once all specific proficiencies have been written, teachers can match each proficiency with an appropriate formative assessment. Assessments might be rubrics or simple checks for understanding such as response cards, whiteboards, graphic organizers, even thumbs-up and thumbs-down, or simple group activities such as turn-to-your-neighbor or think-pair-share.

Behavioral Expectations

In the research on classroom management, the most prominent finding from the past 85 years is that if teachers want students to act a certain way, then they must teach that way to their students. During ILTs, teachers can productively use their collaborative time to list all of the activities and transitions that might occur in their classroom and then create specific behavioral expectations for each.

Randy Sprick, with whom I have collaborated for years, suggests that expectations be built around five key areas, summarized by the acronym CHAMPs (2009). Specifically, expectations for all activities and transitions should address (a) what kind of student conversation, if any, is acceptable; (b) how students should ask for *help*; (c) what the *activity* is that student will be performing; (d) what kind of *move-ment*, if any, is acceptable; and (e) what appropriate *participation* looks like.

Other Teaching Practices

ILTs are not limited to these practices. An ILT may focus on what-ever teachers and district leaders identify as high leverage. At the International School in Monterrey, Mexico, for example, teachers meet to create and share stories they are using in their classrooms using the storytelling practices described in *Instruction That Makes an Impact* (Knight, in press). ILT participants could also look at integrat-ing effective questions, differentiating reading practices, developing quality assignments, and so forth. What matters is that the practices being developed have a very good chance of having a positive impact on student learning.

Planning for Instructional Coaching Support

All of the work of an ILT will not mean much unless it turns into new practices in the classroom. For that reason, coaching plans must be created during ILTs. Specifically, teachers and ICs need to lay out a step-by-step plan that details when the coach will work with each teacher on the team and what components of coaching will be addressed. A copy of a coaching planning form is included in the Impact Toolkit in Resource A.

To make it easier for teachers to implement what has been created, ICs must follow up with teachers immediately to build on the momentum of the ILT. When teachers have used their knowledge and creativity to create new guiding questions and learning maps, they are usually excited about trying out what they have created.

If products have been created and they need to be typed up and disseminated, it is essential that they are made available as soon as possible. The longer time passes, the less enthusiastic teachers will be to implement what they have created.

To Sum Up

- Data teams, professional learning communities, and leadership teams for positive behavior supports are common forms of collaborative learning teams in schools.
- In Impact Schools, teams are grounded in the partnership principles, so all participants have equal input into whatever the team creates.
- Partnership facilitators use a variety of strategies to reduce friction during collaborative learning. They employ dialogue structures that are designed to lead to productive outcomes while also honoring the choices of teachers.
- ILTs bring together teachers who are teaching the same grade or course to write curriculum or to integrate the high-leverage teaching practices described on the Target.

Going Deeper

In 1992, as a graduate student at the University of Toronto, I was fortunate to complete an independent study with Michael Fullan, who was the dean of the University of Toronto Schools at that time. Michael guided me through most of what he had written up to that time, and he also introduced me to other works that he thought would be important for me to read.

One of those books was Peter Senge's *The Fifth Discipline* (1990). *The Fifth Discipline* is now considered the seminal work on the topic of learning organizations, having inspired a generation of writers, including me. I doubt that the books that shaped my thinking for this chapter would have existed as they are were it not for Senge's work. For my own part, I would not have come to see collaborative learning the way I do were it not for *The Fifth Discipline*.

Senge's work was a major influence on the development of professional learning communities, and Shirley Hord and William A. Sommers' *Leading Professional Learning Communities* (2008) and Rick DuFour and Robert Eaker's *Professional Learning Communities at Work* (1998) are seminal works in this area, introducing the idea of professional learning communities (PLCs) in schools.

Nancy Love's *Using Data to Improve Learning for All* (2009) describes a simple but powerful process that can be used in schools by data teams to gather and analyze data, identify concerns, invent possible solutions, as well as test and monitor solutions.

Randy Sprick, Mickey Garrison, and Lisa Howard's *Foundations* (2002) and George Sugai and Rob Horner's "School-Wide Behavior Support" (2000) both describe a process that schools can adopt for schoolwide problem solving, intervention planning, and assessment of interventions to make schools safer and more civil learning communities.

Patrick Lencioni's books embed sound thinking on business leadership in compelling narratives. *The Four Obsessions of an Extraordinary Executive* (2000) describes, among other things, the importance of organizational clarity similar to that provided by an Instructional Target. *Getting Naked* (2010) presents effective practices that consultants, such as those leading intensive learning teams, can use to build healthy productive relationships. Finally, Lencioni's *The Five Dysfunctions of a Team* (2002) is a classic work describing, despite its title, effective practices of teams. The latter is even available in a manga edition illustrated by Kensuke Okabayshi (2008).

Harrison Owen's *Open Space Technology* (2008) and Juanita Brown and David Isaac's *World Café* (2005) introduce the exciting idea of community learning, grounded in and driven by the choices of everyone in the community. Both books are philosophically consistent with the partnership approach, and the process for group dialogue they describe can be employed successfully in many settings.

New Yorker columnist James Surowiecki's *The Wisdom of Crowds* (2004) is an entertaining and thought-provoking book, describing, as its subtitle explains, "Why the many are smarter than the few, and how collective wisdom shapes business, economies, societies, and nations."

Keith Sawyer's *Group Genius* (2007) is a well-researched and interesting description of teams achieving "group flow" and the 10 conditions that are necessary for group flow. In addition, Sawyer explains why traditional forms of brainstorming fail, how the conditions for improvisation can be put in place in any team, and how group think can be avoided.

Susan Sullivan and Jeffrey Glanz's *Building Effective Learning Communities* (2006) and David Straker's *Rapid Problem Solving With Post-it Notes* (1997) both contain dialogue structures that can be used productively with almost any group of learners.

7

Partnership Communication

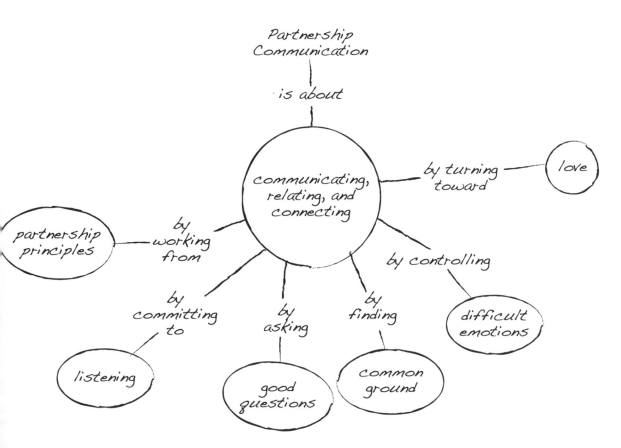

In Impact Schools, all forms of professional learning, including principal observations and leadership, instructional coaching, workshops, and teams are coordinated to have a powerful positive impact on how teachers teach and how students learn. But aligning professional learning is not enough to create the outcomes we all want. If schools are to become Impact Schools, all change leaders—administrators, coaches, teachers, anyone in a school who supports improving instruction—must communicate effectively. A leader will sink or swim, more often than not, based on how effectively she communicates.

What is true in the workplace is true in the rest of our lives. Much of the happiness and sadness we experience flows from our ability to communicate. Many of our most joyous moments involve sharing our ideas, dreams, and love with others, and many of our most painful moments occur when communication breaks down. If we can improve our ability to communicate, we can improve the quality of our relationships. And ultimately, since our lives are lived in relationship, when we improve how we communicate, we improve the quality of our lives.

What can give all of us hope, however, is that there are simple-to-implement communication strategies that can dramatically improve how effectively we communicate. The five simple but powerful strategies described in this chapter can help you communicate more effectively at school, at home, or wherever you interact with others. The strategies of listening, asking good questions, finding common ground, controlling difficult emotions, and finding love are easy to learn, and using any one of these strategies should shorten the gap between us and others.

Partnership Principles and Communication

Taking the partnership approach makes it easier to communicate, relate, and connect with others. Partnership improves our ability to relate as much by what it keeps us from doing as it does by what we do. For example, if we see others as equals, we don't assert our superiority or bully or patronize, at least not intentionally. When we honor the principle of voice, we don't interrupt others or dominate conversations. What we do not do during interactions, in fact, may be as important as what we do.

Acting on the partnership principles naturally leads to other effective communication practices. Honoring voice means that we listen with care and that we are open to others' opinions. When we recognize the importance of reflection and dialogue, we ask better questions and approach others with humility, open-mindedness, and respect. And if we value praxis, our conversations prompt reflection on issues that matter. An important part of effective communication is taking time to say something true or meaningful.

By positioning us as partners with our colleagues, partnership principles set us up to communicate in ways that enrich our lives and the lives of others. However, if we believe in partnership, but communicate in ways that are inconsistent with the principles, others will not see our beliefs in our actions. Like so much in leadership and life, we need to walk the talk. In Impact Schools, leaders—whether they are principals, coaches, workshop leaders, partnership facilitators, teachers, or other educators in a school—give life to the partnership principles by employing partnership communication strategies such as those described below.

Listening

There is a simple way to recognize the importance of listening. Take a second to think of someone whom you consider to be an excellent listener. This is someone who is genuinely interested in your ideas, who really listens to you when you speak, someone who lets you talk, and who makes sure you are the focus of the conversation. Now think of someone who never seems to listen to you. This is someone who is not interested in what you are saying, who frequently interrupts when you are in the middle of a sentence, who seems to be just waiting for his or her chance to jump in when you are talking. More than likely, you have a high opinion of the listener and a low opinion of the non-listener. In Impact Schools, the change leaders are listeners.

Almost any communication and leadership book identifies listening as essential. Nevertheless, authentic listening is a scarce commodity today. Our conversations at home, at work, and in the community are often more about jockeying for airtime than really communicating. Real communication is a two-way process, and for it to be authentic and humane, we need to take in at least as much as we put out. To be good communicators, we need to be good listeners.

Authentic listening is an important way to show respect for others. When we really listen, we have a chance to enter into a deeper form of communication. A conversation characterized by people really listening is humanizing for all parties. When we truly hear people, we see them as human beings who count, whose ideas, heart, and soul matter. When we fail to listen, on the other hand, we treat others as objects put on earth only to help us get what we want.

So how do we become good listeners? We certainly have lots of advice in shelves and shelves of self-help books. Numerous authors offer a long list of suggestions: We should make sure our body language mirrors our partner's. We should make eye contact. We should paraphrase back what we hear. We should make sure we nod frequently to encourage others to communicate. We should get inside our partner's paradigm. We should empathize.

These are all useful ideas, and following some or all of these suggestions will undoubtedly help us listen better or at a minimum help us look like we are listening. I believe we can act ourselves into better behavior, but I also believe a few high-leverage strategies can ensure that we become better listeners. The strategies are simple. They can be mastered by anyone, and when they are applied with discipline, they will make you a much better listener, maybe even a better person.

The Listening Strategies

Make the Decision to Really Listen

Most of the listening techniques listed above will be taken care of if we do one simple thing: commit to really hearing what others are saying. If we genuinely want to hear what the other person is saying, if we are curious, if we care, we won't have to worry about another's paradigm, facial expressions, eye contact, or body language. The outward evidence that we are listening will be taken care of when we care deeply about what the other person says. Trying to listen by looking like we're listening will not work unless we also choose to focus on hearing what others say.

Strategy 1: Simply commit to listen.

Listening, when it is authentic, is something we feel as much as we see. You can tell when your sister who lives 2,000 miles away isn't listening when you are talking with her on the phone. Clearly, you can feel when someone right besides you is or is not listening. Authentic listening causes a connection, almost a chemical connection, between people. If you choose to make sure you are locked in to your partner, really listening, they will know. And so will you.

Be the Listener, Not the Speaker

When two people talk, there are really only two ways the conversation can be structured at any particular point: (a) one person is the speaker and the other one is listener or (b) both are the speaker and neither is the listener (I suppose some might say no one could be talking and no one listening, but that doesn't really seem like a conversation to me.) In the midst of a conversation, train yourself to ask, "Am I the listener, or am I the speaker?" If you find that you are always the speaker, work on taking on the alternate role.

There are many ways you can shift to being the listener. You can make a decision to care about what your partner has to say (Strategy 2). You can also dramatically improve your listening and communication skills by choosing to ask questions about the person you're talking with rather than telling them what you have to say. See every interaction as a chance to let the other person tell you something you don't know. See each conversation as a learning opportunity, not a telling opportunity, and use questions to learn about your conversation partner. A great conversationalist, as Susan Scott has commented in *Fierce Conversations* (2002), is one who lets the other person have the conversation.

As your conversation progresses, check the situation and ask, "Am I the speaker, or am I the receiver?" If you're the speaker, then make a point to ask a question that hands the conversation back to your partner.

> **Strategy 2:** Make sure your partner is the speaker.

Pause and Think Before You Respond

Even if you listen with all your heart, mind, and soul, there is still a possibility that you will be perceived as a terrible listener. Careless words in response to what someone says can negate another person's comment and create the same impact as not listening at all. Let's say someone comes to me with a suggestion or idea, and without thinking, I quickly respond, "Oh, that will never work. We've tried that before, and it always fails." I may have heard what my colleague said, but my comment has the same impact as not listening because my words communicate that my partner's words had no impact on me at all.

A better strategy is to pause before responding and ask yourself, "Will what I'm about to say open up or close down the conversation?" If my comments shut down my partner, then I should find another way to respond—or say nothing. But listening is more than taking words in. You may have had the experience where someone was able to parrot back what you said but who didn't really seem to listen to you. Listening is about hearing the words *and* being sure to process them. When we listen to others, we must make sure we let their words sink in, and then we need to comment in ways that authentically show that we have heard what they have said. There are two techniques here, and both are important. First (a) we pause, and then (b) we think about what we are about to say before we speak.

Strategy 3: Pause before you speak and ask yourself, "Will my comment open up or close down this conversation?"

The Listening Strategies

1. Commit to listen.
2. Make sure your partner is the speaker.
3. Pause before you speak and ask, "Will my comment open up or close down this conversation?"

Good Questions

More than a decade ago, I had the pleasure of working with two visionary corporate leaders in Canada, Jim Chestnutt and Tony Lamantia. Jim and Tony had worked together for decades for a major Canadian retail company, Eatons, and Jim, Tony, and I worked together with many other good people at Ryerson University in Canada to create communication and leadership courses for retail managers.

One of my colleagues at Ryerson, Francis Gunn, was an outstanding teacher. One day when Francis, Tony, Jim, and I had lunch together, Francis turned to the two men and asked a simple question: "I bet you two have had some great adventures together. What have been some of your most interesting experiences?" Francis' simple question led to a wonderful conversation during which Jim and Tony told us about their travels around the world to buy goods for the national chain, their brushes with famous Canadians, and their shared experience moving up through the Eatons organization. One simple question opened up the entire conversation, Francis and I learned a great deal about our colleagues, and in one brief conversation we came to feel more affection for them as they regaled us with stories about trips to India and encounters with famous hockey players.

Good questions, like Francis', can open up conversations, generate respect, accelerate learning, and build relationships. Questions are the yang to complete the yin of listening. If we don't ask questions, we won't have the opportunity to listen. If we don't listen, our questions won't serve much purpose. When we see others as equals, we usually give them at least equal time at the center of our conversation, and that requires asking questions that allow our conversation partners to say what they wish. By asking good questions, we demonstrate what Tony Stoltzfus in *Coaching Questions* (2008) calls "conversational generosity." There are three simple and powerful strategies we can use to ask good questions.

Be Curious

Much has been written about the techniques that good questioners should use. Technique, however, is not as important as the mindset you bring to questioning. As literacy coaching expert Cathy Toll said to me, we shouldn't ask questions to which we think we already know the answer. Rather, we should ask questions because we authentically want to hear what our partner has to say. When we are curious, when we really want to know what others think, we communicate respect for them, and that respect greatly increases the likelihood that our partners will speak freely with us.

Curiosity is the embodiment of the principle of reciprocity. When we view conversations as reciprocal, we enter

Strategy 1: Be curious.

into conversations as learners not talkers. When we are curious, we see a conversation as a living interaction that we co-construct with our partner, not a means to tell someone something or an opportunity to control somebody.

If we are curious, that means we genuinely want to hear what the other person has to say. Therefore, when we ask good questions out of curiosity we are 100 percent present in the conversation. Good questioners give their conversation partners their undivided attention, and they genuinely empathize. Good questioners also let their partners say what they wish by honoring, what Susan Scott (2010) refers to as the "sweet purity of silence." When you are curious and ask good questions, you communicate respect, build relationships, and you usually learn something important.

Ask Open-Ended, Opinion Questions

Much has been written about types and levels of questions, but two basic distinctions, in my opinion, are most important: (a) closed-ended versus open-ended questions and (b) right-or-wrong versus opinion questions.

Closed-ended questions elicit limited responses, and they always ask for answers to which a complete answer can be given. For example, if I ask you the closed-ended question, "Who is the president?" you can give me a complete answer simply by naming the president. Closed-ended questions usually invite short, yes-or-no, factual, or multiple-choice answers.

Open-ended questions elicit unlimited responses and provide the opportunity for an expansive, extended response. For example, if I ask you the open-ended question, "What do you think about the president?" you can theoretically talk as long as you wish during your reply. Open-ended questions usually invite longer, detailed, knowledge, opinion, or feeling answers.

Closed-ended questions can be used effectively, especially to check student understanding in the classroom during mechanical learning, but they are not especially effective during partnership conversations. If I want to hear what my conversation partner is thinking or feeling, then asking open-ended questions is much more effective.

Right-or-wrong questions, as the name implies, are questions for which there are correct or incorrect answers. On the other hand, opinion questions are questions to which there are no specific correct answers since they prompt people to give their own opinion. The question "Who is the president?" is both a closed-ended and a right-or-wrong question, because there is only one correct answer to it. Similarly, our example of an open-ended question, "What do you think about the president?" is also an example of an opinion question. I may not agree with your answer, but when you tell me what you think, your answer is your opinion, not an attempt to give a correct reply.

Strategy 2: Ask open-ended, opinion questions.

Right-or-wrong questions, like closed-ended questions, can be used effectively for mechanical learning, but they are rarely successful during open conversations. When asked right-or-wrong questions, people are often hesitant to respond for fear of being wrong. However, when asked opinion questions, they are much more forthcoming.

These distinctions between open- and closed-ended questions and right-or-wrong and opinion questions may seem obvious, but in my experience the most common mistake people make during questioning is to use closed-ended or right-or-wrong questions as vehicles for conversation. When a workshop leader or a meeting facilitator asks a question that falls dead, the reason is almost always because the question was not an opinion, open-ended question.

Be Nonjudgmental

Michael Fullan has written about the importance of leaders taking a nonjudgmental stance. In *The Six Secrets of Change* (2008) he writes,

> Nonjudgmentalism is a secret of change because it is so very heavily nuanced. You have to hold a strong moral position without succumbing to moral superiority as your sole change strategy. As [William] Miller puts it,
>
> > When we strive for some great good or oppose some great evil, it is extremely difficult not to spill out some of the goodness onto ourselves and the evil onto our opponents, creating a deep personal moral gulf. It is very difficult, in other words, professing or striving for something righteous, to avoid self-righteousness and moral condemnation. (p. 60)

No matter how skillfully crafted our questions are, they will fail if we judge our conversation partners' responses. Dennis and Michelle Reina in *Trust and Betrayal in the Workplace* (2006) have written about the importance of what they call "communication trust," which they define as "The willingness to share information, tell the truth, admit mistakes, maintain confidentiality, give and receive constructive feedback, and speak with good purpose" (p. 34).

Conversational trust develops, according to the Reina and Reina, "when people feel comfortable and

Strategy 3: Be nonjudgmental.

safe enough to share their perceptions regarding one another's perceptions without repercussions. They trust they will not suffer the consequences of retaliation because they spoke the truth" (p. 47). Passing judgment on the answers others give to our questions almost always destroys conversational trust.

There are two simple things you can do to not be judgmental. First, when asking good questions, you need to listen without assumptions and without prejudging your conversation partner. If you jump to conclusions about what your partner says, chances are they will notice and then be less open.

Second, to remain nonjudgmental when you ask questions, let go of the desire to give advice. For some reason, most of us have an almost uncontrollable desire to tell others how they should go about their business. However, in almost all cases, our partners don't want that advice unless they explicitly ask for it. What people want is someone who listens, values their ideas, and is empathetic and nonjudgmental.

Good Questioning Strategies

1. Be curious.
2. Ask open-ended, opinion questions.
3. Be nonjudgmental.

Good Questions

In the past few years, I have been on the hunt for good questions by asking for advice or attending workshops. Here are some of the questions that I have found to be most helpful and the names of the people who first shared them with me.

- Given the time we have today, what is the most important thing that you and I should be talking about? (Susan Scott)
- What if nothing changes? So what? What are the implications for you and your students? (Susan Scott)
- What is the ideal outcome? (Susan Scott)
- What can we do if we resolve this issue? (Susan Scott)
- When you watch this lesson, what do you feel?
- Tell me a little bit about this . . .
- Say more about this . . .
- What leads you to believe . . . (Robert Putnam)
- What would be the ideal classroom for you?
- What would we see and hear that would be evidence of this? (Bruce Wellman; Lucy West)
- What went well? What surprised you? What did you learn? What will you do differently next time? (Steve Barkley)
- On a scale of 1 to 10 how close are you to your ideal classroom? (Steve Barkley)
- What are you seeing that shows that the strategy is successful? (Steve Barkley)
- What impact would . . . have? (Steve Barkley)
- When have you seen . . . ? Can you make a connection between that time and this time? (Steve Barkley)

Finding Common Ground

In the fall of 2009, I had the pleasure of presenting to a group of teachers in Chennai, India. This was an extremely unique experience, and

I loved every minute. The city was as exotic as you can imagine, with spice and incense in the air, sitar music emanating from buildings, and wonderful local food. As I walked into the workshop the first day, children stood along the entrance holding candles and lotus flowers, and the session began with chanting. The teachers in the workshop couldn't have looked more different than those I am used to, with all the women wearing saris and sporting bindis on their foreheads.

But, after about 30 minutes into my workshop on the Big Four teaching practices, I had a revelation. This was the most exotic setting in which I had ever presented, and yet it felt just like any other workshop I had led. As different as everyone looked, we were all educators, we all wanted our students to be successful learners, and we shared a host of interests, concerns, and passions. We may have looked different, but we were mostly the same.

In our day-to-day experiences, we can easily lose sight of how much we hold in common with others, especially when people let us down, disagree with us, treat us poorly, or stand in the way of us achieving our goals. This is especially true when leading change in schools because we can become frustrated when others' legitimate questions slow down a change initiative we are championing. However, if we label others as resistors just because they need time to think through new learning on their own, we may make change more unlikely by damaging relationships.

One important relationship skill, then, is to notice and remember the similarities we share with others. When we find common ground, we will have healthy relationships and better conversations. Being intentional about finding common ground is an important part of effective communication.

There are wonderful examples of people finding common ground all around us. One organization, Playing for Change (n.d.), creates short movies in which people all over the world are filmed playing the same songs, and then through the wonders of technology, the recordings are edited to create the impression that everyone is playing the song together at the same time. The videos at www.playingforchange.com illustrate how much each of us holds in common with everyone else.

The Milestones Project is another organization dedicated to helping us find common ground. Founded by photographers Richard and Michele Steckel (2010), the project assembles photographs of children from around the world to show, as Richard and Michele say, "a world where what divides us is healed and what unites us is loved . . . by seeing how we are all the same." Their photographs can be found at www.milestonesproject.com. If you have time and are near a computer, I suggest you check out both websites before reading further in this book.

What these two projects suggest for the world, we can do on a smaller scale with the people in our lives. We can seek out similarity rather than notice difference. Each time we try to find common ground with teachers, administrators, students, parents, or anyone in our lives, we contribute to the cause depicted on the websites: we move our world a little closer to unity and a little further away from division. Finding common ground is a powerful communication strategy to help us improve our relationships and communicate more effectively, but it is also a noble act that makes the world a better place.

Several strategies can help us find common ground.

Commit to Finding Common Ground

The first step in finding common ground, like the first step in listening, is to commit to finding common ground. The core belief in this strategy is that we are more alike than we are different, and, therefore, in every interaction, we should attempt to find common ground, especially with those who are and appear different from us. The creators of the Milestone Project described above have developed a pledge that both children and adults can embrace. The pledge puts in words what a commitment to find common ground might look like.

The Milestone Pledge

- I pledge to notice the ways people are like me before I notice the ways they are different.
- I pledge to say only kind things to others and to stop myself before I say mean things.
- I pledge to use respectful words to work out my problems with other people.
- I pledge to encourage my friends to do these things too, because . . . (The Milestones Project, n.d.)

I know that if everyone does these four things we will put an end to intolerance and hatred all over the world.

Seek Common Denominators; Avoid Common Dividers

Another way to find common ground is to consciously look for similarities we share with our conversation partners. Common denominators might include

- interests or passions such as music, particular books, food, local restaurants, or sports teams;
- roles such as teacher, administrator, parent, committee member, Scout leader, or choir leader;
- activities such as cooking, running, singing, or writing;
- beliefs such as religious, political, and intellectual; and
- history such as experiences, schools or universities, people known, and locations lived in or visited.

In their useful book *The Art of Connecting* (2006), Claire Raines and Lara Ewing describe how we might go about finding common ground, even with someone who appears to be quite different from us.

Ana, who is 24 and works in Chicago, tells us about trying to find a way to connect with her client who worked for Allstate. After speaking to each other on the phone, the two met face-to-face for the first time at a luncheon presentation. Ana tried like crazy all through lunch to find common ground. Her client was obviously trying to do the same thing.

Over salad, each of them made quick statements, throwing out offers, but each was blocked. Ana was born in Columbia; her client was born in Columbus. The client was older and plain—jeans, tennis shoes, no makeup. Ana dresses expressively and wears bright dresses and interesting jewelry. One mentioned a favorite restaurant; the other had never heard of it. One talked about a movie she especially enjoyed; the other said she didn't like that kind of movie. One even went out of her way to praise the dessert; the other said she thought it was awful. They fumbled and mumbled and seemed to have nothing in common. . . .

"What did you do in the past for Allstate?" she asked. It turned out her client had worked with computers creating pictures and doing graphics. She said she was really into her Macintosh. Ana didn't know a thing about Macs, but . . . as luck would have it, she had just read about the iPod shuffle.

"So we had a really good time talking about iPods," Ana tells us. "When it was time to say goodbye, I said, 'Let me see where you sit so I'll know where to find you next time I'm here.' She showed me her iPod, her speakers, her playlist, everything. She told me when I got mine I should come in and she'd show me how to download music. She said she'd do it for me. Now we talk on the phone and catch up on whether I've been to the Apple store and what new accessories I've got." (p. 51)

The second half of this strategy is to avoid common dividers. When we find something we share with another person, it can be the stepping stone to establishing an authentic connection or relationship. However, if we call attention to a major difference between us and our conversation partners, it can build a stone wall between us.

Interestingly, all of the potential common denominators listed above (interests or passions, roles, activities, beliefs, or histories) can also be dividers. An obvious example of this is political beliefs. If you and I have the same political bumper sticker on our cars, we can probably find a common bond in our shared political views. But if we have different bumper stickers supporting different parties, we may have a little difficulty relating if I surface that difference. In such a case, it becomes all the more important to seek out common ground.

Use Words That Unite; Avoid Words That Divide

Whenever we speak, we must be aware that our words have the power to instantaneously bring people together or split them apart. We should use words that unite and avoid words that divide. Use *we* instead of *I*, *yes* instead of *no*, and *and* instead of *but*.

Sam Horn, in her simple and powerful book *Tongue Fu!* (1996), writes the following about the power of words to unite:

From this day forth, use the constructive word *and* instead of the destructive word *but*. The beauty of this word is that it builds on, rather than blocks out, what has just been said. It advances discussions rather than anchoring them in argument. . . .

Think about it. Doesn't the word *but* often precede negative news? "You did a nice job on this, but . . ." "I know we said it would take only 15 minutes, but . . ." The word evokes an uh-oh response because listeners know they're about to hear something they'd rather not. . . .

The word *and* lets both statements stand, even if they are diametrically opposed to one another. "You did a nice job on this, and could you please add a sentence asking them if they could . . ." "I know I said it would take only 15 minutes, and I'm sorry it is taking longer. Our computers will be back on line shortly, and then we can. . . ." (pp. 72–73)

A second part of this strategy is avoiding words that carry negative emotional implications. For example, words like *careless, dishonest, lazy*, and *unprofessional* can be very divisive when directed at others—even when they are used indirectly. To say to someone, "It would be dishonest to say that" is not much different from telling someone, "You're lying." We must avoid such language and continually look for language that unifies. A useful online resource is "Forty Inviting Comments" and "Forty Disinviting Comments" identified by William Watson Purkey and John M. Novak (n.d.) at their website *Forty Successes:* http://honolulu.hawaii.edu/intranet/committees/FacDevCom/guidebk/teachtip/40succes.htm.

All attempts at finding common ground will fail if they are seen as manipulative or inauthentic. We have probably all experienced salespeople who have tried to find common ground with us just so they have some leverage for a sale or people who try to force agreement in a meeting by saying, "I'm sure we can all agree . . ." Such phony talk is not what I am proposing.

This strategy is our attempt to build unity with others by seeing how we are alike. It is an attempt to connect with others, especially others who, on the surface, seem a lot different from us. By finding common ground, we open authentic doors to communication, connection, and meaningful relationship; we seek out what William Orville Douglas calls "the common ground binding all mankind together."

Strategies for Finding Common Ground

1. Commit to finding common ground.
2. Find common denominators; avoid common dividers.
3. Use words that unite. Avoid words that divide.

Controlling Difficult Emotions

A basic assumption at the heart of the partnership approach to communication is that our world and each of us in it would be better off if we were more effective at communicating and connecting with others. Destructive emotions can be one major barrier to communication.

Many emotions are constructive. Love, joy, satisfaction, contentment, and many others are nourishing and constructive, but emotions like anger, shame, and fear can tear us down if we don't control them. The following illustrates how destructive emotions can be a major barrier to effective communication. Consider the following two people:

> Bill is a passionate principal who is committed at a deep level to increasing the student achievement scores at his school. In a staff meeting, he proposes that his teachers explore the use of formative assessment and points out that there is a "massive amount of research that says formative assessment can really make a difference for students." For Bill, this is a "no-brainer. Formative assessment can help students, so we should do it."
>
> When Bill makes his proposal to his staff, he is surprised at the push-back he gets. He tries to listen. He tries to understand his teachers and puts on a brave face, but the truth is that he simply cannot believe that his staff are not embracing his idea. "This would help kids," he thinks, "and if it helps kids, we should do it." The more teachers raise their concerns, the more Bill gets frustrated and, eventually, angry. Finally, after one more teacher's comment about how difficult formative assessment is to implement, Bill blows his cool, snaps at the teacher who made the comment, and criticizes all the teachers in the room for not caring about the students. Bill cuts the meeting short, saying, a little ominously, "We will be discussing this further once you all get your priorities straight. I want you all to think about whether you care about kids or not. This meeting is over!" Bill's emotions are a barrier to communication.

> Kate is the victim of a verbally abusive marriage. She attends mediation with her now ex-husband, Todd, to discuss how to cooperate to raise their child. Kate dreads each meeting, fearing that her ex will use the forced time together to say things that she finds humiliating. "I'd rather go to the dentist to have every tooth drilled than go to mediation," she says, "but I have to do it."
>
> One day during mediation Kate and Todd talk about the two-week vacation Todd wants to take their son on. When Kate objects, saying it is too much time off school, Todd tells her, "But you said he could go last September when we talked about this. Now I've made all the plans. Surely you're not going to screw this up too."

Kate is certain that she never agreed to this, and she is just as sure that her ex is simply saying this to get his way in front of the mediator. But when Kate tries to say what she thinks, she is overwhelmed by emotions. Fear, uncertainty, and shame all cloud her brain, and Kate, having had too many confusing conversations just like this in the past, struggles to say anything. Buried under her emotions, she can't find the words to say what needs to be said. Shaped by an extremely painful history, Kate's emotions are a barrier to communication.

When we fail to control our destructive emotions, we may fail to say what needs to be said, or we may say something that we will regret. There are three simple strategies we can use to control destructive emotions. The strategies, name it, reframe it, and tame it, are as follows.

Name It

The first strategy is to recognize when we enter into the kinds of situations that might trigger an emotional response. We will be better able to maintain control of our emotions when we come to recognize what circumstances trigger our responses. Sybil Evans and Sherry Suib Cohen, in *Hot Buttons* (2001), describe these triggers as hot buttons:

> A hot button is an emotional trigger. Hot buttons get pushed when people call you names, don't respond to you, take what you think belongs to you, challenge your competence, don't respect you, give you unsolicited advice, don't appreciate you, are condescending. When someone pushes one of your hot buttons, it makes you a little crazy. That's all it takes. You explode. Not all explosions are loud, and maybe no one can see your eruptions, but you still explode inside. (pp. 1–2)

The first part of controlling destructive emotions, then, is to watch our actions and environment carefully so that we can recognize when there is potential for mayhem. If we recognize that a situation may trigger our negative emotions, that awareness can sometimes be enough to keep us from being overwhelmed.

Reframe It

Naming the situation as one where our emotions can get the better of us is often all that it takes to control our emotions. When we

recognize one of our hot buttons is about to be pushed, we can sometimes stop ourselves from reacting. On other occasions, however, we
need to reframe the interaction to better be able to keep our destructive emotions under control. Reframing involves two steps.

First, in order to control our emotions, we must believe we can do
it. Stanford University researcher Carol Dweck, in *Mindset: The New
Psychology of Success* (2006), suggests that people generally adopt one
of two ways of approaching the world: a growth mindset or a fixed
mindset. If you have a fixed mindset when it comes to controlling
your emotions—that is, you believe "that your qualities are carved in
stone" (p. 6)—you will find it difficult to learn how to control how
you respond to emotional triggers. However, if you have a growth
mindset—that is, you believe that "your basic qualities are things you
can cultivate through your efforts" (p. 7)—you have the potential to
change the way you respond when others push your buttons. Fortunately, Dweck's research suggests that we can change our mindset
from fixed to growth, and she uses herself as the prime example of
someone who has done just that.

Dweck's (2006) ideas echo Martin Seligman's in his classic book
Learned Optimism: How to Change Your Mind and Your Life (1998). "Habits of thinking," Seligman says, "need not be forever. One of the most
significant findings in psychology in the last 20 years is that individuals can choose the way they think" (p. 9). Seligman explains that we
can control how we respond to triggers like hot buttons. The first step
is to recognize the trigger when we see it, name it, and then change
the way we respond to the trigger, reframe it, so that it doesn't control
us. The first step in the reframe it strategy is to recognize that we
control and can change our emotional response to hot buttons.

Second, the heart of this strategy is to reframe a potentially negative situation so that it can become one we can control. Simply put,
we need to change the way we see the interaction so it doesn't eat us
up. Here are some simple ways to reframe a potentially dangerous
conversation:

- *Think of yourself as a listener.* Use your listening skills to let your
conversational partners have the floor. Then, before you share your
thoughts, start by paraphrasing what they have said until they agree
you've got it right. Your goal is to understand fully what they are
saying before you comment. Stephen Covey (1989) refers to this as
"Seek first to understand, then be understood."

- *Think of yourself as a learner.* See a potentially difficult talk as a
chance to understand your conversational partner's point of view

fully so you can explain points of agreement between the two of you. Your goal is to understand fully your partner's paradigm.

- *Have a personal victory.* You can make the conversation a personal challenge and turn the conversation into a game of self-control by striving not to let your emotions control you. Your goal is to stay in control. If you do, you win.

- *Go to the balcony.* William Ury in *Getting Past No* (1991) writes that

> going to the balcony means distancing yourself from your natural impulses and emotions . . . The balcony is a metaphor for a mental attitude of detachment. From the balcony you can calmly evaluate the conflict almost as if you were a third party. You can think constructively for both sides and look for a mutually satisfactory way to resolve the problem. (p. 38)

Your goal is to stay detached.

In summary, two ideas are important for reframing. One is to adopt a growth mindset that opens you to your own potential for controlling your emotions. The second is to maintain control of your emotions during tough conversations by mentally rethinking the conversation and seeing it as an opportunity to (a) listen, (b) learn, (c) have a personal victory, or (d) detach.

Tame It

Reframing the conversation may not be enough, so we need to have a repertoire of strategies to help us stay in control. Some of these are tricks your mom taught you, but they are still helpful. Many of them are proposed by the outstanding thinkers at the Harvard Negotiation Project:

- *Buy time to think.* According to William Ury (1991), "The simplest way to buy time to think in a tense negotiation is to pause and say nothing. It does you little good to respond when you're feeling angry" (p. 45). Simply counting to 10 slowly can work. Even taking a quick break from the conversation, say, to go to the restroom, can help. Ury suggests we "follow the biblical dictum: 'Be quick to hear, slow to speak, and slow to act'" (p. 46).

- *Rewind the tape.* William Ury (1991) writes, "To buy more time to think, try rewinding the tape. Slow down the conversation by playing it back. 'Let me just make sure I understand what you're saying'" (p. 46). We slow down the conversation by paraphrasing what our conversation partner has said.

- *Break vicious cycles.* When it comes to conversation, some common patterns leave no room for graceful exit. For example, Douglas Stone, Bruce Patton, Sheila Heen, and Roger Fisher (2000) describe "what happened" conversations, in which "we spend much of our time . . . [struggling] . . . with our different stories about who's right, who meant what, who's to blame" (p. 9). If we recognize a vicious conversation cycle, the best we can do is stop the cycle by calling attention to it. For example, we might say, "You know, I don't think we can agree on why this happened, but can we talk about what we can do to make sure it doesn't happen again?"

- *Equilibrate the conversation.* Edgar Schein, in *Helping: How to Offer, Give, and Receive Help* (2009), suggests that many negative emotions arise in conversations because of issues related to status. If we are mindful of status, we may be able to decrease our conversation partner's negative emotions or recognize that the source of our discomfort is related to status, as a way to help us control difficult emotions.

- *Don't make assumptions.* Learning not to make assumptions about others' intentions can also help us better control the emotional dynamics of any interaction. Don Miguel Ruiz (2001), in his beautiful little book *The Four Agreements*, writes that

> The problem with making assumptions about what others are thinking is that we believe they are the truth. We could swear they are real. We make assumptions about what others are doing or thinking . . . then we blame them and react . . . We make an assumption, we misunderstand, we take it personally, and we end up creating a whole big drama for nothing. (pp. 63–64)

The antidote to making assumptions is to ask questions. Ruiz (2001), again, offers some powerful suggestions:

> Have the courage to ask questions until you are clear as you can be, and even then do not assume you know all there is to know about a given situation. Once you hear the answer, you

will not have to make assumptions since you will know the truth. (p. 72)

Strategies for Controlling Destructive Emotions

1. *Name It.* Identify situations where your buttons might be pushed.

2. *Reframe It.* (a) Choose to adopt a growth mindset, a belief that you can change the way you react when others push your buttons. (b) Change the way you think about emotionally difficult conversations by adopting a new frame for understanding them. See yourself as a listener, learner, game player, or a detached observer.

3. *Tame It.* Use one of the following strategies to keep your emotions under control: (a) buy time, (b) rewind the tape, (c) break vicious cycles, (d) equilibrate the conversation, and (e) avoid making assumptions. Or, use your own strategies to maintain control of your emotions.

Love Your Partners

Two years ago, I stayed at the Sylvia Beach Hotel in Newport, Oregon, a hotel with a wonderful dining room where visitors eat together at common tables. Over dinner I naturally ended up chatting with my tablemates. Everyone was very friendly, and the conversation just flowed from one topic to another. As we talked about our life experiences, we discovered that a kindly gentleman sitting with us had lost his wife to a terrible disease a year and a half earlier. He told us that he had nursed her every day for more than a year, and each day she had been in excruciating pain. He had watched her suffer a great deal just to stay alive.

We all expressed our sympathy, and one of the people at our table commented that it must have been terribly difficult to live through each of those days, watching his wife in such pain. Without pausing for a second, he smiled gently and said, "I wouldn't have traded a minute of that time for the world."

I've thought a lot about that conversation and the purity and beauty of loving someone so selflessly. We live, I think, to love like this. I believe our lives are impoverished, terribly, more by lack of love than anything else. It is love that carries us through any disaster and love that gives meaning to our days. With love, we can get through almost anything. Without love, nothing means all that much.

The poet and novelist Margaret Atwood has famously said, "The Eskimo has 52 names for snow because it is important to them; there ought to be as many for love." As it turns out, there aren't really 52 words for snow, but Atwood's statement is nonetheless true. Love has many colors and hues. There is the love of a parent and child. The love of a sibling. The love we feel in an emergency room, worried about a loved one, and the love we feel at a wedding. There is the love between lovers, the love of longtime friends. There is the love of a married couple, which can include many of the other kinds of love.

I think we are afraid to talk about love, and I'm not sure why. Maybe the word just sounds soft. Maybe the idea of love makes us more vulnerable than we want to be. Maybe we just don't understand it, so we avoid it. Maybe we have been hurt and don't want to open old wounds. Nonetheless, if we are going to explore healthy relationships, we simply have to suck it up and talk about love, even love at school.

Michael Fullan in *The Six Secrets of Change* (2008) has named "love your employees" as one of the six secrets, referencing the work of Rahendra Sisodia, David Wolf, and Jaqdish Sheth to support his claim. The researchers report on their analysis of a group of companies they refer to as "firms of endearment"—a list of companies that includes Whole Foods, Timberland, Costco, Southwest Airlines, L.L.Bean, New Balance, the Container Store, Patagonia, and Toyota. Not only are these organizations nice places to work; they also significantly outperform the companies identified by Jim Collins in his famous study of great companies, *Good to Great* (2001).

Sisodia and his colleagues include the comments of several outstanding leaders who recognize the importance of love in the workplace. Herb Kelleher, the longtime CEO of Southwest Airlines, comments that "a company is much stronger if it is bound together by love rather than by fear" (Fullan, 2008, p. 156). Tim Sanders, formerly the chief solutions officer of Yahoo!, states, "I don't think there is anything higher than love . . . Love is so expansive . . . Love is the selfless promotion of the growth of the other" (2008, p. 101). Kevin Roberts, CEO of Saatchi & Saatchi, is similarly quoted:

> At Saatchi & Saatchi, our pursuit of Love and what it could mean for business has been focused and intense. Human beings need love. Without it they die. Love is about responding,

about delicate, intuitive sensing. Love is always two-way . . . Love cannot be commanded or demanded. It can only be given. (2008, p. 101)

For Sisodia, Sheth, and Wolfe, "love is the antidote for . . . dehumanization" (2008, p. 103). Indeed, after studying the incredibly successful organizations they describe as Firms of Endearment (FOEs), the researchers come to the following conclusion:

It is not possible to fully understand how FOEs outperform their closest competitors without understanding the role of love in their success. FOE executives lead with strong spines and dedicated resolve, but they retain the capacity to love and inspire love—in the workplace, in the marketplace, and across the full spectrum of their stakeholder groups. (2008, p. 103)

If love is the defining characteristic of airlines, food stores, running shoe companies, and carmakers, surely it has an important place in schools. Most educators talk about loving their students, but that is about as far the conversation goes. If Roberts is right, that without love we die, then leaders need to understand how to create settings where positive relationships will flourish. Loving your employees, Fullan explains, is about creating the conditions for people to succeed, increasing their skills, and empowering them to find meaning by fulfilling goals. However, in order to translate the idea of love into reality, change leaders also need to know how to communicate in ways that foster emotional connection. To create more loving schools, we need to be more loving.

Making Emotional Connections

John Gottman and Joan DeClaire (2001), one the world's leading experts on relationships and a researcher at the University of Washington, don't mention love in particular, but I believe that is what they are talking about when they explain that emotional connection is the primary goal of relating to others. Gottman and DeClaire write,

whether people are struggling to save a marriage, to cooperate in a family crisis, or to build rapport with a difficult boss, they usually have one thing in common: They need to share emotional information that can help them feel connected. (p. 3)

Gottman and DeClaire's research provides us with a simple strategy for observing behavior and monitoring how well we and people we know build up or tear down emotional connection (Gottman and DeClaire's synonym for *love*). According to Gottman and DeClaire, emotional connection is fueled or frustrated by how we reach out to connect (*bids*) and how we respond (turning toward, turning away, turning against) to those who respond to us. I've described each of these responses below, along with a fourth type of interacting, "fuzzy" bids and responses.

Bids

Gottman and DeClaire (2001) describe the bid as "the fundamental unit of emotional communication . . . A bid can be a question, gesture, a look, a touch—any single expression that says 'I want to feel connected to you'" (p. 4). "Even our best efforts to connect can be jeopardized," Gottman and DeClaire state, "as a result of one basic problem: failure to master . . . the bid" (p. 4).

When someone makes an emotional bid, according to Gottman and DeClaire, we can respond in one of three ways: (a) turning toward, (b) turning away from, or (c) turning against. How we respond can make or break a relationship.

Turning Toward

When we turn toward someone who offers us an emotional bid, we respond positively toward that invitation. If someone shakes our hand, we might pat them on the back. If we are invited out to dinner, we say yes, or we acknowledge the thoughtfulness of the invitation. If someone smiles, we smile back. Gottman and DeClaire (2001) put it this way, "To turn toward one another means to react in a positive way to another's bid for emotional connection" (p. 16).

Turning Away

When we turn away from a bid, we fail to respond to the bid for emotional connection. Often, this means we don't even notice that someone has made a bid for connection. For example, an overwhelmed administrator might be too preoccupied by the countless work-related demands on her time and turn away by failing to notice or acknowledge a colleague's compliments. Gottman and DeClaire observe that turning away "is rarely malicious or mean-spirited. More often we're simply unaware of or insensitive to others' bids for our attention" (2001, p. 5).

The impact of turning away can be devastating. According to Gottman and DeClaire,

> When somebody turns away from a bid, the bidder loses confidence and self-esteem . . . people almost seem to "crumple" when their partners turn away. The bidders don't get puffed up with anger; they don't get indignant; they just seem to fold in on themselves. On video we can see their shoulders sag slightly as if they've been deflated. They feel defeated. They give up. (2001, p. 47)

Turning Against

When people turn against bids, they react in argumentative or hostile ways. If someone makes a bid by offering to cook dinner, for example, a person turning against might respond by saying, "Are you kidding? I've tasted your cooking!" For me, the perfect example of a couple that turns against is George Costanza's parents on *Seinfeld.* Each conversation between George's parents proceeds like a verbal boxing match in which both partners throw disdainful comments at each other. When we watch these conversations on TV, we might laugh, but when we experience them in our own lives, they can be far from funny—the results can be profoundly destructive.

Fuzzy Bids

The way in which we make emotional connections is complicated by the messy way in which people bid for connection and respond to those bids. Gottman and DeClaire (2001) point out that people often offer "fuzzy" bids and "fuzzy" responses to bids for many reasons, but the most common reason is to avoid emotional risk.

> Openly bidding for connection can make us feel vulnerable. (p. 32)

> By the time people reach adulthood, they've typically mastered the subtle dynamics of bidding, making all sorts of challenging social situations easier to negotiate. How often, for example,

have you heard someone offer a vague invitation like "Let's get together some time"? (p. 33)

Bids can also be hard to decipher when the bidder doesn't acknowledge his or her own needs for connection. (p. 34)

To bring more love into our life, we need to train ourselves to be sensitive to the ways in which others extend emotional bids for connection and the way in which we respond to those bids. We also need to make more bids. There are three simple strategies for building more emotional connection with others.

Pay Attention

We will be more effective at building emotional connections, we will bring more love into our lives, if we are mindful of others' emotional bids for connection and if we respond in ways that enrich emotional connection with others. As Gottman and DeClaire (2001) observe, "if you don't pay attention, you don't connect" (p. 66).

Gottman and DeClaire suggest that if we are mindful of emotional connection, especially when people do not appear to want to connect with us, we can go a long way toward building healthy relationships.

Strategy 1: Pay attention.

If you can see past a person's anger, sadness, or fear to recognize the hidden need, you open up new possibilities for relation. You're able to see your coworker's sullen silence as a bid for inclusion in decisions that affect his job, for example. Or you can recognize that your sister's agitation says she's feeling alienated from the family. You can even see the bid in your three-year-old's temper tantrum: He not only wants the toy you can't buy for him, he wants your comfort in a frustrating situation, as well. (2001, p. 36)

By paying more attention to how we connect, we can do so much more effectively. And more connection should mean we experience much healthier relationships and much more love.

Make Lots of Bids; Respond to Lots of Bids

We can increase the emotional connection we feel with others if we are intentional about reaching out to connect with them. This can be done in many different ways. We can make a point of showing interest in people's lives and families. We can find out what our conversation partners are interested in and ask them about their interests. We can write thank-you notes and place them in people's mailboxes.

When I work with coaches, we often talk about "being a witness to the good," that is, watching for actions that our colleagues do well and then telling them what we see. A coach or principal observing a teacher, for example, should always be watching for what goes well (student behavior or teaching practices) and communicate that to the teacher. There are thousands of ways in which we can extend bids to our partners in school, and to build emotional connections, we need to be constantly trying out new ways to connect.

> **Strategy 2:** Make lots of bids, and respond to lots of bids.

Our bids for connection will fail if they aren't authentic. Most of us are quite savvy about spotting phony praise or bids for connection. What counts is that our bid for connection is based on something real, and is not a trick or technique. If we praise someone, but in our heart we don't believe in the praise, we're not being a witness to the good. Authentic bids arise when we see something that truly impresses or pleases us and we tell others what we see. If people believe we are buttering them up because we want to manipulate them, they will keep their distance. However, if they sense that we genuinely are interested, that we care, that we see the good they do, and if we communicate that awareness to them, that can be the start of a beautiful friendship.

If we find innovative ways to make bids for connection, and if we are mindful of how bids shape the emotional landscape of our schools, homes, and communities, we should find many opportunities to turn toward bids from others. To do this, we need to take the time to listen, observe, and interact. Taking the time to connect with others is just as important as taking the time to observe in the classroom. People long for connection, and that takes time. Emotionally intelligent leaders are constantly watching for opportunities to respond positively to others' bids for connection.

Let It Go

Imagine you are driving to the airport to catch a plane, a little behind schedule. You encounter a traffic jam that puts you even further behind, and you start to realize that there is a very good chance that you will miss your flight. At that point, you have two options. One, you can try to roar past the traffic on the shoulder, annoying and endangering the other drivers, and then drive well above the speed limit, with the hope that your dangerous and reckless action will get you there on time; or two, you can let it go.

When you let it go, you decide that you can't control the traffic, and that it is too dangerous to speed, dodge traffic, and so on, and to let the plane go, and you'll try to catch the next one. (The good news is that since airlines are frequently behind, you still have a good chance of catching your flight!) When you let it go, you stop trying to control the situation, you stop doing actions that are dangerous, and you let the situation take care of itself.

Letting it go is just as important for communication as it is for driving, and not letting go can also be just as dangerous for our relationships as reckless driving can be for driver safety. When we let it go in relationships, we stop trying to control how other people feel or act. To let it go means to respect others enough to truly let them make their own choices about what they do and feel.

This is important when communicating one-to-one or with groups. For example, trying to control how someone feels about us,

> **Strategy 3:** Let it go.

for example, is a surefire way to make it more difficult for that person to actually feel affection for us. At its extreme, trying to control how others feel about us is emotionally abusive, but the need for control can show up in other rather innocent kinds of personal interactions, and it almost always has a negative impact.

At its most innocent, not letting go is manifested in sharing our positive feelings and expecting something in return. Reducing love to an economic exchange (I've praised you, now you owe me praise) is often to remove authentic love from the relationship. To let it go, on the other hand, is to share kindness, praise, or other generosities of the spirit without expecting anything in return. Authentic love occurs because we care about what is best for our colleagues and friends, not because we expect to get something in return for whatever we give.

The irony is that the people who love most selflessly, who give gifts with no strings attached, are the people who are the most loved. Indeed, there are few things more attractive than kindness, generosity of human spirit, and warmth toward fellow human beings. To encourage love at home, at work, or in the community, begins with letting go of trying to control how others feel about us.

Letting it go also applies in group settings, such as team meetings, for example. For me, this is much more challenging than letting it go in one-to-one conversations. When we work on something that really matters to us with a project team, we often come to the table with an enormous amount invested in the team's outcome. For example, I sit on research teams where we discuss methods, measures, and practices for something I have spent my professional career studying, and where the outcome of our conversation can really shape what happens to my work in the future. Everyone else on the team comes to the meeting with the same kind of commitment.

What I have learned is that if I try to control the outcome of the meeting by talking more than others, pushing for my ideas, directly confronting those who appear to disagree with me—or worse—my actions make it less likely that I will get my way. A better tactic is to let go of the need to control the meeting. This doesn't mean that we silence ourselves. However, it does mean that we go into meetings open to being persuaded. Our goal should be to come up with the best plan, rather than to come up with our plan. If we let go of the need to control the meeting and focus on helping the voices of everyone be heard, more often than not, our ideas will be implemented. When they're not, it is probably for good reason.

Strategies for Nourishing Love

1. Pay attention.
2. Make lots of bids; turn toward lots of bids.
3. Let it go.

Partnership Communication Strategies

1. Listen

- Commit to listen.
- Make sure your partner is the speaker.
- Pause before you speak and ask yourself, "Will my comment open up or close down this conversation?"

2. Ask Good Questions

- Be curious.
- Ask open-ended, opinion questions.
- Be nonjudgmental.

3. Find Common Ground

- Commit to finding common ground.
- Find common denominators; avoid common dividers.
- Use words that unite. Avoid words that divide.

4. Control Difficult Emotions

- Name it.
- Reframe it.
- Tame it.

5. Love Your Partners

- Pay attention.
- Make lots of bids; turn toward lots of bids.
- Let it go.

To Sum Up

- The kind of change we hope to see in Impact Schools demands that educators are excellent communicators.
- We can be become better listeners if we (a) commit to listen, (b) make sure our partner is the speaker, and (c) pause and ask, "Will my comment open up or close down this conversation?"
- To ask good questions, we should (a) be curious; (b) ask open-ended, opinion questions; and (c) be nonjudgmental.

- We can find common ground by (a) committing to finding common ground, (b) finding common denominators and avoiding common dividers, and (c) using words that unite and avoiding words that divide.
- We can control difficult emotions by using the strategies of (a) naming it, (b) reframing it, and (c) taming it.
- To bring more love into our relationships, we should (a) pay attention, (b) make lots of bids and turn toward lots of bids, and (c) let it go.

Going Deeper

The best books about listening are about so much more than listening—they are about human interaction in all its complexity and richness; they are about hope that better communication can create a better world. The book that has been most useful and inspiring for me is Margaret Wheatley's *Turning to One Another* (2002), a beautiful statement about the importance of authentic communication between all of us and the potential that respectful interaction has for humanity.

Susan Scott is another outstanding author writing about communication. Her books *Fierce Conversations* (2002) and *Fierce Leadership* (2009) contain powerful stories about the importance of honest, authentic communication. Scott does a better job than anyone I've read of explaining how to respectfully but directly discuss difficult information.

John Gottman's books all provide excellent suggestions for how to establish and maintain emotional connections. I find his writing particularly useful because he gives us a vocabulary and way of understanding the interactions we see around. I recommend his book *The Relationship Cure* (Gottman & DeClaire, 2001) if you are interested in books about relationships in general. *Ten Lessons to Transform Your Marriage* (Gottman, Gottman, & DeClaire, 2006) is more relevant if you are interested in issues related to your marriage.

In general, the numerous other communication books available are helpful by reminding us, often in compelling ways, to engage in such simple acts like listening to others or remembering people's names. For me, the two classic works along these lines are Stephen Covey's *The 7 Habits of Highly Effective People* (1989) and Dale Carnegie's

(1936) *How to Win Friends and Influence People*. If you haven't read these classics, I encourage you to do so. They are guaranteed to pay you back for the time you invest in reading them.

Final Thoughts

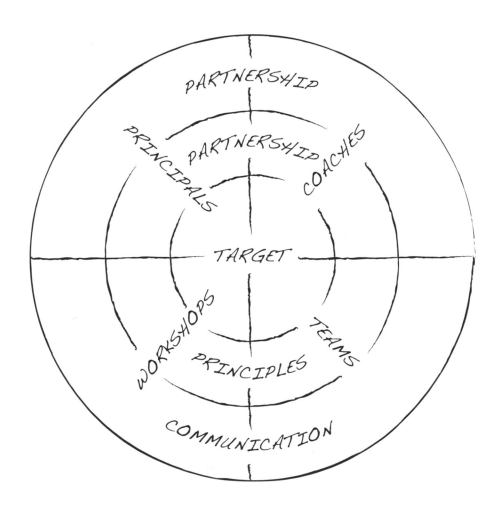

Creating an Impact School is not for the faint of heart. It requires reconstructing the entire way in which professional learning is organized and delivered. In Impact Schools, everything—teacher evaluations, workshops, teams, and coaching—is coordinated for maximum positive effect. Additionally, the scope of professional learning is narrowed so that what is learned can be learned well—first by coaches and administrators and eventually by all teachers in a school. In an Impact School, there is no gap between learning and doing. As Michael Fullan says, "the learning is the work" (2008, p. 79) and in an Impact School everyone learns so that they can do a better job right away.

Leading an Impact School asks a lot of everyone in the school. Principals need to embrace being instructional leaders, and they must develop the self- and project-management strategies that allow them to make instruction their top priority. Central office staff must make instruction a priority and become actively involved in the nuts and bolts of professional learning. Instructional coaches, workshop leaders, and team facilitators must master a host of new skills and attain a deep, practical understanding of all the practices on the Target. Teachers and all other educators need to learn, implement, and master the new teaching practices and engage in honest conversations about what is working and what is not working. In addition, teachers need to seek out and act on the precise feedback that can come from instructional coaches and from watching themselves on recordings of their teaching.

Impact Schools also demand that everyone works together to create a new kind of school culture, one based on partnership rather top-down directives, a culture based on love more than bullying and fear. Impact Schools start from the default assumption that teachers are smart, good people who more than anything else want to help their students succeed.

The work is hard, but the rewards are great. A fully realized Impact School is characterized by the quality and respect of the conversations taking place there and embodies a love of learning that is modeled by everyone in the district. Love of learning is infectious; it is energizing, joyous, and humanizing. In schools where professional learning is at the core, teachers come to work excited by the prospects of what new idea or practice they might do every day. In this way, each day, an Impact School moves closer to the goal: every student receives excellent instruction, every day, in every class.

Resource A

Impact Toolkit

Resource A: Impact Toolkit can also be accessed at the *Unmistakable Impact* companion website at www.corwin.com/unmistakableimpact

Core Questions for Impact Schools

School

- Do we have a one-page instructional improvement plan that clearly describes the critical teaching behaviors that are most important for our students and teachers?

Principal

- Do I know precisely what it looks like when the teaching practices on the instructional improvement plan are used effectively by teachers?
- Do I know exactly how well each teacher is doing in implementing those practices?
- Do I know how to prompt teachers to use the school's professional learning opportunities to master the teaching practices in the Target?
- Do I know how to communicate clearly and positively so that staff are motivated to implement the Target?

Teacher

- Is the content I teach carefully aligned with state standards?
- Do I clearly understand how well my students are learning the content?
- Do my students understand how well they are learning the content being taught?
- Do I fully understand and use a variety of teaching practices to ensure my students master the content being taught in my class?
- Do my students behave in a manner that is consistent with our classroom expectations?

Workshops

- Do workshops focus exclusively on the teaching practices in the instructional improvement plan?
- Do workshop facilitators use effective teaching practices?
- Does each workshop conclude with teachers planning how to use their coach to implement the practices learned during the workshop?

Teams

- Do teams and professional learning communities focus exclusively on the teaching practices in the instructional improvement plan?
- Do teachers use coaches to help them implement the methods and materials developed during team meetings?

Coaches

- Do I have a deep understanding of *all* of the teaching practices in the instructional improvement plan?
- Can I provide sufficient support (precise explanations, modeling, observation, feedback, and questioning) so teachers can implement the practices?

Instructional Improvement Target

(T) = Teacher
(S) = Students

Community Building

(T) Posts expectations and ensures they are followed by students

(T) Interacts with at least a 3:1 ratio of interaction

(S) Are on task at least 90 percent of the time or more

(S) Keep disruptions to no more than four per each 10 minutes

Content Planning

(T) Creates and shares unit questions with students effectively

(T) Fully understands the standards for the course being taught

(T) Has created a learning map and shares it with students effectively

(S) Can paraphrase the guiding questions

(S) Can describe the plan for the unit as laid out on the map

(S) Have the questions and map open on their desk before class starts

Instruction

(T) Uses intensive-explicit teaching practices appropriately

(T) Uses constructivist teaching practices appropriately

(T) Uses cooperative learning, stories, effective questions, thinking prompts, challenging assignments, experiential learning, and similar practices appropriately

(S) Maintain a pass rate of 95 percent or higher

(S) Enjoy learning in the classroom

Assessment for Learning

(T) Uses informal assessments effectively

(T) Knows how each student's learning is progressing

(S) Understand the learning targets for all learning

(S) Know how their personal learning is progressing

Community Building

- ❑ Time on task: _____ percent
- ❑ Opportunities to respond: _____/minute
- ❑ Ratio of interactions: Reinforcing _____:_____ Corrective
- ❑ Disruptions: _____/minute
- ❑ Expectations posted: Yes _____ No _____

Comments:

Big Four
Observation Tools

Content Planning

❑ Instruction is aligned with state standards.

❑ The day's lesson is shaped by guiding questions.

❑ The teacher and students refer to a learning map for the unit's content.

❑ Percentage of students who have the learning map out when class starts: _____ percent.

❑ The learning map and guiding questions are used to provide an advance organizer for the day's lesson.

❑ A review of the critical content and student thinking occurs at the end of the class.

Comments:

Big Four
Observation Tools

Instruction

❑ Direct instruction is used appropriately.

❑ Constructivist instruction is used appropriately.

❑ Questions are appropriate for the learning occurring.

❑ Instruction includes a variety of appropriate teaching practices:
   ❑ Stories
   ❑ Thinking prompts
   ❑ Cooperative learning
   ❑ Experiential learning

❑ Student assignments are optimally challenging.

Comments:

Big Four
Observation Tools

Assessment for Learning

❏ The teacher clearly describes the lesson's learning target.

❏ The teacher effectively checks for understanding.

❏ The teacher can precisely describe how well all students are learning.

❏ Students can precisely describe how well they are learning.

Comments:

Big Four
Observation Tools

Introduction

Purpose

The teacher progress map (TPM) is a simple, comprehensive tool administrators can use to overlook and monitor teacher improvement in the Big Four areas of classroom management, content planning, instruction, and assessment for learning.[1]

The TPM is designed to be used by principals in conjunction with the Big Four Teacher Evaluation Tool and the Big Four Mini-Coaching Manuals. Thus, principals can use this map to keep track of how effectively teaching is occurring, basing their observations on data they gather while observing teachers using some or all of the components of the Teacher Evaluation Tool.

Additionally, professional learning (which might include workshops, instructional coaching, and professional learning communities) can focus on teaching practices that specifically address the Big Four. Mini-Coaching Manuals have been created for all of the specific areas within the Big Four framework.

How to Use the TPM

The teacher progress map is a simple five-column table administrators can use to record how their teachers are progressing. Column one, on the left-hand side of the table, should be used to list the names of all teachers described on the progress chart. The four other columns of the table should be used to document how completely each teacher has mastered each of the Big Four areas of classroom management, content planning, instruction, and assessment for learning. We suggest the following criteria:

L = Limited use of the targeted teaching practices

S = Some use of the targeted teaching practices

M = Mastery of the targeted teaching practices

Specific criteria for each of the Big Four areas are included in this short manual. In addition, a hard copy of the teacher progress map is

Teacher Progress
Map (TPM) Resources

---

1. To protect the non-administrative nature of coaching, we suggest that coaches do *not* use the teacher progress map.

included, and an electronic copy of the map can be downloaded from www.instructionalcoach.org/tools.html. We suggest administrators create a new map whenever they see improvements in teachers' implementation of the Big Four. For this reason, the electronic version of the map may be more convenient, and the tool can be kept confidential with password protection on a computer.

Teacher Progress
Map (TPM) Resources

Classroom Management

Limited Use

Code your teacher as *limited use* if any of the following factors is observed.

- Time on task is less than 80 percent.
- The teacher has not created and posted expectations.
- The ratio of interaction is less than 1:1.
- Disruptions are more than 10 in 10 minutes.

Some Use

Code your teacher as *some use* if none of the limited use factors is observed and at least one of the following factors is observed.

- Time on task is above 80 percent but less than 90 percent.
- Expectations are posted but are not followed by students.
- The ratio of interaction is more than 1:1 but less than 2:1.
- Disruptions are five to nine each 10 minutes.

Mastery

Code your teacher as *mastery* if the following factors are observed.

- Time on task is 90 percent or greater.
- Expectations are posted and followed by students.
- The ratio of interaction is 3:1 or more.
- Disruptions are zero to four each 10 minutes.

Teacher Progress
Map (TPM) Resources

Content Planning

Limited Use

Code your teacher as *limited use* if either of the following factors are observed.

- The teacher has not created unit questions.
- The teacher has not created a learning progress map.

Some Use

Code your teacher as *some use* if any of the following factors are observed.

- The teacher has created unit questions but has not shared them with students effectively.
- The teacher has created a learning progress map but has not shared it with students effectively.

Mastery

Code your teacher as *mastery* if the following factors are observed.

- The teacher has created unit questions and has shared them with the students effectively.
- The teacher has created a learning progress map and has shared it with the students effectively.

Instruction

Limited Use

Code your teacher as *limited use* if either of the following factors are observed.

- The teacher uses the same one or two teaching practices during entire lesson.
- The teacher does not know about constructivist teaching practices.
- The teacher does not use constructivist teaching practices when appropriate.
- The teacher does not know about intensive-explicit teaching practices.
- The teacher does not use intensive-explicit teaching practices when appropriate.

Some Use

Code your teacher as *some use* if any of the following factors are observed.

- The teacher understands but doesn't use intensive-explicit teaching practices appropriately.
- The teacher understands but doesn't use constructivist teaching practices appropriately.

Mastery

Code your teacher as *mastery* if the following factors are observed.

- The teacher understands and uses intensive-explicit teaching practices appropriately.
- The teacher understands and uses constructivist teaching practices appropriately.

Teacher Progress Map (TPM) Resources

Assessment for Learning

Limited Use

Code your teacher as *limited use* if any of the following factors are observed.

- The teacher does not clearly identify Instructional Targets.
- The teacher does not use informal assessments during instruction.
- The students do not know how well their own learning is progressing.
- The teacher does not know how well each student's learning is progressing.

Some Use

Code your teacher as *some use* if some but not all of the following factors are observed.

- Students understand the learning targets.
- The teachers utilize informal assessments effectively.
- The students know how well their personal learning is progressing.
- The teacher knows how well each student's learning is progressing.

Mastery

Code your teacher as *mastery* if *all* of the following factors are observed.

- The students understand the learning targets.
- The teacher utilizes informal assessments effectively.
- Students know how well their personal learning is progressing.
- The teacher knows how well each student's learning is progressing.

Teacher Progress Map (TPM) Resources

Teacher Progress Map

Date:

Teacher	Behavior	Content	Instruction	Formative Assessment
Teacher				
Teacher				
Teacher				
Teacher				
Teacher				
Teacher				
Teacher				
Teacher				
Teacher				
Teacher				
Teacher				
Teacher				
Teacher				
Teacher				
Teacher				
Teacher				
Teacher				
Teacher				
Teacher				
Teacher				
Teacher				
Teacher				
Teacher				
Teacher				

Teacher Progress
Map (TPM) Resources

Teacher	Behavior	Content	Instruction	Formative Assessment
Teacher				
Teacher				
Teacher				
Teacher				
Teacher				
Teacher				
Teacher				
Teacher				
Teacher				
Teacher				
Teacher				
Teacher				
Teacher				
Teacher				
Teacher				
Teacher				
Teacher				
Teacher				
Teacher				
Teacher				
Teacher				
Teacher				
Teacher				
Teacher				
Teacher				

Step 1: Enroll

Goal: To establish a coaching partnership with a teacher

Actions: Consider using some or all of these practices:

1. One-to-one interviews

2. Large-group presentations

3. Small-group presentations

4. Principal referral

5. Workshops

6. Informal conversations

Time: 5–40 minutes

Coach Resources:
What Coaches Do

Step 2: Identify

Goal: Teacher and coach will identify a compelling, specific, measurable goal for coaching interactions

Setting the Goal: Goal setting is a delicate dance, so the process needs to be personalized to each teacher and his students' unique needs. Therefore, these are guidelines—not a rote process to be followed.

1. Ask questions that prompt teachers to discuss the best aspects of the video, such as "What went well?" Listen. Respect what Susan Scott (2002) calls the "sweet purity of silence."

2. Ask questions that prompt teachers to explore other aspects of the video such as "What surprised you? What did you learn?" Listen.

3. Probe further by asking good probing questions such as "What do you mean when you say . . . ?" "Tell me more about . . ." or "What will happen if . . . ?"

4. Identify a student behavior on which the teacher would like to focus by asking questions such as "What would you like to see more of?" "What change would you like to see in your students?" or, "If things were ideal in your class, what would be different? What would you see and hear?"

5. Target data that can be used to measure the desired behavior. This may involve gathering more data, revisiting the data, or meeting again.

6. Collaborate with the teacher to name the compelling, specific, goal that will usually be measured by student data (such as time on task or other forms of engagement data, disruptions, correct responses, students responding to questions, student products, or teacher's anecdotal data).

Coach Resources: What Coaches Do

Step 3a: Explain

Goal: To explain and modify how the new teaching practice will be taught so that it is tailor-made for a teacher's students' unique needs

Actions:

1. Meet the teacher one to one.

2. Give the teacher a copy of a checklist (when appropriate) for the teaching practice being learned.

3. Go through the checklist item by item, and explain each one.

4. After discussing each item, ask the teacher whether or not the item is okay with them or would they like to modify it (95 percent of the time, the teacher will not want to modify it).

5. Modify the form to reflect the teacher's concerns if they wish to change it after discussing the reason why the form is organized as it is.

6. Co-construct an observation protocol for additional teaching practices.

7. Confirm an already scheduled date for you to model in the classroom.

Time: 15–40 minutes

Coach Resources:
What Coaches Do

Step 3b: Mediate the Content

Goal: To prepare and adapt teaching practices (such as content maps, guiding questions, formative assessments, and graphic organizers) being implemented so that they are tailor-made for a teacher's students' unique needs

Actions:

1. Get a copy of the teacher's curriculum materials (textbooks, state and/or school curriculum, state standards, etc.).

2. Look for ways you can speed up coaching by proposing ways the teacher can incorporate a new teaching practice into their teaching routine.

3. Share your list of concepts.

4. Co-construct a lesson plan that integrates the new teaching practices.

Time: 5–30 minutes (excluding preliminary activities)

**Coach Resources:
What Coaches Do**

Step 4: Model

Goal: To ensure the teacher knows what the new teaching practice looks and sounds like when it is employed effectively

Actions:

1. Arrive in the class well before the lesson is to be given.

2. Give the teacher a copy of the co-constructed checklist (when appropriate) for the teaching practice being learned.

3. Explain how the teacher should use the checklist.

4. Ask the teacher if they would like to record it.

5. Speak to students informally before the class begins.

6. Have the teacher introduce you.

7. Prompt the students to create name tents if you don't know their names.

8. Model the lesson, doing everything on the checklist.

9. Involve the teacher in the lesson, and authentically praise the teacher.

10. Keep your model short by focusing on the practice being learned.

11. Offer to download a copy of the lesson to the teacher's computer.

Time: 15–40 minutes

Step 5: Observe

Goal: To gather accurate data on the effectiveness of a teaching practice as a method for achieving the goal

Actions:

1. Arrive in the classroom well before the lesson to confirm that the teacher wants you to observe the lesson.

2. Find an inconspicuous spot in the classroom where you can watch the teacher and the students.

3. Position the video camera so that you will be able to record the entire lesson.

4. Set up the camera on a tripod so your hands are free to take notes.

5. After the teacher begins to use the new practice, be especially attentive for anything the teacher does well.

6. Write brief descriptions of all the positive aspects of the lesson in the comments column.

7. Put a checkmark in the OBS (observe) column beside each teaching practice you see the teacher use, and leave a blank space in the OBS column beside any teaching practices that you do not see.

8. Before leaving the classroom, confirm that you will meet at your predetermined time to discuss the lesson.

9. Download a copy of the lesson onto the teacher's computer before you leave the classroom.

Time: 15–40 minutes

Coach Resources:
What Coaches Do

Step 6: Explore the Lesson

Goal: To identify what went well during the practice attempt and what adjustments need to be made if the goal has not been met

Actions:

1. Prior to meeting, review the recording of the lesson and identify at least three sections that you think are excellent and two sections that you think would be meaningful to discuss.

2. Ask the teacher to also identify three sections that they think are excellent and two sections that they have concerns about.

3. Give the teacher a copy of the observation protocol or protocols.

4. Review the video.

5. Identify at least three clips you think are well done and plan direct, specific, nonattributive feedback.

6. Identify sections that you think would be profitable to discuss.

7. Choose questions (review the question sheet on page 260) that you think will open up the conversation.

8. Meet with the teacher to review the teacher's and your clips.

9. Pause the recording when you talk.

10. Use open-ended nonjudgmental questions to open up meaningful conversation.

11. Identify a SMART goal for the next step.

Time: 20–60 minutes

Coach Resources:
What Coaches Do

How to Get the Most Out of Watching Your Video

Goal: Identify two sections of the video that you like and one or two sections of the video you'd like to further explore

Getting Ready

Watching yourself on video is one of the most powerful strategies professionals can use to improve. However, it can be a challenge. It takes a little time to get used to seeing yourself on screen, so be prepared for a bit of a shock. After a little time, you will become more comfortable with the process.

- Find a place to watch where you won't be distracted.
- You may find it helpful to read through the teacher and student surveys and/or the big-ticket items to remind yourself of things to keep in mind while watching.
- Set aside a block of time, so you can watch the video uninterrupted.
- Make sure you've got a pen and paper ready to take notes.

Watching the Video

- Plan to watch the entire video at one sitting.
- Take notes on anything that is interesting.
- Be certain to write the time from the video beside any note you make so that you can return to it should you wish to.
- People have a tendency to be too hard on themselves, so be sure to really watch for things you like.
- After watching the video, review your notes and circle the items you will discuss with your coach (two you like and one or two you would like to further explore).
- Sit back, relax, and enjoy the experience.

Additional Tools

Watch Your Students

Date:

After watching the video of today's class, please rate how close the behavior of your students is to your goal for an ideal class in the following areas:

	Not Close					*Right On*	
1. Students were engaged in learning (90 percent engagement is recommended).	1	2	3	4	5	6	7
2. Students interacted respectfully.	1	2	3	4	5	6	7
3. Students clearly understand how they are supposed to behave.	1	2	3	4	5	6	7
4. Students rarely interrupted each other.	1	2	3	4	5	6	7
5. Students engaged in high-level conversation.	1	2	3	4	5	6	7
6. Students clearly understand how well they are progressing (or not).	1	2	3	4	5	6	7
7. Students are interested in learning activities in the class.	1	2	3	4	5	6	7

Comments:

Watch Yourself

Date:

After watching the video of today's class, please rate how close your instruction is to your ideal in the following areas:

	Not Close						*Right On*
1. My praise to correction ratio is at least a 3-to-1 ratio.	1	2	3	4	5	6	7
2. I clearly explained expectations prior to each activity.	1	2	3	4	5	6	7
3. My corrections are calm, consistent, immediate, and planned in advance.	1	2	3	4	5	6	7
4. My questions are at the appropriate level (know, understand, do).	1	2	3	4	5	6	7
5. My learning structures (stories, cooperative learning, thinking devices, and experiential learning) were effective.	1	2	3	4	5	6	7
6. I used a variety of learning structures effectively.	1	2	3	4	5	6	7
7. I clearly understand what my students know and don't know.	1	2	3	4	5	6	7

Comments:

Additional Tools

Big-Ticket Items

Content Planning

- Guiding questions
- Learning maps
- Introducing, daily use, and end of unit review
- Lesson planning

Assessment for Learning

- Developing specific proficiencies
- Identifying informal checks for understanding
- Using assessments in the classroom effectively

Instruction

- Stories
- Effective questions
- Cooperative learning
- Thinking prompts
- Challenging assignments
- Experiential learning

Community Building

- Expectations for all activities and transitions
- Reinforcing appropriate behavior (ratio of interaction)
- Correcting behavior fluently
- Increasing interactions (opportunities to respond)
- Physical environment creates a positive and productive learning environment
- Students communicate respectfully
- All students contribute to class discussion

Additional Tools

Coaching Planning Form

Activity	Date	Location	Time
Film the class			
Identify a goal			
Explain the new teaching practice			
Model			
Film/observe the class			
Explore			

Seventh-Grade Math Leadership Team Workshop

Schedule of Activities

8:00–8:05: Welcome

Workshop leader welcomes everyone, thanks them for coming, and articulates our belief that if we tap all the knowledge and expertise of everyone in the group, we can do great things.

8:05–8:25: Introductions

Workshop leader explains that after introductions, we'll review our plan of action for the day.

Procedure for Introductions

- Explain that one person is going to introduce everyone at the table to the group, so that person should take notes.
- Tell everyone that we have a unique way to figure out who will introduce everyone.
- Ask everyone to close their eyes.
- Then, they should point at the person who'll do the introductions. The person who gets the most fingers pointed at becomes the spokesperson.
- Then, they open their eyes and find out who will introduce everyone to the group.
- At the tables, everyone introduces themselves to each other—stating their name, what school they teach at, and some other interesting fact about themselves.
- Then, the designated introducer introduces each person at his or her table to the larger group.

8:25–8:30: Introduction to Unit Organizer

Workshop leader goes through the unit organizer describing events, times, and outcomes.

8:30–9:00: Vignettes

Workshop leader reads each vignette; then, people at each table discuss (a) whether the vignette is accurate, (b) whether something was left out of the vignette, (c) and how the vignette makes each person feel.

9:00–9:45: Team Norms

Workshop leader explains the importance of norms and explains that if we create the right kind of team culture, we will accomplish a great deal. Then, the workshop leader explains the activity.

- Participants at each table write down some of the norms that they think are important.
- They lay their cards on the table and explain to their table groups why they think these norms are important.
- The instructional coach (IC) at the table leads a discussion in which the group at the table synthesizes the norms into key ideas—these ideas are written on a flip chart and reported back to the larger group. The IC reports back for the group.

(These norms will be refined by the leader and returned to the group, desktop published.)

9:45–9:50: Revisit Unit Organizer

Workshop leader revisits the unit organizer and previews what the next activity will be.

9:50–10:00: Break

10:00–11:30: Developing New Scope and Sequence

Workshop leader explains the plan and oversees activities.

Finding Key Indicators in the Text (45 minutes):

- Participants are given pieces of paper that list the 24 key indicators (each group gets either four or five key indicators).

- Participants are directed to find where the key indicators are located in the new text and write the page numbers on the pieces of paper.
- Participants report back to the group, guiding them through the key indicators and where they're located in the text (the person reporting back is someone who hasn't spoken to the group yet).

Placing Key Indicators on a Timeline (45 minutes):

- Participants take their 24 key indicators and place them on the line.
- Each group takes turns placing individual indicators.
- The group discusses the location until they are satisfied with the location.
- Then, another group places another indicator.

11:30–12:00: Lunch

12:00–12:45 Developing Unit Organizers

- Workshop leader explains the plan and oversees activities.
- Each of the five groups picks a unit they want to develop.
- The group brainstorms all ideas, concepts, vocabulary, skills, and big ideas that need to be taught in the unit.
- Each piece of information is written on a sticky note and added to a flip chart.
- When all the pieces of information are on the flip chart, the group arranges them into no more than seven categories.
- The groups of stickies are given headings (which might be a word from a flip chart).
- These groupings will be the unit organizers.

12:45–1:30: Carousel Review of the Draft Unit Organizers

- As with a jigsaw cooperative learning activity, the original groups break into five new groups made up of participants from each group (Groups 1–5); each new group must contain at least one member from each old group.
- The groups rotate through each unit organizer, adding terms and making adjustments to the groupings until everyone has visited and contributed to all five organizers.

1:30–1:45: Break

1:45–2:30: Portfolio Smorgasbord

Workshop leader explains that a key outcome from our work is the development of portfolios containing activities, formative assessments, expectation sheets for activities and transitions, learning sheets, and other good stuff.

Workshop leader explains the activity.

- The large group will self-organize into three groups.
- Three different learning situations will be set up.
  - *Expectations.* Tricia will give a 15-minute overview of expectations, explaining the activity and transition planning sheets and whatever else she can cram into 15 minutes.
  - *Formative Assessment.* Workshop leader will give a 15-minute overview of some of Richard Stiggins' ideas about formative assessment.
  - *New Textbook.* Workshop leader will give a 15-minute overview of some of the features of the new textbook.
- Each group will rotate through and listen to each of the three 15-minute presentations.

2:30–3:15: Teachers' Guide

Workshop leader explains that one of the outcomes of this project will be the development of a teaching guide for math. The teaching guide will be written largely by this group, so we can all learn the good teaching practices that individuals among us are using.

Workshop leader explains and oversees the activity.

- In each group, participants take 15 minutes to note down all of the things they consider best teaching practices.
- First, each member makes a personal list of teaching practices on teaching cards (label these cards as *teaching practices*).
- Then, the list is synthesized by the table group and noted on a flip chart.
- A member of the table group who hasn't presented yet explains what the group recorded on the list.
- The workshop then, essentially, ends with an upbeat discussion of effective teaching practices.

Workshop leader explains the next steps.

- We'll be meeting on April 22.
- At that time, the following will be shared:
  o A values statement that embodies the norms identified by the group
  o A draft course organizer based on the identified scope and sequence
  o Five draft unit organizers based on the work completed today
  o A rough draft of the Teachers' Guide

Intensive Learning Teams

Vignettes

A Magical Moment

Moments happen with kids that are just incredible. I had one grade schooler who had never written, and it was my first year in the classroom. Well, all kids at our school get to make choices, and he could choose not to do things that are hard. But I said to him, "It's okay to do things that are hard." Eventually, that little boy decided to take a risk and write something down. I looked at what he'd written, and it looked kind of poetic, and I told him, "You're a poet; did you ever know that?" He said no. I said, "You mean this is your first time writing, and you didn't know you were a poet?"

From that moment on, he started to believe in himself. All of a sudden, this kid started feverishly writing. It was a magical moment. Those kinds of things happen all the time. There's artfulness around teaching, helping kids to build identities for themselves that they didn't really know they could build. It's exciting.

A couple of months later, one of the teachers talked to him and said, "Gee, you're so different this year."

He said, "Well, I'm a poet."

Precious Cargo

I really came to teaching through the back door, watching what was happening with my kids. I guess that's why I became a teacher: Because, watching them, I realized that education should be an amazing experience.

At my school, it's been really wonderful, empowering. I know I've made a difference, and I know I respect the kids that come into my room. It's been an amazing four years here. Just to be able to work so individually, to have small class sizes, to be in a small school where you know everyone by name and you have a sense of responsibility for each other, to see how kids have grown, that's a magical thing to watch.

I feel privileged. I feel that seriously. It's about the most important work a person can do. I'm just one of the people who can wake up each morning and say I love what I do and look forward to what I do. I feel just really fortunate, and it's wonderful. I think it's critical how I react, and how I support the kids, and help create an environment.

They are precious cargo.

Everything I Stand For

You've got to believe in these kids because a lot of them don't have anyone else who believes in them. But that doesn't make it easy. We face a lot of challenges. We've seen that when parents get involved in kids' education it works like a charm, but too often parents don't have the time or inclination to give that support. There are discipline problems, and too many kids seem unmotivated. And we don't have time to do everything we need to do. It's more of a challenge to teach these kids, but that's why it can be more satisfying.

I love the diversity, the fact that they come from all these levels and backgrounds. A lot of the time, the kids don't realize their potential, and they might have jack squat for friendship at home. If I can help them feel hope, if I can help them feel respected, I can do something really important. I've taught in other places, and I like the relationships I get to have with my students. They give back to me. People have tried to get me to move to other schools and districts where the kids are more affluent and there are fewer challenges. I just don't know how to tell them that that kind of move goes against everything I stand for.

Empathy, Compassion, and Kinship

I think emotional safety is a core need for kids. I think that they need to feel like they're accepted, not going to be judged, teased, or harassed. You know, kids can be quite mean to each other. I can't imagine how learning can take place if that emotional safety isn't present. Yet often that is not prioritized. Often what is prioritized is classroom behavior. I don't know if this is something a kid would be able to articulate, but I do know that my happy days in school were when I felt loved and supported. And I also had days when I wasn't sure.

So when I talk about a partnership school, I'm going to start with what you shouldn't see. I don't want trivial celebrations where we do the Mexican hat dance and now we've got Mexico. What I don't want is that diversity is about you celebrate Hanukah, and I celebrate Kwanzaa. It's not just about cultural rituals! It's about racism; it's about fat kids and thin kids; it's about homophobia; it's about power and who actually has lunch every day and who doesn't. Who gets a car when they turn 16, and whose family can't even afford shoes. I think a partnership school should be about helping kids to feel empathy and compassion and kinship.

Ether

Racism can be like ether at my school: it's floating, and you catch a whiff of it.

There is too much of institutional racism at my school. I am really appalled that in the year 2010 I hear racist comments in school from my colleagues. Sometimes, the racism is less obvious. Maybe teachers categorize people based on race. Maybe they skirt the issue of race. Maybe they ignore racial issues, saying, "I treat everyone equally." Well, not everyone is equal; not everyone is the same.

There is a dire need for training in this area in my school. It's not right that such narrow-minded individuals teach our children. Too many people are unaware or do not care about the struggles of all ethnic groups. These teachers are doing a disservice to children, the community, the district, and the profession of teaching.

I Teach

I keep coming back to teach every year so that I can experience the light-bulb moment. I teach to instill a love of learning and a spirit of inquiry. I love seeing them learn, move forward, gain confidence. That gives me a great sense of accomplishment. I teach because I know I'm making a difference in the lives of students.

I teach because I love the fellowship of the staff. I love the friend-ship and the support, working with the faculty throughout the school. I love it when the teachers have the same spirit of inquiry that I want to see in my students.

Just a simple event makes it all worthwhile. I love it when a student comes back and says, "I remembered what you said about being a gentleman," when a student comes back and says, "I'm reading more now." I love it when a mom says, "I'm glad you're teaching my daughter, because you really helped my son."

I teach because I learn a great deal from the kids. I love how I feel when things are going great with a class. Nothing is better that when you're flying, and they're flying with you.

Seventh-Grade Math Leadership Team Workshop

Workshop Evaluation Form

Date:

Please rate today's program by circling the appropriate number.

	Disagree						*Agree*
1. I feel that my knowledge and expertise were validated today.	1	2	3	4	5	6	7
2. People were listening to me when I spoke today.	1	2	3	4	5	6	7
3. We are creating practical, useful materials on this team.	1	2	3	4	5	6	7
4. I am committed to this project.	1	2	3	4	5	6	7
5. The chance to work with my peers, provided by this session, will help me reach more students.	1	2	3	4	5	6	7
6. I had sufficient opportunities to give input today.	1	2	3	4	5	6	7
7. I like the materials we're creating.	1	2	3	4	5	6	7
8. I enjoy working with the people on this team.	1	2	3	4	5	6	7
9. I plan to implement what we're creating.	1	2	3	4	5	6	7
10. I know what the state standards are for seventh-grade math.	1	2	3	4	5	6	7
11. The work we did today was worth the time and effort.	1	2	3	4	5	6	7
12. I am excited about this project.	1	2	3	4	5	6	7

Comments:

Dialogue Structures

Talking Cards

Talking cards allows everyone to participate anonymously in a group. Each member of a group is given an index card and a marker that is the same color. Someone poses a question, and each member records their response (one idea per card). A participant can contribute as many responses as they want, but each is on a separate card. Cards are then collected and laid out so everyone can see the responses. Members of the group then sort the cards into themes or clusters as a way to make sense of all the ideas presented and label each one. This process promotes lots of invaluable conversation among the participants. If there are multiple questions to be addressed, use different-colored index cards for each (York-Barr, Sommers, Ghere, Montie, 2006, pp. 187–188).

Video Club

Video club (Wallace, 1991, p. 8, cited in Bailey, Curtis, & Nunam, 1998, p. 553) provides an opportunity for teachers to review and reflect on what actually goes on in their classrooms. Groups of four teachers gather monthly to review and reflect on short segments of videotapes of themselves teaching (approximately 10 minutes). The value here is that the teachers do not have to attend to the whole class but only to the dynamics that are taking place on the video. The intent is not to evaluate but to provide an opportunity for the teacher (whose video is being watched) to reflect on how they responded, why they responded the way they did, and what they might want to change in the future. It also provides an opportunity to pay more attention to student responses during instruction (York-Barr et al., 2006, p. 192).

Synectics

Synectics is a specific type of metaphor that elicits higher-order thinking and application. Have each group write down four nouns— for example, *dog, window, truck, fence.* Then ask them to select one of their nouns and complete a given sentence using the format *X is like Y because . . .* Here is an example: "Teaching is like a window because it allows you to see things more clearly and opens your mind to many possibilities." Other words like *discipline, standards, mission, knowledge,* and *professional,* to name just a few, promote higher-level thinking about participants' experiences as teachers. It also enhances their understanding of the professional life of colleagues.

Another way to use metaphors in groups is to reflect on how the group members view something currently, and how they hope to view it at the end of the year. When the individual results are shared, it provides insight not only into themselves but also into others who are traveling the same road. Teachers rarely talk with one another about their profession in such a reflective way (York-Barr et al., 2006, pp. 186–187).

One-Minute Papers (or Half-Sheet Response)

One-minute papers (also known as the half-sheet response) focus on the content of a day and provide feedback to the leader as well the rest of the group. There are two questions that need to be answered, "What was the most important or useful thing you learned today? What important question do you still have?" (Angelo & Cross, 1993, p. 148). The participants are given one minute and are timed. Answers can be written on index cards or half-sheets of scrap paper. These can be used to begin the next day's discussion, to facilitate discussion within a group, or provide the leaders feedback on the participants' understanding (Angelo & Cross, 1993, pp. 148–153).

Muddiest Point

Muddiest point is a very simple technique to use. It is also very efficient, as it provides a high information return for a very low investment of time and energy. This strategy consists of asking participants to jot down a quick response to the following question: "What was the muddiest point in _____?" (Angelo & Cross, 1993, p. 154). A procedure that could be used is to reserve a few minutes at the end of the presentation. Have index cards at each table for each member to write their responses on. Allow each person time to respond, and then have them put the cards in the center of the table. Give the group a short break; when they return, have them discuss what each person wrote. If further clarification is needed, perhaps the presenter or members of other groups could provide input. Depending on the organization and schedule, muddiest points might have to be addressed the next day. However, immediate feedback would be better (Angelo & Cross, 1993, pp. 154–158).

One-Sentence Summary

One-sentence summary is a simple strategy that allows participants to answer the questions, "'Who does what to whom, when, where, how, and why?' (represented by the letters WDWWWWHW) about a given topic'" (Angelo & Cross, 1993, p. 183). Next, members need to synthesize their answers into a grammatical sentence that follows the WDWWWWHW pattern. If the group is small enough, have members share orally with one another, and have someone record the responses. These could then be shared in a whole-group setting (Angelo & Cross, 1993, pp. 183–187).

Pro and Con Grid

A pro and con grid has probably been used by all of us at one time or another as individuals or in groups in an effort to clarify our thoughts about a question, issue, decision, or dilemma that has important implications for a particular situation. Given a prompt, asking groups to come up with a minimum number of pros and cons might be suggested as well was trying to view the problem from more than one viewpoint—such as those of an administrator, teacher, parent, and school board member. Prior to beginning, it should be determined if phrases are adequate, or if the pros and cons should be expressed in complete sentences.

Pros and cons listed by each group can be compared in a whole-group setting to see if they have some in common. This provides an excellent opportunity for looking objectively at something and then being able to look at the value of competing ideas (Angelo & Cross, 1993, pp. 168–171).

Stickies

Stickies is similar to a technique called "chalk talk" (Sullivan & Glanz, 2006, p. 131) except that the ideas and comments of the group leader are written on large pieces of chart paper that are taped to the wall. Small pads of sticky notes are made available, so participants can add their ideas, comments, questions, and so forth, to those statements or questions written on the large sheets of chart paper. These can be left on the wall for a while, so people can continue to add comments. A way to share all the input with everyone is to have each main topic or question and the accompanying comments typed up and shared with the whole group (Sullivan & Glanz, 2006, p. 132).

Application Cards

Application cards provides an opportunity for a small group to think about something they have just learned or from a prompt given.

If a prompt is used, make sure everyone is responding to the same prompt. Index cards or sticky notes are passed out, and each person is asked to write at least one real-world application for their particular prompt or what they just learned. Group members then share their ideas among themselves. All ideas can then be posted on a large chart tablet or other space for the whole group to view. Given time, particular items of interest can be discussed in a whole-group setting, or small groups could select their favorite idea in their particular group and then share it with the whole group (Cross & Angelo, 1993, pp. 236–239).

Nominal Group Process

Nominal (in name only) group process involves groups of four to six. Everyone involved will be working on a written statement of the problem to be addressed. Each person spends about five minutes writing out ideas about or responses to the problem. Once everyone has done this, small groups are formed, and each member contributes one idea to be put on a chalkboard or chart tablet. The process continues around the group until all the ideas are on the chart. No ideas are eliminated at this point, but clarification may be asked for. If there are time constraints, this whole process can take place in a group setting, going round robin. Participants then rank their top three choices, and the facilitator circles the ideas with the most votes.

This process is very democratic. Everyone's ideas are recognized and validated, and individual members are more likely to accept the group's preferences (Sullivan & Glanz, 2006, pp. 130–131).

Post-Up

Post-Up, using sticky notes, is a great way to collect all kinds of pieces of information about a problem situation or question. It enables a group to collect all this information in one place and actively involves everyone, as each individual probably has pertinent information. Because everyone is involved, rather than a mere few, focus on solutions to the problem is increased. It is also a more efficient way than conventional brainstorming to generate lots of ideas.

Each person, without talking, has their own pad of sticky notes on which they write statements or ideas that help solve the question or problem. Since ideas may be considered as facts, opinions, or guesses, each person should indicate which they think applies by putting an F, O, or G in the lower right-hand corner of each sticky note. Different-colored notes can be used for each letter as well. When everyone is done, leave the notes in place for a while. New and useful information might appear later. At the appropriate time, the group can then evaluate the usefulness of items posted (Straker, 1997, pp. 27–34).

Swap Sort

The swap sort, using sticky notes, is a way to help you prioritize a list of items generated by a group, all of which relate to a specific problem or objective. They are usually not organized and need to be sorted into order of importance. The goal may be to rank all the items in order of importance, perhaps choosing only one or two to address. A list of 10 or fewer items is suggested, as sorting a longer list can be very time consuming. It is also helpful to see if there are notes that can be combined or that repeat one another. Another way to shorten a longer list is to select a given number of notes (five, for example), and transfer them to a shorter list.

Before shortening a list or prioritizing a final list, the group needs to decide what criteria make one item more important than another. This is an important step so that there is a consistent way of judging each item. After putting all notes selected vertically above one another, begin at the top of the list, and compare the first two. If the second one is determined to be more important than the first, swap them. Compare the next two and follow the same procedure. Continue this process until there are no more pairs that need to be swapped, and the group is satisfied with the final list (Straker, 1997, pp. 35–37).

Keynote Review

Keynote review requires chart paper and colored markers—one color per group. The following is a modified version of the original. Following a presentation at a conference, inservice, or seminar, participants are divided into groups. Each group is given a piece of chart tablet paper and a colored marker. A recorder in each group records 5 to 10 points members gleaned from the session, and each group either shares their information orally, or the sheets are posted on the wall for other participants to review on their own. If charts are going to be posted for others to view, provide time for members to circulate and view the items identified by each group (Solem & Pike, 1998).

Resource B

Research

Research on Coaching

We have been studying instructional coaching at the Kansas Coaching Project since 1996, though we didn't realize that was what we were studying when we started on this journey. Initially, my goal was to provide ongoing support for professional learning. It was clear to me that traditional professional development—usually one-day workshops—was not leading to real change, and I wanted to find a way to provide the kind of support teachers needed.

Our initial studies explored the concept of learning consultants, onsite staff members who provided support for teachers. In 1999, we began experimenting with instructional collaborators, onsite staff developers who explained, modeled, and supported teachers as they implemented new practices. In 2003, instructional collaborators became instructional coaches, and we continued to refine our approach to coaching. In 2004, I published my first article on instructional coaching in the *Journal of Staff Development*.

Between 1999 and 2007, I conducted several informal studies as I refined our coaching model. These studies included surveys of teachers, interviews with teachers, dozens of interviews with coaches, and feedback from coaches on implementation rates. Many of these informal studies are included in *Instructional Coaching: A Partnership Approach to Improving Instruction* (Knight, 2007). Others are available online at www.instructionalcoach.org/research.html.

In 2009, Jake Cornett and I published a chapter on research on coaching in a book I edited, *Coaching: Approaches and Perspectives*. Although there were few rigorous, published studies of coaching, in each study we reviewed, we found that professional development without coaching did not make an impact on teaching practices. Professional learning that involved coaching, however, did lead to improvements in teacher efficacy and teaching practice.

Implementation Study

Jake Cornett and I also conducted a more rigorous study of the impact of coaching, and we presented the findings at the American Educational Research Association (AERA) in San Diego in 2009. The paper from that presentation is available at www.instructionalcoach.org/research.html. For the study, we offered an afterschool workshop on the *Unit Organizer* (Lenz, Bulgren, Schumaker, Deshler, & Boudah, 1994). The unit organizer is a planning and teaching routine that guides teachers through the development of guiding questions and a map for planning a unit, and then guides teachers on how to share the map and questions throughout a unit of instruction with students.

Instructional coaches in the Topeka School District indentified 50 teachers from the district who were interested in learning the unit organizer. All the teachers attended an afterschool workshop on the unit organizer. Then, the names of everyone attending the workshop were placed in a hat, literally, and 25 names were drawn. The 25 teachers whose names were drawn were assigned a coach to assist with implementation. The 25 other teachers, whose names were not drawn, did not receive coaching support.

The instructional coaches (ICs) used most of the components of coaching described here. ICs helped teachers adapt the material to meet their students' needs, modeled in teachers' classrooms, observed teachers teaching the unit organizer, and provided feedback. We observed all the teachers to see whether coaching had an impact on teaching practices.

To conduct our observations of all teachers in the study, we trained research assistants to observe for specific teaching practices. We created checklists describing effective teaching practices for using the unit organizer. These practices were (a) reviewing previous content learned prior to starting the day's lesson, (b) introducing new content to be learned that day, (c) adding new content to the unit organizer when appropriate, and (d) using the device to end each lesson. Then our army of observers (a total of 23 research assistants) visited the classes of all 50 teachers. Most of the classes taught were observed by research assistants for one entire unit of instruction. We also conducted follow-up interviews with most of the participants to see if they continued to use the unit organizer.

The results suggest that coaching made a significant difference (see Figure B.1). In classes of teachers who did not receive coaching, observers saw evidence of implementation 36 percent of the time. In classes taught by teachers who received coaching, observers saw evidence of use 92 percent of the time.

Further, as Figure B.2 indicates, there was a dramatic difference in the quality of instruction in classes with coaching versus those who did not have coaching. When we placed average scores on a 10-point scale, the effective teaching practices were more than twice as common in coached classrooms than they were in classrooms where teachers did not receive coaching.

Finally, our follow-up interviews were also telling. When we asked teachers who were coached whether or not they thought the

Figure B.1   What We Found

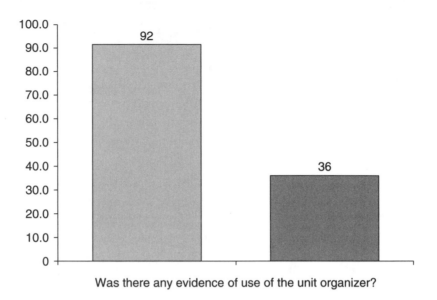

Was there any evidence of use of the unit organizer?

Figure B.2   What We Found

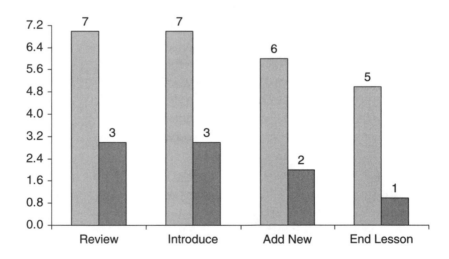

unit organizer helped their students learn, fully 100 percent—22 out 22—agreed, whereas only 12 of 17 of the non-coached teachers agreed. Also, when we asked teachers whether they continued to use the new practice, 15 of 22 coached teachers said they continued, whereas only 3 of 17 non-coached teachers continued use. The results strongly suggest that coaching increases teacher implementation, increases the quality of teacher implementation, and increases the likelihood that teachers will continue to implement what they have learned.

Other Studies

At the Kansas Coaching Project, we continue to study who coaches are, what they do, and how they should best proceed. Recently, my colleagues Barbara Bradley, Irma Brasseur-Hock, Mike Hock, Tom Skrtic, and I have been conducting a design study of instructional coaching, and many of the practices described in this book grew out of this work. Also, my colleagues Belinda Berry Mitchell, Jake Cornett, Michael Kennedy, Leslie Novosel, Tom Skrtic, and I have been conducting qualitative analysis of the characteristics of effective coaches. Much of the data from that study inform the description of coaching attributes included in this book. For more information on our research on instructional coaching, visit www .instructionalcoach.org/research.

Research on Workshops

Design and Method

I conducted a careful study of the partnership approach to presenting and shared the findings of the study at the American Educational Researcher Association in 1999. A complete copy of the findings can be downloaded from www.instructionalcoach.com. To look at the impact of the partnership approach, I used what researchers call a counterbalanced design, which works well in education because the same groups experience two different approaches, so each group is its own experimental and control group.

In the experiment, I compared two approaches to leading a workshop—the partnership approach and a traditional approach. The partnership approach was grounded in the partnership principles, and throughout the session I used stories, reflection learning, thinking prompts, experiential learning, cooperative learning, and effective questions. The traditional approach was based on the expert model, with an emphasis on the importance of fidelity, and I delivered the content in lecture format, pausing every 15 minutes for questions. We video recorded each session, and I and another person checked to make sure that the same content was covered in the two different sessions and that each session was the same length.

Two groups of teachers attended workshops, and each group attended two different workshops. Each group received a two-hour workshop on the *Visual Imagery Strategy* (Schumaker, Deshler, Zemitzsch, & Warner, 1993) followed by a two-hour workshop on the *Self-Questioning Strategy* (Schumaker, Deshler, Nolan, & Allen, 1994).

For one group—let's give them the sexy name Group A—I delivered the visual imagery workshop using the partnership approach to presenting. Then in Group A's second workshop, I used a traditional approach. For the second group, let's call them Group B, I again presented visual imagery in the first workshop and self-questioning in the second workshop. For Group B, however, I switched the order in which I used the partnership approach and the traditional approach. Then, once both groups had attended both workshops, I compared the results of the partnership approach with the results of the traditional approach (see Table B.1).

Table B.1 Counterbalanced Design

Group	First Session	Second Session
Group A	Visual imagery	Self-questioning
Training Model	Partnership learning	Traditional learning
Group B	Visual imagery	Self-questioning
Training Model	Traditional learning	Partnership learning

Research Questions, Measures, and Results

The study was built around four research questions.

1. Engagement. Were participants engaged in one workshop more than the other?

I tried to determine an answer to this question by giving every participant a form with numbers on a scale from one to seven, which participants used to self-assess their level of engagement (1 = *not engaged*, 7 = *very engaged*). During the workshop, a timer rang every 10 minutes, and participants circled the appropriate number at each ring. I then calculated median scores and compared the results from the two approaches. As Figure B.3 shows, the participants in the partnership workshop were much more engaged.

2. Comprehension. Did participants better comprehend the content taught in one workshop than the other?

To answer this question, I gave participants a workshop evaluation that asked them questions about their comprehension of the content (such as, "Am I ready to teach this strategy?"). On evaluation forms from the partnership workshop, 81.1 percent of scores were in the agree to stongly agree range, but on the traditional workshop forms, only 46.3 percent of the scores were in the agree to strongly agree range—almost 35 points lower. I also answered this question by giving everyone a test to see how much they had learned at the end of each workshop. On average, participants in the partnership workshop scored 5 percent points higher than did those in the traditional workshop, a statistically significant difference.

Figure B.3   Engagement Form/Median Scores

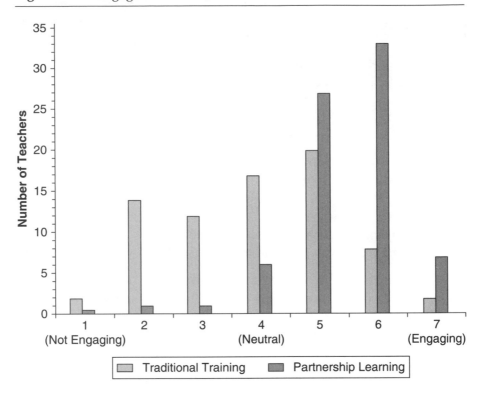

3. Implementation. Were participants more likely to implement what they learned after one workshop than another?

To answer this, at the end of the second workshop, I gave everyone a simple question: "Now that you have learned about two strategies, which of the two do you believe you are most likely to teach?" Teachers chose a strategy explained through the partnership approach over a strategy explained through traditional training by more than a 4:1 ratio. Fifty-nine teachers stated that they were more likely to teach a strategy that they had learned through partnership learning, and 14 teachers stated that they were more likely to teach a strategy that they had learned through traditional training.

4. Enjoyment. Did participants enjoy themselves in one workshop more than another?

To answer this question, I used the workshop evaluation form and asked questions about how much participants enjoyed the workshop. On evaluations of the traditional workshop, 40.59 percent of the participants' median scores were in the agree range on the evaluation form. On evaluations of the partnership workshop, 78.2 percent of the scores were in the agree range—a difference of close to 40 percent. Clearly, during the partnership workshop, teachers had more fun.

Conclusion

All the scores analyzed suggest that the partnership approach, compared with the traditional approach, is more enjoyable and engaging, more likely to encourage implementation, and more likely to offer learning experiences that will be remembered.

Research on Intensive Learning Teams

More recently, I have been studying intensive learning teams (ILTs), and my research on this approach to professional learning is at this point informal. During intensive learning teams, as outlined in Chapter 6, I bring together groups of teachers from across a district who are all teaching the same class. In most cases, my colleagues and I have worked with mathematics teachers, but we have also worked with reading teachers.

The process for ILTs was originally the result of my collaboration with Dr. Ethel Edwards when Ethel was the associate superintendent for mathematics in USD 501, Topeka, Kansas. I have subsequently refined the process in several other districts in the United States. In each situation, intensive learning teams have been used as a vehicle for teachers to write a new curriculum. ILTs have always included general and special education teachers.

The ILT process varies each time, but it also has common features. Specifically, all ILTs have involved (a) enrollment interviews, (b) identifying team values, (c) identifying where key indicators for standards will be taught, (d) developing guiding questions, and (e) creating learning maps. The curriculum is always developed by small groups of teachers working on three to five units at a time and then refined as all other teachers have input into the draft units. Many of the dialogue structures I've described in the book are used during ILTs.

In May 2010, I facilitated a five-day ILT with sixth-grade mathematics teachers in Cecil County, Maryland. The sessions included mathematics teachers and special education teachers. During the five days, spread over one month, the participants created a new curriculum for sixth-grade mathematics by unpacking the standards to be taught during the year, identifying an appropriate instructional sequence for units, and by creating guiding questions and learning maps for each unit. Additionally, participants unpacked each guiding question to identify specific proficiencies (precise, discrete statements that answer each question) and checks for understanding for each specific proficiency.

Participants completed the survey at the end of the workshop, and identified their level of skill prior to the ILT and their level of skill at the end of the ILT. In total, 29 participants answered at least some of the questions. The items on the survey and the raw scores from respondents are included in Table B.2.

Table B.2 Intensive Learning Teams: Pre- and Post-Assessment, May 2010

Completely Skilled	Somewhat Skilled	Slightly Skilled	Somewhat Unskilled	Novice		Completely Skilled	Somewhat Skilled	Slightly Skilled	Somewhat Unskilled	Novice
6	11	9		3	I know how to create a unit organizer.	21	8			
	1	5	8	15	I know how to write specific proficiencies.	11	14	4		
8	8	8	2	3	I know how to teach the unit organizer in my class.	15	12	1	1	
1	4	10	7	7	I understand how to teach the concept mastery routine.	4	17	7	1	
10	8	5	3	3	I fully understand the content to be taught in sixth grade.	17	9	1	1	1
12	10	3	3	1	I completely understand the state standards.	20	7	2		
9	11	4	4	1	I know where our curriculum addresses state standards.	18	9	2		
5	8	8	5		The scope and sequence of the curriculum is appropriate for my students.	13	11	2		
7	8	8	3		I am ready to teach the curriculum as it stands.	17	9			
6	8	10	3		I am well prepared to frequently assess student learning.	20	7			

In order to better depict the impact of the ILT, I have reproduced the above data, including only the scores for completely skilled. The data suggest that teachers see themselves as having expanded their skills in all areas. Those results are depicted in Table B.3. You may want to review the table with all raw scores to see additional areas of growth, from slightly skilled to somewhat skilled, for example.

The results suggest that teachers at least believe that they know more about their content, are better prepared to teach it, and that they better understand high-leverage teaching practices (unit organizers,

Table B.3 Intensive Learning Teams: Pre- and Post-Assessment, May 2010: Snapshot

	Number of Participants	Completely Skilled—Pre-Assessment	Completely Skilled—Post-Assessment
I know how to create a unit organizer.	29	6	21
I know how to write specific proficiencies.	29		11
I know how to teach the unit organizer in my class.	29	8	15
I understand how to teach the concept mastery routine.	29	1	4
I fully understand the content to be taught in sixth grade.	29	10	17
I completely understand the state standards.	29	12	20
I know where our curriculum addresses state standards.	29	9	18
The scope and sequence of the curriculum is appropriate for my students.	26	5	13
I am ready to teach the curriculum as it stands.	26	7	17
I am well prepared to frequently assess student learning.	27	6	20

concept mastery routine, formative assessments, etc.) they can use to ensure students master the content.

The data on ILTs are just a beginning. We will be conducting ongoing research on ILTs to determine whether the perceived deeper knowledge translates into increased student achievement and changes in teaching. We will also continue to do research on other forms of professional learning. As we uncover new findings, we will post the results on www.instructionalcoach.org/research.html.

References and Further Readings

Ainsworth, L. (2003). *Unwrapping the standards: A simple process to make standards manageable.* Englewood, CO: Lead + Learn Press.

Allen, D. (2001). *Getting things done: The art of stress-free productivity.* New York: Penguin.

Allen, D. (2008). *Making it all work: Winning at the game of work and the business of life.* New York: Penguin.

Alliance for Excellent Education. (2005). *About the crisis.* Retrieved December 7, 2009, from http://www.all4ed.org/aboutthecrisis.

Amos, J. (2008). *Dropouts, diplomas, and dollars: U.S. high schools and the nation's economy.* Washington, DC: Alliance for Excellent Education.

Anderson, J. R. (1976). *Language, memory, and thought.* Hillsdale, NJ: Erlbaum.

Angelo, T. A., & Cross, K. P. (1993). *Classroom assessment techniques* (2nd ed.). San Francisco: Jossey-Bass.

Babauta, L. (2009). *The power of less: The fine art of limiting yourself to the essential . . . in business and in life.* New York: Hyperion.

Bailey, K., Curtis, A., & Nunan, D. (1998). Undeniable insights: Collaborative use of three professional development models. *TESOL Quarterly, 32*(3), 546–556.

Bain, A. (2007). *The self-organizing school: Next-generation comprehensive school reforms.* Lanham, MD: Rowman & Littlefield Education.

Barkley, S. G. (2010). *Quality teaching in a culture of coaching.* Lanham, MD: Rowman & Littlefield.

Barth, R. (1990). A personal vision of a good school. *Phi Delta Kappan, 71*(7), 512–516.

Belsky, S. (2010). *Making ideas happen: Overcoming the obstacles between vision and reality.* New York: Penguin.

Bernstein, R. J. (1983). *Beyond objectivism and relativism: Science, hermeneutics, and praxis.* Philadelphia: University of Pennsylvania Press.

Block, P. (1993). *Stewardship: Choosing service over self-interest.* San Francisco: Berrett-Koehler.

Bloom, G. S., Castagna, C. L., Moir, E., & Warren, B. (2005). *Blended coaching: Skills and strategies to support principal development.* Thousand Oaks, CA: Corwin.

Bohm, D. (1996). *On dialogue.* London: Routledge.

Brown, J., & Isaacs, D. (2005). *The world café: Shaping our futures through conversations that matter.* San Francisco: Berrett-Koehler.

Brown, T. (2009). *Change by design: How design thinking transforms organizations and inspires innovation.* New York: HarperCollins.

Brubaker, J. W., Case, C. W., & Reagan, J. G. (1994). *Becoming a reflective educator: How to build a culture of inquiry in the schools.* Thousand Oaks, CA: Corwin.

Buber, M. (1970). *I and thou.* New York: Walter Kaufmann.

Buckingham, M. (1999). *First, break all the rules: What the world's greatest managers do differently.* New York: Simon & Schuster.

Burkins, J. M. (2009). *Practical literacy coaching: A collection of tools to support your work.* Thousand Oaks, CA: Corwin.

Carnegie, D. (1936). *How to win friends and influence people.* New York: Simon & Schuster.

Chapuis, J. (2009). *Seven strategies of assessment for learning.* New York: Allyn & Bacon.

City, E. A., Elmore, R. F., Fiarman, S. E., & Teitel, L. (2009). *Instructional rounds in education: A network approach to improving teaching and learning.* Boston: Harvard Education Press.

Collins, J. (2001). *Good to great.* New York: Harper Collins.

Collins, J., & Porras, J. I. (1994). *Built to last: Successful habits of visionary companies.* New York: HarperCollins.

Cornett, J., & Knight, J. (2009). Research on coaching. In J. Knight (Ed.), *Coaching: Approaches and perspectives* (pp. 192–216). Thousand Oaks, CA: Corwin.

Costa, A., & Garmston, R. (2002). *Cognitive coaching: A foundation for renaissance schools* (2nd ed.). Norwood, MA: Christopher-Gordon Publishers.

Covey, S. (1989). *The 7 habits of highly effective people: Powerful lessons in personal change.* New York: Simon & Schuster.

Csikszentmihalyi, M. (1990). *Flow: The psychology of optimal experience.* New York: Harper Collins.

Csikszentmihalyi, M. (1994). *The evolving self: A psychology for the third millennium.* New York: Harper Collins.

Danielson, C. (2007). *Enhancing professional practice: A framework for teaching.* Alexandria, VA: Association for Supervision and Curriculum Development.

Davenport, T. H. (2005). *Thinking for a living: How to get better performance and results from knowledge workers.* Boston: Harvard Business School Press.

Decker, B. (2008). *You've got to be believed to be heard: The complete book of speaking in business and in life* (rev. ed.). New York: St. Martin's Press.

Denning, S. (2005). *The leader's guide to storytelling: Mastering the art and discipline of business narrative.* San Francisco: Jossey-Bass.

Downey, C. J., Steffy, B. E., English, F. W., Frase, L. E., & Poston, W. K. (Eds.). (2004). *The three-minute classroom walk-through: Changing school supervisory practice one teacher at a time.* Thousand Oaks, CA: Corwin.

Duarte, N. (2008). *Slide:ology: The art and science of creating great presentations.* Sebastopol, CA: O'Reilly Media.

DuFour, R., DuFour, R., Eaker, R. E., & Karhanek, G. (2010). *Raising the bar and closing the gap: Whatever it takes.* Bloomington, IN: Solution Tree.

DuFour, R., & Eaker, R. E. (1998). *Professional learning communities at work: Best practices for enhancing student achievement.* Bloomington, IN: National Education Service.

Dweck, C. S. (2006). *Mindset: The new psychology of success.* New York: Random House.

Eisler, R. (1988). *The chalice and the blade: Our history, our future.* New York: HarperCollins.

Erickson, H. L. (2007). *Concept-based curriculum and instruction for the thinking classroom.* Thousand Oaks, CA: Corwin.

Evans, S., & Cohen, S. S. (2000). *Hot buttons: How to resolve conflict and cool everyone down.* New York: HarperCollins.

Fearofphysics.com. (n.d.). *What is friction?* Retrieved August 30, 2010, from http://www.fearofphysics.com/Friction/frintro.html.

Friedman, S. (2008). *Total leadership: Be a better leader, have a richer life.* Boston: Harvard Business School Publishing.

Freire, P. (1970). *Pedagogy of the oppressed.* New York: Continuum.

Fromm, E. (1941). *Escape from freedom.* New York: Farrar & Rinehart.

Fullan, M. (1993). *Change forces: Probing the depths of educational reform.* New York: Falmer Press.

Fullan, M. (2008). *The six secrets of change: What the best leaders do to help their organizations survive and thrive.* San Francisco: Jossey-Bass.

Fullan, M. (2010a). *All systems go: The change imperative for whole system reform.* Thousand Oaks, CA: Corwin.

Fullan, M. (2010b). *Motion leadership: The skinny on becoming change savvy.* Thousand Oaks, CA: Corwin.

Gallagher, W. (2009). *Rapt: Attention and the focused life.* New York: Penguin Group.

Gallo, C. (2006). *Ten simple secrets of the world's greatest business communicators.* Naperville, IL: Sourcebooks.

Gallo, C. (2009). *The presentation secrets of Steve Jobs: How to be insanely great in front of any audience.* New York: McGraw-Hill.

Gawande, A. (2007). *Better: A surgeon's notes on performance.* New York: Henry Holt.

Gawande, A. (2010). *The checklist manifesto: How to get things right.* New York: Metropolitan.

Godin, S. (2000). *Unleash your idea virus.* New York: Fast Company.

Godin, S. (2001). *Really bad PowerPoint (and how to avoid it).* Adobe Reader. Do You Zoom, Inc.

Godin, S. (2010). *Linchpin: Are you indispensable?* New York: Portfolio.

Goffee, R., & Jones, G. (2009). *Clever: Leading your smartest, most creative people.* Boston: Harvard Business School Press.

Goldsmith, M. (2010). *Mojo: How to get it, how to keep it, how to get it back if you lose it.* New York: Hyperion.

Goldsmith, M., Laurence, L., & Freas, A. (2000). *Coaching for leadership: how the world's greatest coaches help leaders learn.* San Francisco: Jossey-Bass.

Goleman, D. (2007). *Social intelligence: The new science of human relationships.* New York: Random House.

Goleman, D., Boyatzis, R., & McKee, A. (2004). *Primal leadership: Realizing the power of emotional intelligence.* Boston: Harvard Business School Press.

Gottman, J. M., & DeClaire, J. (2001). *The relationship cure: A 5 step guide to strengthening your marriage, family, and friendship.* New York: Three Rivers Press.

Gottman, J. M., Gottman, J. S., & DeClaire, J. (2006). *Ten lessons to transform your marriage: America's love lab experts share their strategies for strengthening your relationship.* New York: Random House.

Guggenheim, D. (Director/Producer), & Gore, A. (Writer). (2006). *An inconvenient truth* [Motion picture]. United States: Paramount Classics.

Guilford, J. P. (1967). *The nature of human intelligence.* New York: McGraw-Hill.

Hargrove, R. (2008). *Masterful coaching.* San Francisco: Jossey-Bass.

Hattie, J. (2009). *Visible learning: A synthesis of over 800 meta-analyses relating to achievement.* New York: Routledge.

Haynes, M. (2007). *From state policy to classroom practice: Improving literacy instruction for all students.* Alexandria, VA: National Association of State Boards of Education.

Heath, C., & Heath, D. (2007). *Made to stick: Why some ideas survive and others die.* New York: Random House.

Heath, C., & Heath, D. (2010). *Switch: How to change things when change is hard.* New York: Random House.

Heifetz, R. A., Grashow, A., & Linsky, M. (2009). *The practice of adaptive leadership: Tools and tactics for changing your organization and your world.* Boston: Harvard Business School Press.

Heifetz, R. A., & Linsky, M. (2002). *Leadership on the line: Staying alive through the dangers of leading.* Boston: Harvard Business School Press.

Hord, S. M., & Sommers, W. A., (Eds.). (2008). *Leading professional learning communities: Voices from research and practice.* Thousand Oaks, CA: Corwin.

Horn, S. (1996). *Tongue fu: How to deflect, disarm and defuse any conflict.* New York: St. Martin's Press.

Hussey, J., & Allen, J. (2006). *The American education diet: Can U.S. students survive on junk food?* Washington, DC: The Center for Education Reform.

Isaacs, W. (1999). *Dialogue and the art of thinking together.* New York: Doubleday.

Iyengar, S. (2010). *The art of choosing.* New York: Grand Central.

Jensen, W. D. (2000). *Simplicity: The new competitive advantage in a world of more, better, faster.* Cambridge, MA: Perseus.

Jones, C., & Vreeman, M. (2008). *Instructional coaches and classroom teachers: Sharing the road to success.* Huntington Beach, CA: Shell Education.

Kadlac, A., & Friedman, W. (2008). *Opportunity knocks: Closing the gaps between leaders and the public on math, science, & technology education.* Kansas City, MO: Public Agenda.

Kegan, R., & Lahey, L. (2001). *How the way we talk can change the way we learn.* San Francisco: Jossey-Bass.

Killion, J., & Harrison, C. (2006). *Taking the lead: New roles for teachers and school-based coaches.* Oxford, OH: Learning Forward.

Killion, J., & Roy, P. (2009). *Becoming a learning school.* Oxford, OH: Learning Forward.

Killion, J., & Todnem, G. R. (1991). A process of personal theory building. *Educational Leadership, 48*(2), 14–16.

Kirsch, I., Braun, H., Yamamoto, K., & Sum, A. (2007). *America's perfect storm: Three forces changing our nation's future.* Princeton, NJ: Educational Testing Service.

Kise, J. A. G. (2006). *Differentiated coaching: A framework for helping teachers change.* Thousand Oaks, CA: Corwin.

Knight, J. (1998). *The effectiveness of partnership learning: A dialogical methodology for staff development.* Lawrence: University of Kansas Center for Research on Learning.

Knight, J. (2007). *Instructional coaching: A partnership approach to improving instruction.* Thousand Oaks, CA: Corwin.

Knight, J. (Ed.) (2009a). *Coaching: Approaches and perspectives.* Thousand Oaks, CA: Corwin.

Knight, J. (2009b). Instructional coaching. In J. Knight (Ed.), *Coaching: Approaches and perspectives* (pp. 29–55). Thousand Oaks, CA: Corwin.

Knight, J. (in press). *Instruction that makes an impact.* Thousand Oaks, CA: Corwin.

Lambert, C. (1998). *Mind over water: Lessons on life from the art of rowing.* New York: Houghton Mifflin.

Lencioni, P. (2000). *The four obsessions of an extraordinary executive: A leadership fable.* San Francisco: Jossey-Bass.

Lencioni, P. (2002). *The five dysfunctions of a team: A leadership fable.* San Francisco: Jossey-Bass.

Lencioni, P. (2010). *Getting naked: A business fable about shedding the three fears that sabotage client loyalty.* San Francisco: Jossey-Bass.

Lencioni, P., & Okabayshi, K. (2008). *The five dysfunctions of a team, manga edition: An illustrated leadership fable.* San Francisco: Jossey-Bass.

Lenz, B. K., Bulgren, J., Schumaker, J., Deshler, D. D., & Boudah, D. (1994). *The unit organizer routine.* Lawrence, KS: Edge Enterprises.

Liu, E. (2004). *Guiding lights: How to mentor—and find life's purpose.* New York: Random House.

Loehr, J., & Schwartz, T. (2003). *The power of full engagement: Managing energy, not time, is the key to high performance and personal renewal.* New York: Simon & Schuster.

Love, N. B. (2009). *Using data to improve learning for all: A collaborative inquiry approach.* Thousand Oaks, CA: Corwin.

Lummis, C. D. (1996). *Radical democracy.* Ithaca, NY: Cornell University Press.

Maeda, J. (2006). *The laws of simplicity (Simplicity: design, technology, business, life).* Cambridge: MIT Press.

Maister, D. H., Green, C. H., & Galford, R. M. (2000). *The trusted advisor.* New York: Simon & Schuster.

Martin, R. (2009). *The design of business: Why design thinking is the next competitive advantage.* Boston: Harvard Business School Publishing.

Medina, J. (2008). *Brain rules: 12 Principles for surviving at work, home, and school.* Seattle, WA: Pear Press.

Mellon, N. (2006). *Storytelling and the art of imagination.* Cambridge, MA: Yellow Moon Press.

Miles, K. H., & Hornbeck, M. (2000). Rethinking district professional development spending to support a district CSR strategy. *Resource Reallocation, 3.* Arlington, VA: New American Schools.

Milestones Project, The. (n.d.). *The Milestones Project pledge.* Retrieved September 24, 2010, from http://milestonesproject.com/index.php/caring _adults/milestones_pledge.

Miller, G. (1956). The magical number seven, plus or minus two. *Psychological Review, 63*(2): 81–97.

Miller, W. R., & Rollnick, S. (2002). *Motivational interviewing: Preparing people for change* (2nd ed.). New York: Guilford Press.

Mooney, N. J., & Mausbach, A. T. (2008). *Align the design: A blueprint for school improvement.* Alexandria, VA: Association for Supervision and Curriculum Development.

Moran, M. C. (2007). *Differentiated literacy coaching: Scaffolding for and teacher success.* Alexandria, VA: Association for Supervision and Curriculum Development.

Owen, H. (2008). *Open space technology: A user's guide, revised and expanded* (3rd ed.). San Francisco: Berrett-Koehler.

Palmer, P. J. (1998). *The courage to teach: Exploring the inner landscape of a teacher's life.* San Francisco: Jossey-Bass.

Palmer, P. J. (2004). *A hidden wholeness: The journey toward an undivided life.* San Francisco: Jossey-Bass.

Palmer, P. J. (2007). *The courage to teach: Exploring the inner landscape of a teacher's life* (10th ed.). San Francisco: Jossey-Bass.

Passone, A. (Producer), & Radford, M. (Director). (1994). *Il postino* [Motion picture]. Italy: Miramax.

Patterson, K., Grenny, J., Maxfield, D., McMillan, R., & Switzler, A. (2008). *Influencer: The power to change anything.* New York: McGraw-Hill.

Payne, C. (2008). *So much reform, so little change: The persistence of failure in urban schools.* Cambridge, MA: Harvard Education Press.

Pfeffer, J., & Sutton, R. I. (2000). *The knowing-doing gap: How smart companies turn knowledge into action.* Boston: Harvard Business Review.

Pink, D. H. (2005). *A whole new mind: Why right brainers will rule the future.* New York: Berkley.

Pink, D. H. (2009). *Drive: The surprising truth about what motivates us.* New York: Penguin.

Playing for Change. (n.d.). *Playing for change.* Retrieved August 30, 2010, from http://www.playingforchange.com.

Popham, J. (2008). *Transformative assessment.* Alexandria, VA: Association for Supervision and Curriculum Development.

Prochaska, J. O., Norcross, J. C., & DiClemente, C. C. (1994). *Changing for good.* New York: Avon Books.

Purkey, W. W., & Novak, J. M. (n.d.). *Forty successes.* Retrieved August 31, 2010, from http://honolulu.hawaii.edu/intranet/committees/FacDevCom/guidebk/teachtip/40succes.htm.

Raines, C., & Ewing, L. (2006). *The art of connecting: How to overcome differences, build rapport and communicate effectively with anyone.* New York: American Management Association.

Reeves, D. B. (2009). *Leading change in your school: How to conquer myths, build commitment, and get results.* Alexandria, VA: Association for Supervision and Curriculum Development.

Reina, D. S., & Reina, M. L. (2006). *Trust and betrayal in the workplace Building effective relationships in your organization* (2nd ed.). San Francisco: Berrett-Koehler.

Reynolds, G. (2008a). *Presentation Zen: Simple ideas on presentation design and delivery.* Berkeley, CA: New Riders.

Reynolds, G. (2008b). *Presentation Zen design: Simple design principles and techniques to enhance your presentations.* Berkeley, CA: New Riders.

Rifkin, J. (2009). *The empathic civilization: The race to global consciousness in a world in crisis.* New York: Penguin.

Rosenholtz, S. J. (1991). *Teacher's workplace: The social organization of schools.* New York: Teachers College Press.

Ruiz, D. M. (2001). *The four agreements: A practical guide to personal freedom.* San Rafael, CA: Amber-Allen.

Sawyer, K. (2007). *Group genius: The creative power of collaboration.* New York: Basic Books.

Schein, E. H. (2004). *Organizational culture and leadership.* San Francisco: Jossey-Bass.

Schein, E. H. (2009). *Helping: How to offer, give, and receive help.* San Francisco: Berrett-Koehler.

Schön, D. A. (1991). *The reflective practitioner: How professionals think in action.* New York: Perseus.

Schumaker, J. B. (with Sheldon, J.). (1985). *Proficiency in the sentence writing strategy: Instructor's manual.* Lawrence: University of Kansas Center for Research on Learning.

Schumaker, J. B., Deshler, D. D., Nolan, S. M., & Alley, G. A. (1994). *The self-questioning strategy: Instructor's manual.* Lawrence: University of Kansas Center for Research on Learning.

Schumaker, J. B., Deshler, D. D., Zemitzsch, A., & Warner, M. M. (1993). *The visual imagery strategy: Instructor's manual.* Lawrence: University of Kansas Center for Research on Learning.

Schwartz, B. (2004). *The paradox of choice: Why more is less.* New York: HarperCollins.

Scott, S. (2002). *Fierce conversations: Achieving success at work and in life one conversation at a time.* New York: Berkley.

Scott, S. (2009). *Fierce leadership: A bold alternative to the worst "best" practices of business today.* New York: Random House.

Seligman, M. (1998). *Learned optimism: How to change your mind and your life.* New York: Simon & Schuster.

Senge, P. (1990). *The fifth discipline: The art and practice of the learning organization.* London: Random House.

Senge, P. (2006). *The fifth discipline: The art and practice of the learning organization* (rev. and updated ed.). New York: Currency Doubleday.

Senge, P., Kleiner, A., Roberts, C., Ross, R., Roth, G., Smith, B. (1999). *The dance of change: The challenges of sustaining momentum in learning organizations.* New York: Currency Doubleday.

Showers, B., & Joyce, B. (1996). The evolution of peer coaching. *Educational Leadership, 53*(6), 12–16.

Showkeir, J., Showkeir, M., & Wheatley, M. J. (2008). *Authentic conversations: Moving from manipulation to truth and commitment.* San Francisco: Berrett-Koehler.

Simmons, A. (2006). *The story factor: Inspiration, influence, and persuasion through the art of storytelling* (2nd rev. ed.). Cambridge, MA: Basic Books.

Solem, L., & Pike, B. (1998). *50 Creative training closers: Innovative ways to end your training with impact!* San Francisco: Jossey-Bass.

Sparks, D. (2006). *Leading for results: Transforming teaching, learning, and relationships in schools.* Thousand Oaks, CA: Corwin.

Sprick, R. (2009). *CHAMPs: A proactive and positive approach to classroom management* (2nd. ed.). Eugene, OR: Pacific Northwest Press.

Sprick, R., Garrison, M., & Howard, L. (1998). *CHAMPs: A proactive and positive approach to classroom management*. Longmont, CO: Sopris West.

Sprick, R., Garrison, M., & Howard, L. (2002). *Foundations: Establishing Positive Discipline and Schoolwide Behavior Support*. Eugene, OR: Pacific Northwest Press.

Steckel, R., & Steckel, M. (2010). *Millstone project*. Retrieved August 30, 2010, from http://milestonesproject.com.

Stiggins, R., Arter, J., Chappuis, J., & Chappuis, S. (2009). *Classroom assessment for student learning: Doing it right—using it well*. New York: Allyn & Bacon.

Stoltzfus, Y. (2008). *Coaching questions: A coach's guide to powerful asking skills*. Pegasus Creative Arts.

Stone, D., Patton, B., Heen, S., & Fisher, R. (2000). *Difficult conversations: How to discuss what matters most*. New York: Penguin.

Stout, D., & Pear, R. (2008, July 30). Bush seeks budget of $3.1 trillion. *New York Times*.

Straker, D. (1997). *Rapid problem solving with Post-it Notes*. New York: Da Capo Press.

Sugai, G., & Horner, R. (2000). School-wide behavior support: An emerging initiative. *Journal of Positive Behavior Interventions*, 2, 231–232.

Sugai, G., Horner, R. H., Dunlap, G., Hieneman, M., Lewis, T. J., Nelson, et al. (2000). Applying positive behavioral support and functional assessment in schools. *Journal of Positive Behavior Interventions*, 2, 131–143.

Sullivan, S. S., & Glanz, J. G. (2006). *Building effective learning communities: Strategies for leadership, learning, and collaboration*. Thousand Oaks, CA: Corwin.

Surowiecki, J. (2004). *The wisdom of crowds*. New York: Random House.

Toll, C. (2009). Instructional coaching. In J. Knight (Ed.), *Coaching: Approaches and perspectives* (pp. 56–69). Thousand Oaks, CA: Corwin.

Ury, W. (1991). *Getting past no: Negotiating your way form confrontation to cooperation*. New York: Bantam Books.

U.S. Department of Education, National Center for Educational Statistics. (2007). *The nation's report card: Reading 2007; The nation's report card: 8th grade reading 2007*. Washington, DC: U.S. Government Printing Office.

West. L. (2009). Instructional coaching. In J. Knight (Ed.), *Coaching: Approaches and perspectives* (pp. 113–144). Thousand Oaks, CA: Corwin.

West, L., & Staub, F. C. (2003). *Content-focused coaching: Transforming mathematics lessons*. Portsmouth, NH: Heinemann.

Wheatley, M. (2002). *Turning to one another: Simple conversations to restore hope to the future* (2nd ed.). San Francisco: Berrett-Koehler.

Wheatley, M. (2009). *Turning to one another: Simple conversations to restore hope to the future*. San Francisco: Berrett-Koehler.

Wheatley, M., & Kellner-Rogers, M. (1996). *A simpler way*. San Francisco: Berrett-Koehler.

Whitworth, L., Kimsey-House, K., Kimsey-House, H., & Sandahl, P. (2007). *Co-active coaching: New skills for coaching people toward success in work and life* (2nd ed.). Palo Alto, CA: Davies-Black Publishing.

Williams, J. (2009). Federal accountability. In S. C. Carter (Ed.), *Mandate for change: A bold agenda for the incoming government* (pp. 7–12). Washington, DC: The Center for Education Reform.

York-Barr, J., Sommers, W. A., Ghere, G. S., & Montie, J. K. (2006). *Reflective practice to improve schools: An action guide for educators* (2nd ed.). Thousand Oaks, CA: Corwin.

Index

CORWIN

A SAGE Company

The Corwin logo—a raven striding across an open book—represents the union of courage and learning. Corwin is committed to improving education for all learners by publishing books and other professional development resources for those serving the field of PreK–12 education. By providing practical, hands-on materials, Corwin continues to carry out the promise of its motto: **"Helping Educators Do Their Work Better."**

Advancing professional learning for student success

Learning Forward (formerly National Staff Development Council) is an international association of learning educators committed to one purpose in K–12 education: Every educator engages in effective professional learning every day so every student achieves.